Democratic Policy Implementation
in an Ambiguous World

Democratic Policy Implementation in an Ambiguous World

LUKE FOWLER

SUNY
PRESS

Cover image from Shutterstock.

Published by State University of New York Press

For information, contact State University of New York Press, Albany, NY
www.sunypress.edu

Library of Congress Cataloging-in-Publication Data

Name: Fowler, Luke, author.
Title: Democratic policy implementation in an ambiguous world / Luke Fowler.
Description: Albany : State University of New York Press, [2023] | Includes
    bibliographical references and index.
Identifiers: ISBN 9781438493596 (hardcover : alk. paper) | ISBN 9781438493602
    (ebook) | ISBN 9781438493589 (pbk. : alk. paper)
Further information is available at the Library of Congress.

10 9 8 7 6 5 4 3 2 1

To Whitfield "Field" Fowler,
the best research assistant one could ask for.

Contents

Illustrations

Figures

Tables

Introduction

Policy-in-Theory Is Not Policy-in-Practice

One of the biggest myths of government is that passing new laws solves problems. Policymakers and the public treat laws as if they are magic wands or silver bullets that, once written into the books, automatically change society or make problems go away. However, time and time again, policies fail to achieve their stated goals, fail to be complied with, fail to be enforced, or fail to solve the underlying problem they were designed to solve. Of course, policymakers are vested in this myth, as it creates the illusion that they have the power to solve problems. If one believes that policy magically changes the world, then policymakers are the gatekeepers of that magic, making them the most revered and important participants in government. The public buys into this myth because it is easy. It presents a clear end point, after which they can move on to the next problem. Most often, the public shifts attention to the next issue once a new law has been passed, but rarely do they stick around to watch what happens next (Downs, 1991; Peters & Hogwood, 1985). This provides the luxury of not worrying about what happens after policy is enshrined in law. In other words, it saves them from worrying about the hard part.

Yes, the hard part is not passing new laws; the hard part of policy and governance is implementation. It is where the high-minded ideas of policymakers have to be pushed and prodded into the chaos that is the real world. It is like fitting a proverbial square peg into a round hole. Those changes that policy hopes to make in the world are not magic or automatic. They follow a complicated pathway when being put into practice—practice being the actual application of the idea as opposed to the theory behind it. If done correctly, this results in a shifting of behaviors

1

among target populations (i.e., the sub-populations of a community that policies target for change), leading to improvements in the social or environmental conditions that policy is designed around (Fowler, 2019b, 2022; Smith & Larimer, 2016). In other words, problems are not solved through policies-in-theory, but through changes in how people behave in practice. Policies just set out guidance for what should happen. While nothing is automatic, there can be something magical about it when one realizes the sheer miracle it is that policy works at all (Pressman & Wildavsky, 1984). This is chiefly because people have a natural inclination toward doing the same thing over and over again—that is, maintaining the status quo. Creating change requires people to break out of those patterns and do something different, which at times feels unnatural (Nicholson-Crotty, Nicholson-Crotty, & Webeck, 2019; Samuelson & Zeckhauser, 1988).

While anecdotes about broken government are a dime a dozen, when I was researching this book, an interviewee shared two stories that help illustrate how important status quos are for how government works. In the first, an entomologist was contracted to review the pest control practices at a local school. The custodial staff had been using a particular type of ant spray for some time. When asked why, they responded, "Well, that's what the guy who trained me used." Unfortunately, over the decades, the active ingredients in that ant spray had been phased out of common use, because of the risks associated with exposure. Of course, this would likely explain why those school children had higher-than-usual rates of asthma and other respiratory illnesses, which was the reason the entomologist was brought into to investigate. In the second, a regional office of a state agency had stopped issuing open burn permits over a few weeks. When staff from headquarters inquired as to why, the regional office explained that they used magnets to mark a map in order to keep track of where permits had been issued. However, they recently ran out of magnets, so they stopped issuing permits. While neither of these stories is indicative of broader policy failures, they do highlight the dysfunctions that occur when people continue to follow a pattern of behavior without thinking about what they are doing and how it may look in the bigger picture.

In contrast, another interviewee described her experiences in a federal agency under three presidents, remarking that even where new administrations pushed new policy initiatives, the day-to-day work remained the same; it was just rebranded. This by no means equates to a failure, because the policy changes at hand were superficial to begin with. It was not until a non-incremental budgetary change brought significant new resources and expectations that a rethinking of how policy works was undertaken. This is notable because it tells us that status quos may be entrenched but they can also be altered with the right tools. Creating change, as to break away from the "way things have always been done" is ultimately what policy implementation is concerned with; it is certainly why new policies are adopted. But, as stories and experiences of bureaucrats often tell us, new policies are not always met with new actions. Change is necessary to improve the conditions and circumstances of our society, though, particularly as it applies to the dynamic wants and needs of citizens in a democracy. Of course, this change can be targeted at what public services are provided, how they are provided, to whom they are provided, or when they are provided.

By creating the right change, there is a shift in how government and society interact that is built on hopes of solving public problems, and those changes do not happen just because policy says so. For instance, *Brown v. Board of Education* (1954) is most famous for the phrase "separate is inherently unequal" in ordering schools to be desegregated; but a subsequent ruling in *Brown v. Board II* (1955) ordered this to occur "with all deliberate speed." The latter phrase ended up being more important for explaining how schools were desegregated. While *Brown* is a policy statement carrying the weight of law and ordering a social change in how education is provided in the US, it relied on states to implement those changes. Consequently, Southern states used the ambiguity of acting "with all deliberate speed" to rationalize their resistance, and integration in many states did not occur on any substantial level until the late 1960s. This followed several additional court rulings, including *Green v. County School Board of New Kent County* (1968), dealing directly with how school integration was implemented, as opposed to the merits of integration, which were decided upon in previous cases (Ogletree, 2004; Daugherty & Bolton, 2008).

Unfortunately, this is a relatively common story, where it is not a revolution of ideas that is needed, but the implementation of ideas that already exist. Take for instance the national debt that the US federal government has amassed (estimated at around $30 trillion in June 2022) (US Department of the Treasury, 2022). While many have put forth proposals that require a fundamental shift in how money is spent, one of the simplest ways of reducing annual budget deficits is by enforcing existing tax code (Yarrow, 2008). An Internal Revenue Service (IRS) report examining tax revenues from 2008 to 2010 indicates that about $400 billion a year (or about 16% of tax revenue) is not collected (IRS, 2016). This is mostly due to the American tax system's reliance on voluntary compliance (Christian, 1994; Manhire, 2015). While the IRS does have mechanisms to punish tax evaders and recoup tax losses after the fact, it has to catch them first. However, between 2010 and 2020, the IRS conducted audits on between 0.45% and 1.11% of taxpayers (Picchi, 2020), meaning the IRS is typically unaware of whether 99 out of 100 taxpayers are complying with tax code. Of course, this is why President Biden floated increased support for the IRS as a means to pay for his broader economic agenda during his first year in office, as it is likely to create new revenues without changing tax policy (Tankersley & Rappeport, 2021).

Or take the global pandemic brought on by COVID-19. Although there has been significant controversy surrounding what policy solutions are available, one of the most common tools at the local level is mask mandates, which require individuals to wear a face covering while in public. But again, this largely relies on citizens following the rules. In Boise, Idaho, a mask mandate was put in place in July 2020, but the city's plan rested wholly on voluntary compliance. As one can imagine, this did little to quell the number of COVID-19 cases, which continued to increase through community spread over the following months (Frankel, 2020; Harding & Scholl, 2020; Idaho Press Staff, 2020). In November 2020, the city took a more aggressive approach, and decided they would in fact begin enforcing the mask mandate—but only in response to complaints. That is, law enforcement and public health officials would not actively patrol or look for non-compliance; they would only respond if someone not wearing a mask was causing alarm for others. While reports suggest that mask wearing increased, there was by no means universal compliance with the mandate (Berry, 2020; Beck, 2020). Thus, a simple solution to a devastating pandemic was thwarted by how to make it work in practice as local leaders navigated controversial politics during a crisis, as a polarized political environment made it difficult to find functional solutions.

Implementation challenges even arise where policies are largely successful. For instance, the Servicemen's Readjustment Act of 1944 (commonly known as the GI Bill) established benefits for veterans returning from World War II, including low-interest mortgages or business loans, unemployment compensation, and educational assistance. The overall goal was to help veterans readjust to civilian life. This was largely met through greater educational attainment and economic security, as well as more civic participation and volunteerism. This focused on household economics as opposed to macroeconomics, which was a shift in thinking from previous social benefit programs, such as the New Deal. Problems with implementation occurred almost immediately, and many of these were tied to administrative procedures and the reliance on states to determine eligibility of service members, leading to institutional barriers to access. This inevitably contributed to racial discrimination and low participation rates for women, as the same problems that existed in other social programs seeped into veteran services. While the success of this policy is contemporarily accepted by academics and the public, one could still question how effective implementation was (Mettler, 2005; Compton, 2019).

Again, stories of great ideas hashed out by policymakers being dashed when they crash into the real world are so common that "business as usual" is a fitting label (Peters, 2015). Given this, the motivation for this volume is twofold. First, and primarily, how policies are implemented is a cornerstone to the quality and character of democratic governance, but too little is known about why it happens the way it does. Far too often, what happens after policies are adopted is taken for granted, or swept under the rug of broader questions of government that provide too little depth to the specific challenges associated with translating policy into practice (deLeon & deLeon, 2002; Hill & Hupe, 2014; O'Toole, 2000). But policy implementation sits as the core mission of public service organizations and warrants a complex investigation to understand why policies do not always work or why they take on unexpected forms in practice. Second, by doing so, I also hope to explain how collective choices translate into collective action across broad networks of policy actors and ultimately transform social and environmental circumstances. This hits at the heart of questions of democratic governance through multi-level institutions with pluralistic interests, and opens the door to providing better advice to practitioners on how to achieve the public interest (and not just talk about it) (Hill & Hupe, 2014; Ostrom, Cox, & Schlager, 2014; Peters & Pierre, 1998).

While these are ambitious motivations, the coming chapters will unpack an argument of how and why patterns of policy implementation manifest the way they do. The core of this argument rests on policy implementation being the process of altering status quos in what normal behaviors are. Thus, the research question here is: how are norms in these behaviors constructed and deconstructed? In this volume, I will explain how policy serves as a cue to what behaviors are wanted (or at least, which ones are unwanted), but implementers still have to figure out how to accomplish it in the best way possible and how to institutionalize behaviors so that they become the new normal. Complicating this process is the fact that implementers are often operating in ambiguous environments, so that the world is only partially comprehensible. Using the multiple streams framework (MSF) as theoretical framework, I analyze how and where implementers look for decision cues about problems, solutions, and stakeholder values in deciding how or if to shift their behaviors. Based on those decision cues, implementers translate ideas into actions. Of course, this is not the end of it, and the actions of implementers feed into a larger process by which social and environmental conditions are impacted by human behavior (i.e., governance, and more importantly, democratic governance).

Implementation, Policy, and Failure

Now, let us consider an important question: does bad implementation lead to policy failure or is policy failure part of a broader question about bad policy? In other words, does the blame lie with policymakers who come up with ill-fated ideas or with administrators who fail to effectively or efficiently operationalize those ideas? When policy fails, any politician would tell you that it is clearly the fault of bureaucrats. This trope of attacking the bureaucracy is so common in American politics that it is almost cliché (Hall, 2002). Elected officials often argue that they have got it all figured out, but everything falls apart when lazy, self-interested, or incompetent bureaucrats get in the way. Although bureaucrats tend to hesitate to publicly defend themselves, most will say privately that it is the politicians, who are disconnected from reality and more concerned with re-election, who adopt bad policies and force bureaucrats to retrofit those bad policies to meet the needs and wants of their communities. The truth likely lies somewhere in between. Legislators have a bad habit of writing policy that only makes sense in their closed-door sessions and that suffers from too many cooks in the kitchen, and bureaucrats do not always get it right when it comes to implementation (Pressman & Wildavsky, 1984; Hudson, Hunter, & Peckham, 2019).

The phrase "policy failures" (also referred to as "fiascos," "disasters," or "blunders") is used relatively frequently by journalists, commentators, and politicians to grab attention as these issues are examined. In fact, it is no secret of politics and government that failures are far more interesting than successes, to the point that most often when government programs are discussed in media or in academia the focus is on failure, rather than success. To this end, Peters (2015) argues that "for most developed political systems [policy failure] is indeed 'business as usual,' with the system as a whole performing reasonably well, but individual policies failing and then being replaced" (p. 270). However, in the common lexicon, policy failure has taken on a range of meanings, including government policies or programs that fall short of expected outcomes (e.g., Hurricane Katrina response); prove difficult or unwieldy in their functions (e.g., unemployment application processing during COVID-19); produce unintended results (e.g., US Forest Service timber management policies' impact on wildfires); generate immoral, unethical, unpopular, and/or corrupt practices (e.g., immigrant family separation policy); or are met with significant opposition (e.g., racial profiling by police). Thus, policy failure includes some combination of not meeting goals and/or creating unexpected consequences so that no program can be successful if the unintended negative effects are sufficiently greater than any positive outcome created (Bovens and 't Hart, 1996; Gray, 1998).

Of course, there is also an implication here that failures are avoidable. That implication is important, because with it, we assume that every policy has the potential to be successful; that every policy is capable of moving the needle in the direction that we want it to move. But avoiding policy failure often rests on the shoulders of policy implementers, as they are tasked with interpreting and applying the ideas adopted by policymakers to the complexities of the real world. When they do their job "right," policies achieve their goals as originally envisioned. Doing the job "right," though, sometimes means going off script and reinterpreting ideas to keep up with unexpected or unanticipated challenges. Of course, if implementers do their job "wrong," policies will inevitably fail, because ideas mean little without appropriate action to bring them to life. Simply put, implementation may lead to failure, but often failure involves far more than implementation (Peters, 2015). In contrast, policy success is likely to occur only where policy and implementation are both done well; that is, good ideas that are mobilized by an organized group of professionals that connect the dots between policy and behaviors. As policy failures and success exist on a spectrum (McConnell, 2010), the question is more often "To what extent has policy succeeded or failed?" as opposed to "Has this policy failed or not?"

Following this logic, if policy success or failure is marked by the misalignment of intended goals and expected outcomes (i.e., policy design) on the one hand, and the reality of policies in practice on the other, then the extent of policy failure or success can be measured by the gap between policy-in-theory and policy-in-practice. While public policy tends to be most associated with laws and legislation, policy is more complex than it. Policy is a body of ideas and practices that govern our societies (Smith & Larimer, 2016). In most cases, policies appear in formal, written statements (i.e., policy-as-written) that communicate a theory of how a phenomenon should play out under foreseen circumstances. That is, policy-as-written represents how a group of policymakers have charted the ideal pathway for specific activities to occur, and for which they have articulated in so many words the guideposts for what should and should not happen in hopes of presenting a well-defined conceptualization of the acceptable way to engage in that activity. But theories are just ideas, and while they may be based in practice, they are not bound to it, nor are practices wholly bound to theories (Bushouse, et al, 2011; Walker et al., 2019).

For instance, a local ordinance governing road safety presents a theory of the safest maximum speed one should drive along a stretch of road (i.e., speed limit). But this does not guarantee compliance, nor do the associated fines or punishments. Rather, what drives the degree of compliance is how the policy-as-written is enforced, so that drivers come to understand the policy as practiced and what behavioral norms they should be following. In other words, policy is articulated as a theory (ideally, in writing), which influences how policy is practiced; policy-in-practice, then, becomes what is recognized as the functionality of the policy theory. For instance, while a speed limit may be 45 miles per hour (mph), for the sake of argument, let us say that it is uncommon for a traffic cop to stop someone for driving 46 mph (1 mph over the theoretical limit), and it is common is for a traffic cop to stop someone at 50 mph (5 mph over the theoretical limit). Over time, drivers are likely to learn that they can drive up to 50 mph without getting a traffic citation. Thus, while the speed limit in theory is 45 mph, it is 50 mph in practice. While 5 mph may seem to be a negligible difference, it is representative of the gap between policy-in-theory and policy-in-practice, and it is the latter that defines how people behave in our society.

This gap exists for three core reasons, representing the constraints on the theoretical basis of policy. First, policy-as-written is never a perfect articulation of policy-in-theory, so it is often left open to interpretation. To a certain extent, this is a result of the limitations of human language and the ability to convey complex thoughts (Habermas, 1998). As those who are tasked with turning policy-in-theory into actions rely chiefly on the written policy statements as a formalization of requirements, they are often left to make sense out of ideas that are incomplete on paper. While some may seek further guidance through informal interactions with policymakers or stakeholders, formal policy statements are the primary source from which understanding flows. Of course, this is further complicated by the need to compromise in order to reach agreement, which tends to produce less clarity in order to reduce conflict. Consequently, policy-as-written is rarely free of ambiguity, as policymakers choose to leave controversial issues undefined (Zahariadis, 2003). This places responsibility for making sense out of policy in the hands of implementers. Unsurprisingly, the ideas of policymakers are often misunderstood, misinterpreted, or misapplied as a result.

Second, the real world is often different from the world envisioned when grand policy goals are set out. When policies are designed in theory, assumptions are made about how people behave and the circumstances in which they make decisions. If these assumptions align with the real world, then things play out as assumed and policy works as designed; but if these assumptions misalign, then things go off the rails. For instance, in the 1920s, Congress assumed that people would cease consuming alcohol if it was prohibited, causing alcohol-related crimes (e.g., domestic abuse) to decrease. But, as history often tells us, banning something does not always mean that people stop doing it. While alcohol consumption declined initially, it rose to approximately 70% of pre-prohibition levels by the early 1930s, and while some alcohol-related crimes declined, black markets and criminal undergrounds that fueled organized crime and gangland violence rose (Miron & Zwiebel, 1991; Hall, 2010). These types of unintended consequences are common, and many apocryphal stories exist (e.g., cobra effect) (Chollette & Harrison, 2020). Furthermore, things change and evolve over time. As one person interviewed for this book explained, "laws are written to address a perceived need at the time, but a lot of times it is impossible to project into the future and see how things are going to evolve and craft legislation to address those things . . . so in a lot of ways [we/administrators] are always playing catch up to innovation in the marketplace."

Third, policy tends to take a negative form insofar as it outlines what not to do, rather than a positive form providing guidance on what to do. Particularly in democratic societies where it is implicit that rights and liberties exist unless explicitly stated otherwise, policy is oriented toward the prohibition of certain types of behavior (Farber, 2007). Certainly, it is easier to identify and describe the types of behaviors that one wants to restrict, while leaving individuals free to pursue other behaviors. As a natural extension of this, policies tend to outline all the things that should not be done so stakeholders can identify where implementers or target populations are failing to meet guidelines. In contrast, policy rarely, if ever, articulates specific expectations for what should be done, as doing so creates implicit restrictions on innovation. For instance, speed limits restrict the speed that vehicles may travel, but generally leave it open to drivers to choose the speed they are comfortable with; but a speed "requirement" would imply that drivers should travel at a specified speed and no others. While this approach provides implementers with discretion to choose how to make policies work, it tends to provide only restrictions, as opposed to guidance.

This leaves policy implementers with the complicated task of translating policy-as-written into policy-in-practice, requiring them to figure out not only what the idea is but also how to turn it into action. At its most basic, this hinges on how individual decisions are made in the process of providing public services. That is, how and why does a traffic cop decide to enforce a speeding infraction? Naturally, there are errors in this process as people interpret policy-as-written differently than intended. No further evidence of this point may be needed beyond the body of US Supreme Court cases that debate the intent of the Framers of the Constitution, as people continue to argue about what words and phrases from a 200-year old document mean (Greenhouse, 2012; Grundfest & Pritchard, 2002). For better or worse, a degree of ambiguity in policy-as-written provides implementers with the opportunity to adjust practices as necessary to meet the constraints of the real world as it evolves (Fowler, 2019b; Matland, 1995). This is particularly important as one thinks about policy applied across diverse target populations. However, the risk is that adjusting practices causes policy not to function as theoretically intended, which contributes to policies failing to achieve their goals.

Of course, this is layered on top of challenges of operationalization. Turning ideas into actions is where the plans of mice and men go awry most often. Regardless of how well thought out a theory is, trade-offs must be made when that theory hits the real world. The same is true for policy; implementers have to make trade-offs as they balance resources and responsibilities. For instance, what are the costs of pulling over a driver who exceeds the speed limit? Is it worth the labor or opportunity costs to do so if a driver is only exceeding the limit by 1 mph? How fast can a driver go before they endanger public safety? How often are those going only 1 mph over the limit doing so with a wanton disregard for public safety? From a practical standpoint, does it make sense to focus only on drivers who are in excessive violation? Unfortunately, this is a world of limited resources, which requires trade-offs. Typically, this means that all of our interests cannot be served at once. Thus, in the process of translating ideas to actions, some points must be abandoned in order to secure others. Naturally, this causes actions to be less than a perfect manifestation of ideas.

In the 21st century, it is not diagnosing the sources of social ills or coming up with utopian ideas on how the world ought to be that is lacking. The missing pieces are figuring out how to solve the problems that can be solved and addressing the problems that cannot be solved in practical ways that are feasible given the political and economic realities—that is, figuring out how to implement policies to maximize chances at policy success. It is fitting a square peg of policy into a round hole of reality that has become our biggest societal challenge. Even though the peg is not always square nor the hole always round, lawmakers time and time again try to remake the peg in hopes of finding one that fits, but keep falling short. Often, this is because they cannot see the shape of the hole or they believe the hole will conform to the peg. But the real solution to this challenge is to rework the peg until it fits into the hole that exists, whatever the shape may be, because it is often the peg that is more malleable than the hole. Studying policy implementation opens the door to understanding how this process works and how it can be done better. This is why it is fruitful to study policy implementation: good ideas go nowhere without the action to back them up.

Implementation at an Intersection

So, why does existing scholarship not offer better answers? Despite theoretical conflict and different perspectives on where decision-making power lies and the logical pathways used to examine its flow through organizations, scholars have long been in tacit agreement that policy implementation is ultimately a question of who is making decisions and how they are being made (O'Toole, 2000; deLeon & deLeon, 2002; Hill & Hupe, 2014; Fowler, 2019b). That is, most scholars accept the fact that policymakers shift responsibilities to policy implementers, who are then expected to use their discretion to make choices that best serve the public interest. Of course, implementation scholars have not agreed on everything, and those conflicts can be telling about why existing answers are limited. At least part of the theoretical conflicts here stem from integrating the normative (i.e., what ought to be) and the practical (i.e., what is); that is, some scholars tend to superimpose theory about how things ought to work onto practice, while others tend to develop theory from what they see in practice. Consequently, some disagreement is less about different analytical foci or units of analysis, and more about the vantage point by which implementation is examined. While implementation research has matured both methodologically and theoretically, developments have been incremental and disconnected from a central theoretical debate for years (Winter, 2012; Saetren, 2005, 2014).

In general, this can be attributed to two factors. First, as governance and network theory advanced in explaining public service delivery, policy implementation scholars failed to continue to distinguish it from other research foci, while also propagating prototype theories that failed to gain traction. The result was that implementation theory rolled into emerging areas of inquiry (e.g., public service delivery networks) and lost much of its distinct identity (O'Toole, 2000; Hill & Hupe, 2014; Howlett, 2019). As an offshoot, it became more difficult for scholars in other fields (e.g., education) to draw from implementation theory without engaging in a much broader and more complex academic debate, so these studies became unmoored across fields. Second, while implementation studies advanced scientifically, they stalled in providing guidance to practitioners implementing policies. Of course, this was compounded by the "too many variables" problem and the lack of comprehensive theoretical frameworks, so that the literature was not easily accessible to those looking in from the outside (Goggin, 1986; Meier, 1999; O'Toole, 2000; deLeon & deLeon, 2002). Despite implementation studies becoming disjointed as a sub-field, implementation remains of interest to scholars of both public policy and public administration, even though this has also led to it being perceived in competing ways (Saetren, 2005, 2014).

One of the key challenges that underly these broader trends is that policy implementation serves as an inflection point where different elemental forces converge. Implementation is where policy shifts from being dominated by political branches of government to the administrative institutions of government. Even where policy is made within the executive branch, it shifts from actors who are participants in the political world (i.e., elected officials, political appointees) to those who are chiefly administrators (i.e., civil servants). Consequently, implementation has been examined as both a function of policy and a function of administration, causing confusion on where policy implementation resides within a theoretical framework of government. What makes policy implementation a unique node within these broader fields is of particular importance as we parse out how policy implementation exists in comparison to policymaking and/or administrating public agencies. Specifically, at the intersection of policy and administration, implementation is both an extension of defining the public interest and an aspect of maintaining public institutions. Thus, there is often conflict over what the purpose of implementation is, and how it is thought of as a function of government.

In this light, policy implementation serves as a bridge between public policy and public administration, where the tasks of executing policy are both an extension of defining the public interest and a function of maintaining public institutions. Figure I.1 diagrams this relationship where public policy and public administration exist as two overlapping circles, and in the intersecting portion sits policy implementation. To this end, implementation is the mechanism by which the practices of government ensure both the short-term needs and wants of a community and its long-term viability. On the one hand, implementation is central to how public interest manifests in practical functions of government; this means implementation demands change, is inherently political, and flows from

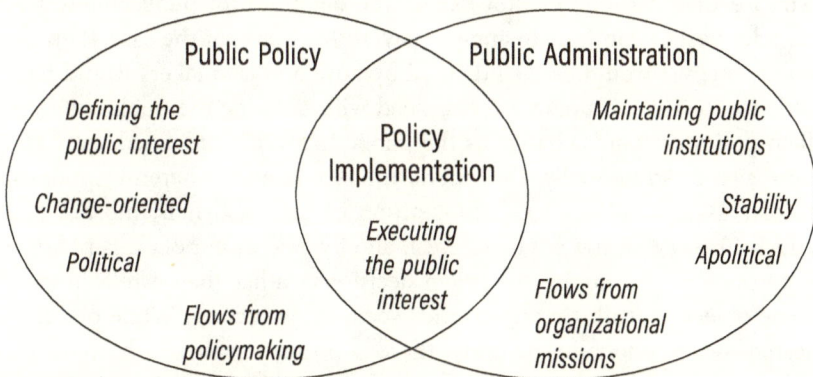

Figure I.1 Venn Diagram of Policy, Administration, and Implementation. *Source:* Author-created image.

policymaking. On the other hand, implementation is also a manifestation of public institutions; this means implementation fuels stability, is grounded in neutral administrative values, and is a function of organizational missions. Of course, this also means there are contradictions at each turn. Implementers are expected to create change but maintain stability, to understand and make value judgments but be neutral, to fuse new policy with existing organizational machinations. Unfortunately, implementation cannot be divorced from either set of demands, and sacrificing one in favor of the other only exposes cracks, that grow every time policies fail, in the foundation of communities and their respective institutions.

Pursuing this further, if one thinks of public policy as being associated with the tasks of defining the public interest, which are inherently political, change-oriented, and focused on how policies are made. While this is most readily represented by the act of passing laws, it also incorporates examining social or community problems, formulating and evaluating ideas on how to improve society, accounting for public opinion and values as well as stakeholder interests, and making choices that represent the interest of communities, among other things, that feed into the process of identifying, understanding, and communicating the public interest in its various forms. Implementation, then, becomes an extension of this, where implementers are working to reflect the public interest in their behaviors and choices during public service delivery. This perspective places implementers as quasi-policymakers who have been delegated responsibilities from officials elected to represent the public.

Importantly, the public interest evolves over time as the state of the world evolves, so one cannot expect the definition of public interest of decades past to continue to apply today. If this were not the case, then the public interest would be well defined by now, and lawmakers would have little to do. Thus, if policy is concerned with defining the public interest, then policy demands change as the public interest is redefined, over and over again. Additionally, the public interest is also inherently political insofar as it is subject to a competition of values, beliefs, morals, and ethics. To say that the public interest, and by extension policy, is political is to say that it is subject to group decisions, rather than a reflection of some objective truth that transcends social construction. While one may search for commonality or unity, there is no universality to how people believe the world ought to be or the wisdom used in determining a proper course of action for bringing it about. Instead, there is a great deal of subjectivity as people debate the virtue in their perspectives on the world (Stone, 2011; Smith & Larimer, 2016).

Of course, this means that policy entails an intensive process with multiple decision points in order to narrow down and define the public interest. To this end, early policy scholars (e.g., Lasswell, 2018 [original edition 1936]) developed the policy stages heuristic to help explain the types of decisions being made. In almost all incarnations, policy stages set policy adoption up as an inflection point whereby the pre-adoption goal is to come to a consensus on what the public interest is and the post-adoption goal is to act on that choice (Smith & Larimer, 2016). From this perspective, one can view policy as existing in two intertwined phases: one focused on defining ideas (policymaking) and the other on defining actions (policy implementation). Prior to adoption, choices are made to refine understandings and options in a complex and chaotic world so that decision points can be narrowed. This typically leads policy adoption to entail binary choices (i.e., yea or nay) by a centralized body of policymakers (e.g., legislature). Thus, choices made pre-adoption flow into adoption. That is, policy-as-written is a formal articulation of how policymakers have defined public interests insofar as they reflect what the public wants and/or needs pertaining to narrow issues, and in coming to that determination, policymakers are likely to collect a plethora of information on the problems, solutions, and politics to understand how choices may or may not align with the public interest.

Thus, implementation as an extension of the policy process is then concerned with defining the public interest in action and deed, where policymakers have done so in ideas and words. Post-adoption, the public interest has been conceptualized, so the goal shifts to acting to manifest the public interest during public service delivery. Additionally, choices become decentralized as implementers make decisions based on the situations they face in applying policies to the real world. While decisions may start out narrow in implementation (i.e., focused choices and few policy actors involved), they become more complex as they flow away from policy adoption (i.e., open-ended options and an indiscrete group with decision-making power). This ultimately means that decisions during implementation take on a different character than those during policymaking. If one thinks of policy implementation as an extension of the policy process, then implementation is how the public interest is defined in action as implementers make choices in a complex array of situations. By virtue of this, implementation is change-oriented and political, and flows from policymaking, as opposed to being a mechanism for maintaining stability.

In contrast to public policy, if one thinks of public administration as associated with the tasks of maintaining public institutions. That is, activities that ensure the institutions of democracy are alive and well. These activities are inherently apolitical, stable, and focused on principles of governance. Implementers, then, become agents of institutions, who are responsible for ensuring their viability. Public institutions are those that are open to the whole of communities and by virtue of that openness impact how people engage in the ordinary activities of life, particularly those of political life. This, of course, means that institutions transcend any particular organization, law, or elected or appointed official. Rather, institutions are made up of a collection of these, and by extension, influence the norms of political, social, and/or economic society over the long term. The importance of institutions, particularly in a democracy, is to ensure that communities adhere to principles of good governance that exist independently of any specific policy or political debate. In other words, institutions persist where individuals and ideas come and go in order to protect the longevity of a community's way of life. By extension, administrative agencies serve as a reflection of the authorities and responsibilities of political institutions, designed to compartmentalize functions within specialized missions.

While administrative agencies engage in budgeting, hiring, and a range of other activities that are common to administrative operations, these are support functions that serve to indirectly advance agency missions that implicitly reflect their institutional responsibilities. For instance, the US Department of Agriculture's Food and Nutrition Service approaches the Supplemental Nutrition Assistance Program (SNAP) as a function of managing the food supply, whereas it would likely be implemented differently if it were treated as a component of welfare policy managed by the Department of Health and Human Services (Gritter, 2015). This means that policy carries the baggage of the organization that is implementing it, so that it is seen as just another function of the same mission, regardless of its original purpose. Implementation in this context becomes an exercise in trying to fit new policy directives into existing processes and practices. Doing so not only helps further the agency's core mission that buttresses the overarching institutions, but also ensures long-term stability. Institutions by their very nature are meant to create stability in political, social, and economic life by embedding a set of norms in people's routine interactions with government, the marketplace, and each other.

In general, administrative institutions push back against change and favor upholding status quos that are proven to be acceptable over time, in order to avoid the risks of alienating parts of the community. Public organizations are notoriously risk averse and bureaucracies are designed to reduce uncertainty by creating predictability pathways for decision-making. When risk is taken on, it tends to be costly, as administrators expend resources to avoid negative outcomes (Williamson, 1999; Brown & Potoski, 2005). This leaves the most common rationalization of behavior as "well, that's the way we've always done it." But this logic also buttresses administrators' roles as conservators of institutional forms, missions, and values that would not be easily reestablished if lost. This conservator role is in contrast to that of entrepreneurs, where administrative self-promotion, risk-taking, advocacy for radical change, and anti-traditionalist attitudes often conflict with democratic theory. In essence, preserving existing institutions is equally as important as building new ones, if not more so, and new is not always better, when new means altering the fabric of institutions. This places administrators as the custodians of shared values from which institutions are built, so that they cannot be easily corrupted (Terry, 1990, 1998, 2003; Terry & Levin, 1998).

At times, this puts administrators at odds with the public and policymakers, who want to see immediate change as issues catch their attention. Although one could argue that all choices are political in a democracy and administrators are political actors as much as anyone, bureaucrats remain neutral in order to preserve confidence in their ability to dutifully and faithfully execute the law. That is, it would be problematic to task someone who overtly lobbied against a policy with its success. While administrators may be asked to offer expertise on policy from time to time, they are expected to be guided by professional responsibility, organizational hierarchies, and the law, over personal politics (i.e., ideology, partisanship), when it comes to its execution (Levitan, 1942; Stewart, 1985; Overeem, 2005; Svara, 1998, 2001; Triantafillou, 2015). This is particularly notable for street-level bureaucrats who deal directly with the public and are distanced from the arenas where policy choices are made. In contrast to the inherently political nature of policy, administration sets a standard of unbiased, rational choices, even though it may not be fully feasible in practice.

Implementation as a component of maintaining public institutions is concerned with how policy fits into the existing organizational schemes proven to uphold the core values and principles of good governance. By doing so, implementation is inherently biased toward stability, rather than change, as administrators search for alternatives that produce the least risk, which often results in implementation of new policies following guidelines and practices already established within organizational rules and culture. Thus, policy-in-practice tends to reflect organizational missions and visions as much as the public interest. Further, implementation becomes less of an exercise in political decision-making and more of an exercise in finding the "best" way to go about the work of the people, so that operations efficiently and effectively achieve their goals. Implementation as administration takes the long view on how to execute the public interest, by favoring established ways of operating that are manifestations of institutional principles over the dynamic want for change that results from political processes. By virtue of this, implementation is stable and apolitical, and flows from institutions, as opposed to being a mechanism for change or a reflection of political choices.

So, how does this affect the practical functions of implementation? Implementation is about how status quos are constructed and deconstructed. There is an ebb and flow here, where on some occasions policy dominates how implementation is approached and on other occasions administration does. When administration dominates, implementation is concerned with upholding the status quo, so behavioral norms embedded in organizations become the framework for putting policy into practice. Administration is a powerful force tied to core public institutions and fortified by patterns of social, political, and economic life that have prevailed over the long term. Business-as-usual is held on to tightly, so it is not an easy task to break away from these status quos. But, at certain opportune times, policy dominates, and implementation becomes about change, where implementers look to policymakers for guidance and choices become political. Of course, those changes then become the new status quo, and embed themselves in organizations to influence how the next policy is implemented (Fowler, 2019b; Fowler & Vallett, 2021). Consequently, both policymakers and administrators are keenly interested in policy implementation, intertwining their responsibilities, and leading to conflict, competition, and cooperation as they navigate where one ends and the other begins.

As such, both policy and administration as fields of study claim ownership of implementation, to a certain extent, but neither places it at the center of the research agenda. For instance, policy scholars tend to examine policy implementation as a natural extension of policymaking and whether policy-in-practice is representative of public interest (e.g., Liang, 2018; Manna & Moffit, 2021); in contrast, administration scholars tend to examine implementation as it pertains to the process of managing institutions by putting implementation into the context of broader issues, such as performance or public engagement (e.g., Long & Franklin, 2005; Henderson, 2013). As a result, neither side sees the full picture of implementation as a push and pull of both policy and administrative forces, so it is treated as a peripheral issue by both. Taking the broad view of implementation, whereby it sits at an intersection, shines a light on why implementation plays out through the construction and deconstruction of status quos in behavioral norms, as "how it has always been done" gives way to change.

Using the Multiple Streams Framework to Examine Implementation

Until the mid-20th century, many scholars believed policy implementation unworthy of study, as it either happened so automatically that it did not warrant investigation or so complexly that it was impossible to study (Pressman & Wildavsky, 1984; O'Toole, 2000). To a certain extent, both are true. There is a bias toward status quos and repetitive behavior that occurs within the administrative branches of government, as well as within society as a whole, that makes policy implementation appear to be mechanized. Underlying this, though, is a complex array of cognitive, social, and institutional processes that shape how people respond to new or existing policies in any given situation. Key to this is understanding that the unit of analysis for policy implementation is decisions, specifically how decisions are made under ambiguous circumstances (Simon, 1997). That is, decisions made by an indiscrete group of policy actors (i.e., implementers) across institutions who must decide how a policy works when the written rules do not provide clear guidance, in the face of competing incentives, and with a high degree of uncertainty about what outcomes are likely to occur (Fowler, 2019b). Thus, a theory of policy implementation is a theory of how implementers make decisions when fitting the proverbial square peg of policy into the round hole that is the reality.

To this end, the multiple streams framework (MSF) provides a theoretical foundation of how policies are implemented by accounting for how status quos for policy-in-practice are built and then dismantled over time. While MSF has most often been used to explain why policies are adopted, this logic can be extended to also understand how an indiscrete group of policy actors make a series of decisions in the process of turning adopted policies into policy-in-practice. Specifically, MSF provides a structure to analyze how policy implementers sort through ambiguous situations when constructing policy-in-practice, or how the decisions they make lead to behavioral norms that are not always connected to policy-in-theory. Further, MSF can also help us understand why new policies are sometimes met with resistance to change and maintenance of status quos, while other times new policy leads to behavioral adjustments. As a model of decision-making under ambiguous circumstances, MSF is well suited to sorting through the key challenges of policy implementation: interpreting policy-as-written and plotting action steps grounded in the underlying policy-in-theory. But it can also further our understanding of the theoretical linkages that tie policy implementation to democratic governance, through the causal pathway that begins with the public interest and ends with social change. Thus, our theory also serves to address the missing links between policy implementation and the democratic foundations of government by parsing out how implementers make choices that both define the public interest and maintain public institutions.

From this perspective, rather than a well-oiled machine, policy implementation occurs within organized anarchies, characterized by ambiguity, so that who pays attention to what and when is the most important determinant of decision-making (Fowler, 2019b; Zahariadis, 2007). The key word here is "ambiguity." Ambiguity exists where circumstances can be interpreted in different ways, so that any two people may come to different but reasonable conclusions about the same situation. Often these ways of interpreting the same circumstances are competing, but not necessarily mutually exclusive (Herweg, Zahariadis, & Zohlnhöfer, 2018). While many like to view institutions and organizations as well-defined hierarchies or markets, in reality, complex sets of regulations create competing incentives layered upon each other over time, that push and pull policy actors in different directions (Cohen, March, & Olsen, 1972). It is, then, typically unclear what information is important, who possesses authority, and/or what the goal is. As a result, most policy actors are trying to make sense out of a world that is only partially comprehensible (Zahariadis, 2007), and are subsequently engaging in competition and/or collaboration in order to gain sufficient power so that others accept their preferred interpretation of these circumstances.

Within these organizations, three types of information become crucial for decision-making. First, problems, or conditions that are undesirable or differing from the ideal and that have attention from stakeholders. Where is the line drawn between an acceptable amount of air pollution or gun violence or joblessness and a problematic amount? Second, policies, or ideas for solving problems. Policy is by its very nature problem-oriented, whether that problem is explicitly stated or not. While policies may trickle up before problems are identified, policies serve as a mechanism to remedy non-ideal conditions through behavioral changes. Third, politics, or how stakeholders believe competing values should be balanced. For instance, should we prioritize preserving the environment or creating jobs? Of course, these streams of information are ambiguous in their own right, and may be interpreted differently depending on what one pays attention to (Fowler, 2019b, 2022; Herweg, Zahariadis, & Zohlnhöfer, 2018). At opportune times, known as policy windows, these streams can be coupled so that decision-makers see a politically acceptable solution to a problem that stakeholders are concerned about. But, for policy implementation, there is no culmination of a single decision. Rather, implementation plays out through a myriad of decisions made across a network of actors connected in various ways, where the decisions of one actor may or may not affect how others do their jobs. These interdependent decisions ultimately aggregate to form the behavioral norms that arise around an activity or problem (Fowler, 2019b).

At a micro level, this is a cognitive process that concerns how individuals make decisions every time they are faced with a question about how to apply policy. There are natural dispensations in information processing, known as cognitive biases, that lend themselves to quick decisions that avoid deep analysis of available information and that favor deference toward a status quo; however, people may engage in deeper, more complex thinking when triggered (Battaglio et al., 2019). Consequently, when conditions seem "normal," people tend to fall back on established ways of doing things, but when conditions seem "abnormal," people are more likely to engage in deliberative calculation of choices, which increases the probability that they will change their behavior. This is, of course, buttressed by the social and institutional environments that choices are made in. Socially, there is an inherent pressure to go along with others to build group cohesion and maintain social bonds, particularly among those that repeatedly interact within the confines of an organization. Furthermore, institutions overlay a set of formal and informal incentives and rules that encourage individuals to comply with a set of pre-defined acceptable behaviors, or face consequences for non-compliance (Hill & Hupe, 2014).

At a macro level, this is an interactive process that concerns how a network of policy actors turn collective choice into collective action. Here, a starting assumption is that as a class, implementers' chief concern is upholding the status quo by maintaining consistent behavioral norms surrounding how policies work in practice. Doing so usually leads to stability in social or environmental conditions, so that problems are unlikely to appear. If those conditions begin to change, there is a risk that policymakers will adopt new policies that shift the spotlight to implementers, who face challenges to their efficacy, legitimacy, or authority. To this end, implementers are generally predisposed to do things as they have been done before or as they are commonly done as experience tells them that it is acceptable to stakeholders. But when problems arise and there are politically feasible solutions available, policymakers use their primary tool (i.e., policy adoption) to send out new "ideas" to implementers. This then forces implementers to take on the burden of figuring out how to turn those new ideas into new actions (Fowler, 2019b, 2022; Fowler & Vallett, 2021).

Given that how policies are articulated in policy statements is rarely unambiguous, there is significant room for interpretation. While implementers tend to resist change and rely on policy interpretations that fortify existing ways of doing things, sometimes they are forced to consider new interpretations. This force often comes when there is a disconnect between policy and implementation, and policymakers, managers, or executives push implementers to address this disconnect. When this happens, the first stage in implementation is making policies "functional" by experimenting with different ways of doing things. Implementers refine these experiments by responding to feedback from stakeholder groups, with target populations being a key source, until they have determined the optimal mechanisms. Of course, what constitutes a functional policy may fluctuate based on the prevailing politics, problem conditions, and interpretation of policy statements. The next stage occurs at the organizational level, whereby these successful experiments in figuring things out are turned into rules and procedures. While making things functional is an exercise in navigating ambiguity, creating processes is an exercise in reducing the uncertainty in how individual implementers respond to any given situation. As such, rules and procedures are used to constrain decision parameters so that implementation decisions become more predictable. Ideally, if functional practices are turned into processes, behavioral norms are established that achieve desirable outcomes and, by default, become the new status quo (Fowler, 2021).

Once status quos are established, they are difficult to break away from. Subsequently, even when the problems, politics, and policy streams fluctuate individually, implementers are likely to uphold the status quo and continue to follow existing patterns when new opportunities to apply policy come up. That is, implementers can rationalize maintaining their behavioral norms when problems are worsening or public concern is increasing. But when both those conditions are coupled with a new policy adoption, implementers are under a substantial amount of pressure to adapt their behaviors or face attacks from other policy actors as the full attention of the policy system focuses on them. With a new policy, implementers first seek out and experiment with alternative ways of interpreting policies that match the local political and problem conditions. Once determined, those interpretations are institutionalized through rules and procedures. But to break away from established status quo, a drastic departure from normal politics, problems, and policy is necessary in order to trigger a wave of new thinking about what is acceptable behavior. Notably, without these specific circumstances, it is most likely that implementers default to the prevailing status quo, rather than risk "fixing what isn't broken" (Fowler, 2019b; Fowler & Vallett, 2021).

Thus, my theory of policy implementation adds theoretical depth to the complex and sophisticated process by which collective choices made during policy adoption become collective action on the part of an interdependent network of policy implementers, and how democratic governance forms a foundation for this process where citizens, policymakers, and implementers all play key roles. It also works to unite disjointed perspectives on policy implementation from public management, organizational theory, policy studies, and other related disciplines. In general, this theory is grounded on the assumption that implementation requires building and maintaining behavioral norms that can later be adapted when warranted by changing circumstances. However, this ultimately represents only part of a larger process by which collective choices become collective action and impact socio-environmental conditions of the surrounding world. Specifically, policy adoption and policy implementation exist as nested sub-processes of a broader process that is often referred to as "governance." There is an inherent codependency where outputs from one process feed into the other, so that it is impossible to separate action from choice or choice from action (and inaction) (Fowler, 2022). Consequently, this theory of policy implementation is also telling of how democratic governance works and why it often breaks down.

Outline of the Book

In this introductory chapter, I have laid out both the underlying reason why examining policy implementation is a worthy focus of study here, and provided a brief overview of my theory of how policies are implemented. In chapter 1, I discuss how ambiguity shapes choices and creates challenges when trying to fit policy into the real world, including what causes ambiguity to arise in different stages of the policy process and its utility as both a political and administrative tool. Ambiguity is a crucial theoretical component here in that it sets the stage for why policy implementers are often faced with difficult decisions about what policy means and what they should do about it. I also discuss how MSF imparts structure to the organized chaos that occurs during policymaking and policy implementation. In particular, I examine how the politics, policy, and problem streams as well as policy windows manifest during policy implementation, as compared to policymaking, in order to understand the conditions necessary for implementers to break away from existing status quos.

In chapter 2, I consider who policy implementers are and how they fit into a system of democratic governance, particularly as ambiguous circumstances often force implementers to make decisions about the nature and quality of public services. Of course, there are arguments for and against implementers having discretion to decide how policies work in practice, which is exacerbated by the growing role of non-governmental organizations (NGOs). Given that a key concern with policy implementation is how representation and responsiveness are weighted against efficiency and effectiveness, this chapter positions implementers in the broader democratic system and considers their responsibilities to citizens and to institutions.

In chapter 3, I examine the cognitive processes that occur at the micro level and how individuals search for and process information. Additionally, I show how cognitive biases often cause people to rely on intuitive judgments that reinforce doing things as they have always been done, but when faced with certain conditions, they engage in a more deliberative thought process. In chapter 4, I discuss how social processes and organizations create an additional layer of influence for implementer behaviors. I also examine how organizations are designed to guide people to certain information and ways of thinking and how managers leverage power to encourage people to conform to behavioral norms.

In chapter 5, I shift focus to functions and processes as the key mechanisms by which behavioral norms are built and maintained within organizations, and how both are designed to deal with ambiguity via experiments in functionality and more formalized process-building. To this end, I differentiate purposes behind functions and processes, the inter-relationship between the two, and their relative effects on policy outcomes. In chapter 6, I consider how policy implementation fits into the broader policy process as a function of democratic governance, and how such a model can help us understand the process by which policy choices are made and those choices become actions, and how those actions lead to social or environmental conditions. Finally, in chapter 7, I contemplate the implications of the preceding chapters on our broader understanding of public policy, public administration, and governance and what advice may be derived for both scholars and practitioners.

1

Adding Structure to Anarchy

One of the clearest signs that things are ambiguous is asking yourself with a sense of both exasperation and confusion: *what's going here?!?* Most policy implementers routinely find themselves doing so, and many times insert a few expletives to punctuate their feelings about once again dealing with a chaotic mess. Rarely, if ever, is what needs to be done or how to do it clear-cut or precise. Most often, things are vague and unclear, leaving one to expend considerable time and mental energy untangling the situation enough to come up with some plan to move forward. Herein lies the essence of policy implementation: trying to make enough sense of what is going on in order to decide what to do and how to do it. While that seems like a simple enough proposition, ambiguity means that situations can be thought of in many different ways and there is often no reliable way to know which is best, so making sense out of it is never straight-forward (Zahariadis, 2003). In most cases, conflicts and disagreement, both internally and with others, are unavoidable as people work through competing explanations for the same circumstances.

Implementers confront ambiguity every day as they figure out what to do in course of making policies work in practice. In trying to comprehend a world that is only partially comprehensible, implementers search for information and ideas on what to do and how to do it, but they must also be cognizant of the purpose of their actions and how those actions are likely to be perceived. Often, this leaves them without clear guidance on what is relevant or irrelevant information, so that who is paying attention to what becomes the most important determinant in in decision-making (Zahariadis, 2014). Thus, making sense out of ambiguity is really about decoding the world, or at least decoding the world to the extent that one can develop a cohesive understanding from which decisions can be grounded. Although people both actively and passively contribute to it, ambiguity is a natural phenomenon, as no one can be quite sure as to the objective relatively of anything they face; rather, all of human knowledge is grounded in a series of epistemological and ontological assumptions and empirical observations of the world (de Paulo, Messina, & Stier, 2005; Rosenberg, 2018). Of course, assumptions evolve and new observations are made, so our understanding of the world changes over time (Kuhn, 2012).

In turn, the meaning that one ascribes to events and how it guides choices also evolves. For instance, drug addiction was long thought of as a moral failing, so policy responses dictated punishment to discourage drug use. In recent years, thinking has evolved and drug addiction is now more commonly thought of as a mental health disorder, so policy encourages treatment to address the underlying problems (Schneider, Ingram, & deLeon, 2018). There is, of course, no objective way to gauge which way of thinking about drug addiction is more accurate or valid, and the debate may never be fully resolved. In either case, how one ascribes meaning to the causes of drug addiction drives how it is responded to, and how one responds to it builds the sociocultural norms that perpetuate ways of thinking about the world (Schneider, Ingram, & deLeon, 2018). The utility of the multiple streams framework (MSF) here is that it adds theoretical depth to these circumstances. While MSF was originally constructed in John Kingdon's *Agenda, Alternatives, and Public Policies* (1984), it has since grown into one of the most widely applied and debated theories of the policy process and provides a framework to understand how one goes about decoding an ambiguous world (see Jones, et al., 2016).

Where the previous chapter lays a foundation for why policy implementation is a compelling point of inquiry, this chapter considers the convoluted and confusing state of affairs that implementers face when ambiguity reigns. The goal of this chapter is to dissect where ambiguity comes from, and how it sets implementers up to muddle through decisions that determine how public services are delivered. To do so, I first discuss ambiguity as a concept in order to examine how it manifests during policy implementation. Then, I discuss the nature of organized anarchies and MSF as a mechanism for adding structure to chaos, and how MSF adds structure and depth to understanding what goes on during policy implementation. Despite the bad rap that ambiguity gets, it is not all bad, so finally, I discuss the pros and cons. The key takeaways from this chapter are that coping with ambiguity is about ascribing meaning to circumstances; and, once status quos are established under this understanding, implementers need a significant jolt to break away from doing things the way they have always been done.

An Ambiguous Concept

What is ambiguity? Ironically, most definitions are left ambiguous. While it is often used synonymously with words like "vague," "imprecise," "inconsistent," "unspecific," or "unclear," most definitions focus on attaching meaning to something, whether it be events, circumstances, or language (Cohen, March, & Olsen, 1972; Zahariadis, 2003; de Paulo, Messina, & Stier, 2005). Specifically, when something is ambiguous, one can never be quite sure of its purpose or significance, as there are multiple potential meanings but no clear indication of which is valid and/or accurate. In the simplest sense, one can think of ambiguity as occurring where there are different ways to think about the same phenomenon. Of course, this is different from a state of not understanding due to a lack of information or knowledge (i.e., awareness or familiarity), because that can eventually be resolved (Zahariadis, 2003). On the other hand, some phenomena remain ambiguous regardless of the amount of information available, or where information that would resolve the ambiguity will never be fully available (e.g., what killed the dinosaurs?). As a topic, it has been examined by social scientists in the context of decision-making (e.g., economists, political scientists, psychologists) as well as by linguistics and communication scholars examining the use of language as a conveyance of meaning and philosophers seeking "truth" in the world (e.g., Ellsberg, 2001; Zahariadis, 2003; de Paulo, Messina, & Stier, 2005).

For better or worse, ambiguity is inevitable in the human condition as meaning, in a philosophical sense, is often elusive and without a universality, particularly in a world shaped by social construction (de Paulo, Messina, & Stier, 2005). From a rational choice perspective, the limits on human cognitive processing ability also mean that one is often faced with situations that one cannot fully comprehend (Simon, 1997; Zey, 1998). Thus, with ambiguity, the act of attaching meaning involves searching for purpose or significance, as people process available information and knowledge. Since more than one meaning can be ascribed to these circumstances that may not be reconcilable in any practical way, one has to either continue in a state in which meaning is clouded or choose a preferred meaning without certainty of its validity or accuracy. This tends to create disagreement, confusion, and stress both for the individual and between individuals as they attempt to work through various meanings and come to some acceptable version that satisfies their interests, or acquiescence to a reality that makes no sense to them. Thus, coping with ambiguity is essentially the process of making meaning or searching to understand the purpose of a phenomenon in as far as it impacts the rationality and/or utility of decisions.

Of course, conventional assumptions of rational choice break down under these conditions, such as preferences being complete (i.e., one can always identify which option they prefer) or transitive (i.e., if option A is preferable to option B and option B to option C, then option A is preferable to option C) that allow people to calculate the optimal choice (Zey, 1998). Under ambiguous conditions, people's preferences are likely incomplete and may shift to the point where transitive properties no longer apply. Further, individuals must at least partially sort through ambiguous circumstances to narrow down decision parameters in order to effectively understand the best choice based on their interests. While some scholars question the utility of rational choice models under these conditions (Zahariadis, 2003, 2014), it is likely best described by bounded rationality, in which people are only rational based on available information and processing capacity (Simon, 1997). In other words, people are not choosing the optimal solution, they are choosing the optimal solution as it appears at that time. Thus, "choice becomes less an exercise in solving problems and more an attempt to make sense of a partially comprehensible world. . . . Who pays attention to what and when is critical" (Zahariadis, 2014, p. 28).

The concept of temporality becomes foundational here, as the sequencing of events is crucial to how decisions are made (Zahariadis, 2014). The dynamic nature of an ambiguous world often ensures that the meanings ascribed to phenomenon can be quickly replaced as new ways of thinking bubble up, shifting the context for choices. That is, things do not just happen because all the right elements are present; things happen because those elements come together in a precise sequence that creates connections that allow it to play out in a certain way. This underlines not just the serendipitous nature of how institutions operate, but also the importance of history within those institutions as status quos and existing precedents are often just as powerful as the contemporary dynamics between actors. Path dependency (i.e., evolving responses to changing conditions) and critical junctures (i.e., crucial moments in institutional formation) help account for both the gradual changes that occur in institutions over time and the radical departures that occur following dramatic events that reshape how people see the world (Thelen, 1999; Mahoney, Mohamedali, & Nguyen, 2016).

In this context, institutions are often described as organized anarchies, which is generally the state that most public and private organizations find themselves in when there is any degree of pluralistic interests, multi-level power structures, decentralized decision-making, and/or shared governance. Rather than a coherent system, organized anarchies can be thought of more as a collection of ideas and circumstances entangled by fluidity, multiplexity, and serendipity in how people connect and decisions are made (Cohen, March, & Olsen, 1972; March & Olsen, 2011). In other words, imagine a state of apathetic disorganization that has not completely boiled over into complete chaos, and then superimpose a logic of decision-making so ambitious individuals can achieve their goals under the guise of a shared mission. This is the quintessential form of an organized anarchy, and it perpetually teeters on the edge of collapse. While not all find themselves in desperate disarray, organizations tend to be described by this state of affairs to one degree or another, with the extent largely depending on the strength of the superimposed logic model and the power of individuals to convince others to follow their lead. Thus, some are able to create a sense of systems and structures that mask the underlying dynamics, but none are able to completely excise anarchy from their organizations.

This means that critical decisions may be triggered by irrelevant factors, and actions shaped by alternative logics tend to be used interchangeably (Christensen & Painter, 2004). Of course, this leads to paradoxes that are often left unresolved. There is also a certain degree of hypocrisy, as the relationship between decisions and actions becomes inversed and values, ideologies, decisions, and actions become misaligned. That is, "it is often wise to make decisions after the actions—when there is no uncertainty about which action has been taken" (Brunsson, 2007, p. 10). Decisions are, then, more than just choices about which actions to take; they are also about mobilizing organizational actors, distributing responsibility, and/ or providing legitimacy (Brunsson, 1990). Underlying these dynamics is a "logic of appropriateness" where "human action [is] driven by rules of appropriate or exemplary behavior, organized into institutions . . . they do what they see as appropriate for themselves in a specific type of situation" (March & Olsen, 2009, p. 2). But what one sees as appropriate may appear inappropriate to others, requiring a degree of collective norms and a shared vision in order to create consistency. Creating that consistency is a key role of organization, as a mechanism to channel collective choice and action into a reality that looks and feels the same for everyone.

Ambiguity contributes to this anarchy as participants search for meaning and are limited in their capacity to make rational choices (Zahariadis, 2003). Individuals that make up organizations are only able to partially understand the world in which they are operating, frequently leading to disorder instead of collective action. In general, there are three sources of ambiguity that fuel this state of affairs: problematic preferences, unclear technology, and fluid participation. First, people often do not have a precise idea of what they want or what choices will best serve their interests (Cohen, March, & Olsen, 1972; Kingdon, 1995; Herweg, Zahariadis, & Zohlnhöfer, 2018). This is not to say that interests are absent; it is just to say that they are unsure how those interests will be served by the parameters of a specific choice opportunity. Rather than entering decision-making processes with a clear idea of what they hope to achieve, they figure out their preferences along with the way and make decisions accordingly, so the end result is not realized until it is arrived at. Of course, this means that participants with problematic preferences are constantly searching for meaning, and by extension, can be manipulated into seeing any choice as aligning with the vague interests that they do have.

Second, technology in the form of organizational processes, rules, procedures, or practices is not always clear or understood, leaving participants to wonder how to do even the most basic things (e.g., how do I order new office supplies?) (Cohen, March, & Olsen, 1972; Kingdon, 1995; Herweg, Zahariadis, & Zohlnhöfer, 2018). This is exacerbated where experiments in different ways of doing things lead to alternative methods across organizations. Often under these conditions it is not fully understood how well any innovation performs in comparison to alternatives, so there is a lack of empirical data to support choices. Of course, managing performance under these conditions becomes highly challenging, as managers try to guide their subordinates toward desirable behaviors (Fowler, 2021). Furthermore, even if participants understand their responsibilities, they may not understand how those responsibilities interact with those of others or support organizational goals. Consequently, few people have a broad perspective of what is happening; instead, most only see the world based on their narrow responsibilities so they prioritize those over all others. On the one hand, this can lead to turf wars and conflicts between those who would ideally work together. On the other hand, organizational actors can often be guided to find meaning in their actions based on one's ability to rationalize contributions to the world.

Finally, participation is fluid as people drift from one decision to another, so one choice opportunity is rarely defined by the same parameters as the previous one. Individual organizational actors are likely to be faced with a constant barrage of new and different decisions. But turnover among employees is often high, and the public is quick to move on to the next issue that garners their attention (Cohen, March, & Olsen, 1972; Kingdon, 1995; Herweg, Zahariadis, & Zohlnhöfer, 2018). Thus, what is met with positive feedback one day may be met with negative feedback or no longer be of interest the next day. In general, this means that experiences from past decisions may not be fully applicable to future decisions; in fact, this may actually create bias by inserting irrelevant information into the equation. Essentially, while individuals try to ascribe meaning to circumstances in order to chart decision paths, the map is shifting along the way, again making it possible for them to arrive at numerous potential conclusions based on reasonable, logical thought processes.

The Multiple Streams Framework

Recognizing the perforating effect of ambiguity in policy processes, John Kingdon drew from Cohen, March, and Olsen's (1972) work on the garbage can theory of organizational choice to explain agenda setting in US national health, transportation, and fiscal policy, laying the foundation for MSF. Appreciating its utility in accounting for the dynamic nature of policy decision-making and its applicability across policy domains, institutions, governmental units, and nations, other policy scholars and political scientists have turned MSF into one of the most applied theoretical frameworks in policy studies over the last several decades. For instance, Jones et al. (2016) identified 311 peer-reviewed journal publications applying MSF between 2000 and 2013 across 65 countries and 22 policy areas (e.g., health, environment), with this trend increasing over time. Furthermore, Jones et al. (2016) also note that within this body of scholarship is the identification of new subcomponents (e.g., macropolitical developments in the political stream or issue opportunists as policy entrepreneurs) and efforts to integrate MSF with other policy theory frameworks, such as punctuated equilibrium theory or advocacy coalition framework. However,

Cairney and Jones (2016) argue that despite the broad, empirical body of work stemming from MSF, much of it only superficially engages with theory because of a low "barrier to entry." Thus, as prominent as MSF is, there is still room for continued application and development.

The basic ideas behind MSF is that within organized anarchies there are five structural elements that account for how decisions are made (see figure 1.1) (Kingdon, 1995). The first three elements are the problems, policy, and politics streams. Problems consist of conditions that deviate from the ideal as envisioned by policymakers and/or citizens and require government intervention to resolve (Beland & Howlett, 2016). Problems are inherently socially constructed, so conditions in one place may be perceived as acceptable while the same conditions in another place may not be (Schneider, Ingram, & deLeon, 2018); for instance, standards of living in the United States or Western Europe versus less developed nations in Africa or Asia. Notably, problems are a function of how issues are perceived and discussed in political discourse, so they are not necessarily objective, even when objective data is used (Herweg, Zahariadis, & Zohlnhöfer, 2018; DeLeo & Duarte, 2022). To this end, any condition

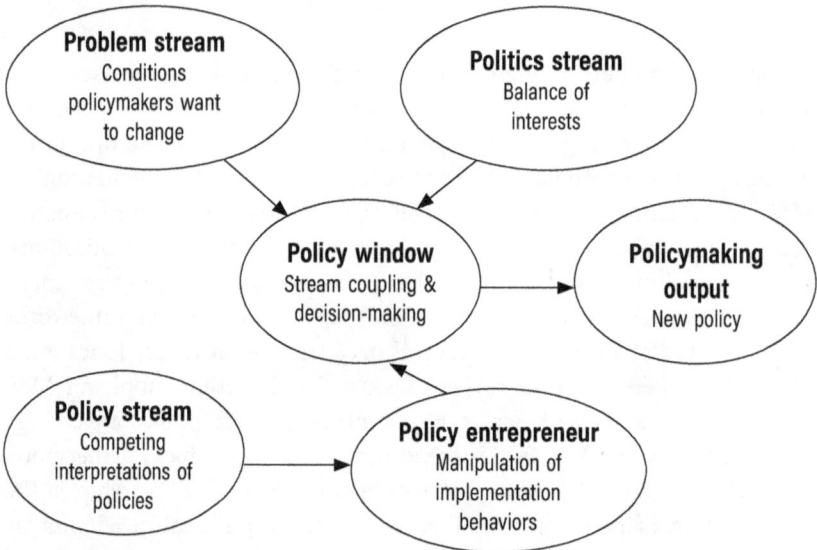

Figure 1.1 Diagram of MSF Structural Elements in Policymaking. *Source:* Herweg, Zahariadis, & Zohlnhöfer (2018).

may be presented as a problem if framed in the right light. Nevertheless, problems tend to be identified via indicators that reflect underlying qualities, focusing events that attract attention, or feedback about program performance, with indicators and focusing events as the most often cited catalysts in problem identification.

Indicators rely on objective measures to track trends over time and make comparisons across space, so that policymakers and citizens understand whether conditions are in fact "normal" (e.g., unemployment rates, violent crime rate) (Herweg, Zahariadis, & Zohlnhöfer, 2018). However, the proliferation of data around certain policy issues can obscure trends and contribute to the amount of irrelevant information available. Interestingly, DeLeo (2018) finds that as the number of indicators increases, so does the likelihood of an issue reaching the policymaking agenda, indicating that as more information becomes available, it becomes likelier that it will draw attention. For better or worse, indicators can also become politicized by entrepreneurs seeking to manipulate how policymakers understand conditions. For instance, DeLeo and Duarte (2022) find that there is a relationship between perceived threats to group interests, changes in indicators, and issue attention. In contrast, focusing events are unexpected, sudden, relatively rare, and potentially harmful events that cause attention to shift. Focusing events can be separated into three types: events that are common but unpredictable (e.g., hurricanes or earthquakes); events that are uncommon and novel so that they seem new (e.g., 9/11 terror attacks); and common events under uncommon circumstances (e.g., particularly brutal vehicle accident) (Birkland, 1997; Fishman, 1999; Birkland & Warnement, 2016). Unfortunately, some scholars have overreached in applying the concept of focusing events, which has obfuscated the term somewhat (Birkland & Warnement, 2016).

The policy stream consists of alternative ideas developed by policy communities (i.e., loose networks of public servants, academics, or consultants) about what should be done within the context of specific policy areas (Herweg, 2016; Herweg, Zahariadis, & Zohlnhöfer, 2018). Policy streams are dominated by experts who work to gain acceptance of their proposed ideas from other experts, as communities internally sort through what are scientifically and/or technically sound solutions. While the number of ideas floating around starts out quite large, ideas are filtered as experts discuss, modify, and debate them (i.e., softening up), so only the most viable receive serious consideration. This process is heavily influenced by the structure of policy communities, so that large, loosely integrated communities that are more competitive operate differently than smaller, tightly integrated communities that are more consensual. Additionally, policies must meet the criteria for survival: technical feasibility, value acceptability, public acquiescence, and financial viability (Kingdon, 1995). If a proposal is unlikely to meet any of these criteria, it is modified during the softening-up process or dropped by the policy community. There is also an element of path dependence here where proposals that diverge from previous paths face more difficulty in surviving (Zohlnhöfer & Rüb, 2016)—for instance, moving from a command-and-control regulation to market-based incentives for environmental protection. The policy stream is ripe when at least one proposal exists that meets the criteria for viability (Herweg, Zahariadis, & Zohlnhöfer, 2018).

The politics stream consists of the dynamic sociopolitical norms that govern what is a palatable course of action within a given community. This tends to be a function of different ways of thinking about how competing values, beliefs, and interests should be balanced. Kingdon (1995) likens this to the "national mood," or "the notion that a fairly large number of individuals in a given country tend to think along common lines and that the mood swings from time to time" (Herweg, Zahariadis, & Zohlnhöfer, 2018). However, some suggest that this is too analytically vague to be useful, while others have used variables like public opinion as an indicator (Zahariadis, 1995; Fowler, 2022). Most often, the politics stream is conceptualized around interest group campaigns or the ideological make-up of governments. Within the politics stream, actors tend to interact through bargaining or compromise building. In general, the MSF literature indicates that those making the decisions are the key element of the politics stream in that those who have the power to set agendas or adopt policies must be satisfied with the acceptability of any policy proposal (Zahariadis, 2003; Herweg, Rüb, & Zohlnhöfer, 2015; Herweg, Zahariadis, & Zohlnhöfer, 2018). These three streams represent the core groupings of information (both relevant and irrelevant) that drive how decision-makers see the world.

Nevertheless, one of the most controversial elements of MSF is how independent the streams are, and MSF is largely based on the assumption that streams develop and exist independently of each other. However, some scholars disagree, and argue that streams can be mutually reinforcing, where what happens in one stream affects the developments of other streams (Herweg, Zahariadis, & Zohlnhöfer, 2018). For example, Robinson and Eller (2010) found that a similar group of political elites participated in both problem identification and solution development in Texas education policy, so that which problems were identified may impact how solutions were developed. Given this, scholars have come to view streams as interconnected but enjoying a life of their own, where streams follow their own dynamics but are not unresponsive to developments elsewhere. For example, policies may be generated to solve a problem that does not exist, and politics changes regardless of whether policies have been adopted or problems solved, but often policies are developed with an eye toward what problems may emerge in the future. To this end, Herweg, Zahariadis, and Zohlnhöfer (2018) argue "the key is to specify when policy is in search of rationale," which requires distinction between the development of problems and solutions as a theoretical device.

The fourth element is policy windows that open at opportune times. During these open windows, there is a willingness among policymakers to consider new policy directions (Kingdon, 1995). This is in contrast to normal circumstances in which policymakers are likely to avoid making decisions for issues that are not ripe, so that the status quo is maintained until the time is right for change. How does a policy window open? During agenda setting, policy windows open through either problems or politics. In the political stream, windows open through turnover in policymakers, interest group campaigns, or shifts in the national mood, all of which bring attention to new ideas. In the problems stream, windows open from negative changes in problem indicators, focusing events, or feedback. Additionally, the more likely that problems threaten the reelection of policymakers, the more likely they are to open a window. Importantly, the emergence of a new policy proposals does not open windows for agenda setting. On the other hand, windows for policy adoption open in response to a proposal reaching the agenda. In all cases, windows are fleeting opportunities, so they must be taken advantage of promptly; otherwise, attention moves on to the next issue (Zahariadis, 2003; Herweg, Rüb, & Zohlnhöfer, 2015; Herweg, Zahariadis, & Zohlnhöfer, 2018).

The final element is policy entrepreneurs, who attempt to couple the policy, problem, and politics streams by manipulating decision-makers via framing and reframing ideas and information. As Zahariadis (2014) puts it, "in a world replete with ambiguity, the most important aspect of entrepreneurial activity is not to pursue self-interest but to clarify or create meaning for those policymakers, and others, who have problematic preferences" (p. 30). Policy entrepreneurs may be individuals with their own agendas or representatives of organizations, and in general, any actor with an interest in policy can become an entrepreneur. Nevertheless, access to policymakers and resources are predictors of success, so not every entrepreneur is effective. Policy entrepreneurs employ manipulation tactics, such as affect priming, using symbols to trigger emotional responses, or manipulating sequential decision-making (i.e., salami tactics) (Zahariadis, 2003; Herweg, Zahariadis, & Zohlnhöfer, 2018). In general, scholarship tends to indicate that entrepreneurs have a positive impact on the likelihood of policy adoption, particularly where they provide new or valuable information (e.g., Anderson, DeLeo, & Taylor, 2020; Arnold, 2021). But research also shows that a variety of strategies and actors are at work and their success often depends on their characteristics and activities as well as the broader context. In other words, there are few broad lessons that are universally applicable (e.g., Frisch-Aviram, Beeri, & Cohen, 2020; Frisch-Aviram, Cohen, & Beeri, 2020).

For instance, Arnold (2021) argues that entrepreneurs tend to fit three archetypes: 1) activists, who are highly active, display entrepreneurial characteristics (e.g., network building, knowledge brokers), and use a range of strategies; 2) advocates, who are similar to activists in terms of characteristics but are less active and tend to focus on one ambitious goal; and 3) concerned citizens, who are less entrepreneurial and lobby with only little effort. In general, activists and advocates tend to have a positive impact on policy adoptions, while concerned citizens are more likely to have no impact. Moreover, Goyal, Howlett, and Chindarkar (2020) contend that multiple entrepreneurs tend to be working simultaneously and serve different functions, such as the process broker, program champion, or technology innovator. In essence, policy entrepreneurs pounce on an opportunity to show decision-makers that there is a policy solution to a problem that has the public's attention and is politically acceptable to key stakeholders. Coupling the streams does not necessarily guarantee success, particularly if entrepreneurs use the wrong window to pursue their goals (Avery, 2004), but it does increase the likelihood of issues reaching the agenda or policies being adopted.

Of course, all of this hinges on two assumptions about policymakers: 1) individuals process serially while institutions process concurrently, so that many issues may exist at the same time but policymakers can only pay attention to a few at once; and 2) there are significant time constraints, so that policymakers do not have opportunity to adequately examine all decision parameters (Zahariadis, 2014). Decision-making is, then, a function of how attention, search, and selection are biased—more specifically, how attention is rationed between competing issues, how search for information and alternatives is conducted, and how selection is manipulated by framing ideas in a manner that allows policymakers to make sense of ambiguous circumstances. Thus, policy entrepreneurs work to push policymakers to pay attention to some issues over others, to find information that supports a certain way of thinking about those issues, and to select policy alternatives based on how they are packaged together with problems and politics. Basically, if choice is an exercise in who is paying attention to what, then policy entrepreneurs couple streams during open windows so that policymakers have a rationale to make decisions that fit the moment (Zahariadis, 2003, 2005, 2014).

Despite the enormous body of research applying and developing MSF, one of the key criticisms revolves around the ability to generate testable hypotheses. Particularly as social science methodologies have advanced in recent decades, critics are concerned that a significant portion of MSF applications are ethnographic descriptions or case studies that emphasize central themes, as opposed to the medium or large n-size quantitative analyses that provide empirical evidence of causal relationships (Jones et al., 2016; Rawat & Morris, 2016; Herweg, Zahariadis, & Zohlnhöfer, 2018; Engler & Herweg, 2019). Of course, Kingdon (1984) offered no hypotheses, and the metaphorical language used is "somewhat difficult to measure and seem to invite storytelling rather than rigorous empirical analysis" (Herweg, Zahariadis, & Zohlnhöfer, 2018). However, Herweg, Zahariadis, and Zohlnhöfer (2018) identify several hypotheses for both agenda setting and policy adoption that have emerged in the MSF literature in recent years (see table 1.1). The most crucial of these is the "coupling" hypothesis, which contends that agenda change or policy adoption is most likely if the policy, politics, and problems streams are coupled by a policy entrepreneur during an open policy window. Other hypotheses address how problems or policies emerge from their respective streams, how policy windows open, or what factors increase the likelihood that a policy proposal successfully advances, among other things.

Two other interrelated critiques of MSF are also common. The first is that the lion's share of MSF research focuses on agenda setting and adoption (i.e., policymaking phases) with few applications to policy implementation (Herweg, Zahariadis, & Zohlnhöfer, 2018; Fowler, 2019b). In fact, of the 311 peer-reviewed studies identified by Jones et al. (2016), only two specifically consider implementation (Riddle, 2009, and Aberbach & Christensen, 2014). As a result, MSF scholarship does little to

Table 1.1. List of Proposed MSF Hypotheses

Coupling hypothesis	• Agenda change becomes more likely if a policy window opens, the streams are ready for coupling, and a policy entrepreneur promotes the agenda change.
Agenda-setting hypotheses	• A problem broker is likely to be more successful framing a condition as a problem the more an indicator changes to the negative, the more harmful a focusing event is, and the more definitely a government program does not work as expected. • Policy proposals that fit the general ideology of a government or the majority in a legislature have a better chance of gaining agenda status. • If a policy proposal does not fulfill the selection criteria, the likelihood of gaining agenda status, and thus being coupled, decreases significantly. • As the integration of policy community decreases, it becomes more likely that entirely new ideas can become viable policy alternatives. • The policy window opens in the problem stream as a result of at least one of the following changes: change of indicators, focusing events, or feedback. • The more a condition puts a policymaker's reelection at risk, the more likely it is to open a policy window in the problems stream. • The policy window opens in the political stream as a result of at least one of the following changes: changes in legislatures, election of a new government, interest group campaigns, or a change in the national mood. • Policy entrepreneurs are more likely to couple the streams successfully during an open policy window if they have more access to core policymakers and they are more persistent.
Adoption hypotheses	• Policy adoption is more likely if the proposal is put forward by political entrepreneurs who hold an elected leadership position in government. • Policy adoption is more likely if the proposal is put forward by a government or majority party that is not constrained by other veto actors. • Policy adoption is more likely if different viable alternatives embraced by different actors can be combined in one package. • Policy adoption is more likely if the problem that the policy is supposed to solve is salient among voters. • The policy adopted will likely differ significantly from the original proposal if actors other than the government have veto power. • The more powerful the interest groups' campaign against the original proposal, the more different the adopted policy is likely to be.

Source: Herweg, Zahariadis, & Zohlnhöfer (2018).

account for what happens after policy adoption or how implementation further impacts agenda setting or adoption (i.e., via problems or through program failure). The second is that MSF has limited utility in examining governance in that governance includes both policy choices and execution, and by extension, it is difficult to distill practical guidance on how to better organize or manage governance processes when execution of policy choices is not fully accounted for. While MSF is very well developed in explaining what happens in policymaking bodies, thus far it has not offered many insights into how policies become practices; consequently, scholars have largely come to view it as only a theoretical framework for policymaking. However, recent developments prove that it is effective in explaining implementation and producing a broader model of policy governance (e.g., Fowler, 2022).

Implementation in Organized Anarchies

In response to the latter set of criticisms, there is a growing body of scholarship that extends MSF to policy implementation in order to close the loop on the policy cycle. For instance, Riddle (2009) examines how the problem and policy streams drive decisions on international cooperation in Burkina Faso, finding that the politics stream is only loosely coupled with the others, and Boswell and Rodrigues (2016) contend that different approaches to implementing policy targets in the United Kingdom are a function of the conditional effects that occur when streams are coupled. Additionally, looking at the roles of policy entrepreneurs in Greek higher education reforms, Zahariadis and Exadaktylos (2016) identify entrepreneurial strategies and political manipulation similar to behaviors seen in the policymaking process. Nevertheless, in most cases, MSF is used as a theoretical device to understand why implementation led to failure for specific policies, as opposed to focusing on theoretical development. Despite that, Howlett (2019) argues that using policy process theory, like MSF, is the best way for implementation theory to develop further. Importantly, my previous work (e.g., Fowler, 2019b, 2022) as well as this volume builds on these initial observations of how MSF can unpack the complex issues that occur in policy implementation.

While the basic structure of MSF can be applied to implementation, the specific dynamics of streams, windows, and entrepreneurs is different within the context of implementation than in policymaking (see figure 1.2). Given that policies already exist at this point, the policy stream is not made up of policy proposals. Rather, it consists of two components: 1) alternative ways of thinking about what policies mean and how those meanings are translated into actions; and 2) mechanisms for directing implementers toward a specific set of behaviors. Policies are often left incomplete, forcing implementers to use their discretion to figure out how to fit the policy into specific practical problems that pop up in the real world. Thus, the policy stream is partially made up of these alternative ways of interpreting policies and their meanings, and by extension, which actions are taken as a logical extension (Fowler, 2019b). In most cases, these interpretations follow the same pathways as policy proposals insofar as experts suggest ways of interpreting policies and how to efficiently or responsively put policies into practice. Implementers often learn what interpretations are acceptable, satisfy competing needs, and/or are successful over time via feedback mechanisms, either as result of individual experiences or through communication with other implementers (May, 1992; Lipsky, 2010).

Although implementers are somewhat independent, it is common for groups to engage in rounds of deliberations to align their behaviors

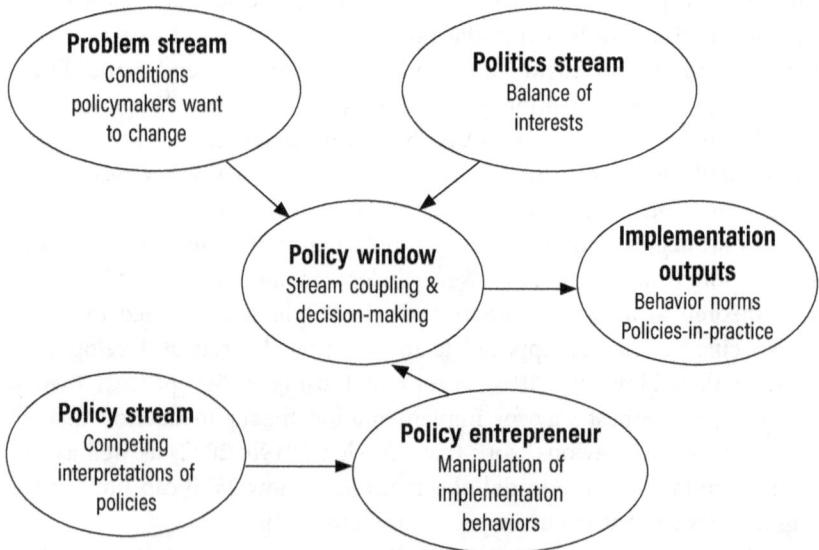

Figure 1.2 Diagram of MSF Structural Elements in Implementation. *Source:* Fowler (2019).

in order to reduce their individual risks by linking actors, resources, and strategies in interactive ways (Zahariadis & Exadaktylos, 2016). Of course, proposed interpretations must meet many of the same criteria as policy proposals in terms of technical, financial, and political viability, so that interpretations that do not stack up are dropped from consideration as implementers work through their options. In this way, groups of implementers function similarly to policy networks when it comes to vetting policy interpretations. Additionally, inherent in the policy stream are also mechanisms to constrain what alternative interpretations implementers consider (Fowler, 2019b; Fowler & Vallett, 2021). For instance, policymakers may use administrative procedures to create institutional barriers or organizations may use informal mechanisms, such as culture, to add layers onto the selection criteria to bound what options are perceived as viable (Wood & Bohte, 2004; Stazyk & Goerdel, 2011). The goal of doing so is to constrain discretion and guide implementers to behave in ways that are consistent with the preferences of policymakers or program managers. The policy stream during implementation is ripe for coupling when there is at least one viable interpretation available, but given that implementers have some autonomy, several interpretations may coexist. In the absence of viable interpretations, implementers will begin considering which alternative is the "least worst," while policies suffer from benign neglect.

The problem stream continues to consist of non-ideal socioeconomic or environmental conditions that are identified via indicators, focusing events, or feedback mechanisms. But identifying problems is much easier for implementers since policymakers have already signaled which problems have their attention, so implementers know what they should pay attention to (Fowler, 2019b, 2022). Bureaucrats inherently focus on what is being measured or monitored, so it is only logical that they would direct their efforts toward problems that policymakers are interested in, rather than seeking out new problems (Brehm & Gates, 1999). However, in order to gain a majority, policymakers often use one policy proposal to solve multiple problems, via mechanisms like package deals, which only serves to muddle how policies should be interpreted (Herweg, Zahariadis, & Zohlnhöfer, 2018). Additionally, policies do not always come with specific performance indicators, so implementers may decide for themselves which measures are the most important or how to construct their understanding of the problem (Chun & Rainey, 2005a, 2005b). Thus, the problem stream is a function of how organizations perceive the problem as much as how policymakers perceive it (Boswell & Rodrigues, 2016).

In any case, the problem stream also serves as a feedback mechanism for both implementers and policymakers; that is, if problems are solved, then policies are working.

The politics stream during implementation is an extension of the politics stream in policymaking, where it is subject to the dynamics of how political leaders and/or the general public mood continue to promote attention to certain issues. Normally, this is a function of competing values and balancing interests that shape how implementers ascribe meaning to policies (Fowler, 2019b). The politics stream may also include whether policymakers or citizens continue to be committed to the policy, which is particularly notable as attention fades after policies are adopted and policymakers move onto the next issue (Downs, 1991; Boswell & Rodrigues, 2016). Implementers must be politically aware and responsive in order to maintain support from governing coalitions, and avoid unwanted attention that may bring questions about performance and whether their choices align with the beliefs of the surrounding community. Thus, implementers are under pressure to be responsive to their environment; if not, they risk challenges to their efficacy or legitimacy, or renewed interest from policymakers who will continue to make policies until they get the response they want (Reed, 2014; Davis & Stazyk, 2015). As such, implementers are likely to shift behaviors if they sense the political climate is for or against certain actions, in response to public opinion, and/or when ideological preferences of elected officials change over time (Fowler, 2019b; Fowler & Vallett, 2021).

While no scholars directly take on the question of stream independence in implementation, most follow the mainstream assumption that streams remain independent before being coupled during an implementation window (Herweg, Zahariadis, & Zohlnhöfer, 2018). The caveat here is that implementation is also thought of a nested process that is interdependent with policymaking, so streams flow from one phase to the next (Howlett, McConnell, & Perl, 2015). Thus, streams during implementation may not be independent of streams during policymaking; rather, streams across phases may be fused together to a certain extent and create a degree of conditionality. For instance, the politics stream in implementation is tied to politics in policymaking, even if it remains independent from problems and policy (Fowler, 2022). Of course, the policy stream presents a more complicated situation since the policy stream during implementation results from coupling of streams during policymaking windows; therefore, it is difficult to say that the policy stream during implementation is completely independent of streams from policymaking. This creates a theoretical problem when parsing through stream dynamics, but one that is likely to remain unresolved for some time.

When streams are coupled during open implementation windows, implementers shift their interpretations of policy and develop new behavioral norms. This requires implementers to be presented with a new way of thinking about their responsibilities that solves a salient problem and does not draw ire from the community, during a time when policymakers and citizens have decided that the current way of doing things is no longer good enough and are paying attention to how policies work in practice. While coupling streams during open windows does not guarantee successful implementation, implementation behaviors are unlikely to change outside of these windows. This means that it should largely be expected that a commonly accepted interpretation of policy will dominate most of the time, so that behaviors are stable and consistent (Fowler, 2019b, 2022; Fowler & Vallett, 2021). Of course, this also means that conditions deemed acceptable are unlikely to become problems and behaviors are unlikely to be challenged on political grounds, so policymakers do not pay attention. Furthermore, "while implementers may be able to withstand challenges to the status quo from any single stream (i.e., shift in public opinion, focusing events), when coupled, implementers have no choice but to respond. Otherwise, they risk a breakdown of political coalitions, challenges to their legitimacy, implementation failures, or issues returning to the policy agendas as policy entrepreneurs shift pressure back to policymakers" (Fowler, 2019b, pp. 7–8).

The primary mechanism for opening implementation windows is through the adoption of policy, which forces implementers to make decisions about what to do in response. New policies create clear opportunities for implementers to reconsider behavioral norms around specific issues (Fowler, 2022). Of course, failure to couple streams during windows opened by policy adoption means that new policies will be either neglected or implemented passively as a byproduct of other activities, rather than active choices about the best way to operationalize that specific policy. Policy windows may also open, although far less commonly, as a result of changes in the politics or problems stream if policies already exist, where implementers rethink their interpretations as a result of emerging threats. Specifically, shifts in political coalitions or focusing events are likely to redirect attention back to old policies, which may lead policymakers to question the efficacy of implementers and/or adopt new policies. In either case, the implementation status quo comes under threat. To stave off these threats, implementers can shift their own behaviors and take the momentum out of the policymaking processes before there is an opportunity to investigate the situation and/or force changes. For instance, police departments may investigate an officer-involved shooting and roll out a community outreach program in order to create the image that existing status quos are salvageable. However, this requires savvy program managers to foresee the situation and develop quick responses.

Some scholars also make a point of differentiating between big and small windows in relation to the magnitude of potential change. Most often, this is thought of in terms of decentralized systems, where big windows are necessary to see changes across the entire system while small windows allow for changes to occur at individual implementation sites (Exworthy & Powell, 2004; Riddle, 2009). For instance, a big window is likely necessary for a wholesale shift in how US federal policy is implemented across states, where a relatively large group of implementers working across different organizations would need to realign behaviors in tandem. On the other hand, a small window would allow for a shift to happen within a specific state or local jurisdiction, while prior status quos remain intact elsewhere. Of course, this contributes to the likelihood that policies are implemented differently across implementation sites. Additionally, the big/little window concept may also apply to the magnitude of the change. Specifically, small windows are likely sufficient for tweaks to existing interpretations that follow the same logical pathway, but big windows may be necessary to abandon existing paths in favor of new ideas.

Policy entrepreneurs play the same core role in implementation as they do in policymaking insofar as their goal is to couple streams during open windows so that implementers find meanings in policy that leads to preferred interpretations (Fowler, 2019b). While scholarship on entrepreneurship in implementation is still unrefined, entrepreneurs want implementers to find the same meanings in policies that they do, so that practices reflect their view on the world. This also allots an opportunity to fundamentally alter the perceived purpose of policies after adoption. On the one hand, this means that entrepreneurs active during policymaking are likely to work to see that streams are not decoupled during implementation; on the other hand, entrepreneurs who are new to the scene or who were unsuccessful during policymaking are likely to attempt to decouple and recouple streams so that policy meanings change from their original intent. Although policy meanings found during policymaking are often carried forward into implementation, the same entrepreneurship strategies used during policymaking can be co-opted to decouple policies from problems and recouple them with new meanings. Of course, this is exacerbated by the entry of new groups of both entrepreneurs and decision-makers (i.e., implementers), so that no one is necessarily committed to choices previously made by other groups of policy actors (Zahariadis & Exadaktylos, 2016).

While some entrepreneurs focus exclusively on policymaking and others on implementation, there are also likely some that stick with the same policy throughout the process from agenda setting to adoption to implementation. To this end, elected officials may be particularly potent entrepreneurs in that their job description often allows authorities to have a voice in administrative decisions (e.g., legislative oversight). In any case, entrepreneur attention is focused on implementers following adoption in order to strategically manipulate decisions at that level. Entrepreneurs may also target program managers rather than individual implementers in order to co-opt organizational rules, structures, or cultures to achieve their goals. Often, this causes program managers to become de facto policy entrepreneurs as they try to guide their subordinates toward certain sets of behaviors. As in policymaking, manipulation is not strictly concerned with persuasion or pursuing self-interest, although those are components. The key aspect of entrepreneurship is to clarify or create meanings for those who are unsure or unaware of how to interpret information by highlighting certain aspects over others. It also must be remembered that implementers are ultimately the ones who decide whether an interpretation of policy is "good enough," even if they are the ones being manipulated by entrepreneurs (Zahariadis, 2005, 2014).

Previous scholarship already offers evidence to support the coupling hypothesis for implementation. Specifically, Fowler (2019b) states it as "Policy implementers continue status quos in implementation behavior by not altering their administrative decisions, but during open windows, implementation behavior is adjusted conditional to coupling of problems, policy, and politics streams" (p. 410). Using data from state implementation of federal environmental programs where core policies being implemented are consistent over time, findings show that if problems, politics, and policy streams reach extreme levels simultaneously, then policy outcomes experience non-incremental changes; but if any of the streams remain at mean levels, then policy outcomes experience only marginal changes. In general, this would imply that abnormal circumstances in all three streams lead to changes in how policies are operationalized, which manifest in changes in environmental conditions over time; but, absent those abnormal conditions, status quos are maintained in implementation, so environmental conditions remain stable.

In building on this work, Fowler and Vallett (2021) test the same hypothesis in the context of Erin's Law, which mandates a training program to educate teachers on how to properly identify and report child abuse. In contrast to implementation practices for federal environmental policies, which have matured and stabilized over decades, Erin's Law involves a new policy that brings with it not only new practices but also a reframing of job responsibilities (i.e., bigger focus on teachers' role as reporter of abuse). Here, findings show a large degree of instability in teacher reporting practices across states prior to Erin's Law, with teachers being sensitive to both problems and politics in absence of a consistent policy framework. After adoption, reporting practices became stable across varied implementation conditions, with reduced effects from problems and politics. Thus, the impacts of coupling streams existed before adoption as the absence of policy made it easier to manipulate how teachers interpreted their role. In sum, where Fowler (2019b) shows that coupling the streams leads to breaking away from the status quos established by existing policies, Fowler and Vallett (2021) show that new policies work to establish status quos and neutralize how much implementers are affected by problems or politics.

Is Ambiguity a Bad Thing?

The conventional wisdom from both scholars and practitioners is that ambiguity has almost universally negative impacts on the execution of efficient, effective operations of a democratic government. Those who are wary of ambiguity see inconsistency and unpredictability in implementation as a barrier to effective policy, and a reason that the public is often critical of the caliber of services provided (Pandey & Wright, 2006; Jung, 2014; Davis & Stazyk, 2015). Furthermore, many point to the normative concerns of whether elected or appointed officials are making crucial decisions about public services, and what that means for the quality of democracy (O'Toole, 2000; deLeon & deLeon, 2002). Of course, this camp also tends to view administration from a principal-agent perspective, assuming the only legitimate role of bureaucracy is as an agent of the political branches and that most bureaucrats are self-interested and predisposed to taking advantage of the system to benefit themselves (Wood & Waterman, 1991; Waterman & Meier, 1998). Thus, there is at least some assumption that because bureaucrats cannot be trusted, ambiguity is a problem. Underlying these criticisms is a wont for simplicity. Specifically, there is a belief that removing or minimizing ambiguity simplifies the process of providing public services, which makes it easier to both find ways to improve performance and to engage the public during decision-making.

But ambiguity should be thought of as a system feature rather than an anomaly to be corrected. Ambiguity is much more than some obstacle to be eliminated in the name of simplicity, as it can also be a powerful tool for dealing with political and administrative challenges, and it is inherent in our institutions. Most importantly, ambiguity is crucial to building consensus around controversial issues by allowing people to find meanings that they are comfortable with (Matland, 1995; Stazyk & Goerdel, 2011). Otherwise, controversy breeds conflict, and implementation grinds to a standstill as warring factions try to push their way of thinking onto others. Ambiguity also allows for decentralized decision-making, so that those closest to the people have the power to decide how policy-in-practice best serves a community's needs. In contrast, centralized decision-making reduces flexibility, which is particularly important as one thinks about the breadth of implementation decisions that occur across time and space. Additionally, this also means that ambiguous policy is more likely to create opportunities for administrators to be responsive to the communities they serve (O'Toole, 2000; deLeon & deLeon, 2002; Frederickson et al., 2015). In order for these benefits to be realized, one must embrace that one-size-fits-all solutions are not possible; rather, implementers must find the moral, conceptual, and practical meanings in policy that best fit their communities. Of course, no one exactly advocates for more ambiguity, but some certainly recognize that there are benefits to it.

Regardless of how one may weigh the relative pros and cons, it is imprudent to think of ambiguity as universally good or bad. Rather, ambiguity should be thought of in terms of which advantages and disadvantages its specific "flavor" (i.e., source, type) creates for the situation at hand. For instance, communicative ambiguity occurs through the application or misapplication of communication techniques, and it can often be remedied with follow-up communication to provide further context and information. While this may seem trivial, courts have spent a significant amount of time and energy arguing over the "letter of the law," and in most cases, ambiguity in policy starts with communication. One particularly egregious example is a 2017 court case in Maine concerning the ambiguity created by the Oxford comma in a state regulation for agricultural production (Willingham, 2017). More complex versions of ambiguity arise in moral, conceptual, and practical forms, though. For instance, moral ambiguity occurs where one may come to different moral or ethical conclusions about whether an action is right or wrong. There may be no better case study of this type of ambiguity surrounding bureaucracy than Hannah Arendt's (1994 [original edition 1963]) study of the banality of evil, examining the role of Nazis, mainly Adolph Eichmann, in the Holocaust. While certainly responsible for reprehensible acts, Eichmann, and others like him, were following orders from their superiors, orders that created their own ethical framework in which to view events.

In contrast, conceptual ambiguity occurs when different understandings of the same events result from the application of theoretical concepts or disagreement over which theoretical concepts apply. In either case, more than one logical conclusion may be valid based on its own internal merits. For instance, there is some disagreement among policymakers on the utility of supply-side versus demand-side (i.e., Keynesian) economics. While studies exist supporting the perspectives of both sides, there is no certainty in which forms the best basis for economic policy, leaving the issue ambiguous (Sowell, 2011; Wright & Zeiler, 2014). Thus, during an economic crisis, economists may come to logical conclusions based on their chosen conceptual understanding of the economy, and be in conflict over their recommended courses of action. Of course, conceptual ambiguity is also furthered by the misapplication or misunderstanding of concepts. On the other hand, practical ambiguity occurs when experience leads to different versions of the same practice. Since practical ambiguity results from experience, it is most likely to occur where people engage in repetitive tasks under different circumstances or experiment with different ways of doing things, so they develop coping mechanisms that may not be universally applicable (Lipsky, 2010).

Furthermore, there is a complex interaction between problematic preferences, unclear technology, and fluid participation that leads to these different types of ambiguity, so that most situations may be ambiguous but rarely are the parameters of ambiguity the same across multiple situations. While every organization faces ambiguity, it is often unique so no two organizations face ambiguity in the same way. Thus, when faced with ambiguous choices, one should start by understanding what makes the situation ambiguous and how that ambiguity can be leveraged so that other people's thinking drives them to behave in a way that leads to desirable outcomes. In other words, one needs to make meaning before one can make sense. Making sense is about rational thinking founded on clear understandings of problem parameters, so in order to make rational choices, one first has to decide what the purposes of actions are. But complete agreement among all interested parties on purpose or meaning is not necessary to achieve the same goals or to find benefit in the same course of action. This is at the essence of fitting the square peg into the round hole: figuring out what the purpose of doing it is so one can decide what to do and how to do it.

In sum, implementers are often faced with ambiguity where events or circumstances do not have a clear, consistent, or discernible meaning or purpose. While this can be confusing, it is not necessarily a bad thing for democratic governance, because it creates opportunities to match actions with the public interest. This occurs as implementers search out meaning to ascribe to ambiguous circumstances so that they can chart action steps. In other words, ambiguity means that the square peg does not always have to be square. This largely describes the challenges and opportunities of policy implementation, where implementers decipher what policies mean in the context of politics and problems. Consequently, ambiguity serves as the cornerstone of a broader theory of implementation as it lays the foundation for why implementers are faced with decisions and why those choices are often difficult and important; MSF then provides the tools for examining why status quos in these choices are constructed and deconstructed. In the next chapter, I turn attention to who implementers are and how they affect the quality and character of democratic governance. While ambiguity is a function of fluid policy communities, unclear technology, and problematic preferences, implementers face decision points because policymakers have adopted incomplete policies, shifting responsibility for making meaning to implementers.

2

Administrators, Citizens, and Democratic Governance

If policy implementation is a bridge between defining the public interest and maintaining public institutions, then who is responsible for building that bridge? One could argue that everyone in a democracy (i.e., elected officials, civil servants, citizens) is responsible, because they have equal ownership of both seeing the short-term interest realized and seeing institutions remain viable over the long term. But it is a maxim of group projects that when everyone is responsible, no one is responsible. One can certainly think of policy implementation as a big group project of which the results are exceptionally consequential for society. Of course, this is one reason it is difficult to understand why policies fail, since it is never clear who is responsible for what, as policy actors shift blame back and forth. While elected officials and citizens play their parts, civil servants are those most often tasked with seeing that policies are put into practice. However, policy implementation is only a subset of what public servants do, even if it is a vital function of administrative agencies. Furthermore, public servants are not the only ones who have power and influence over how ideas become actions.

One of the most complex constraints on policy implementation is that it is a function of democratic governance, so that many have an interest in what happens but few are performing the crucial tasks that it requires. In other words, while everyone watching may have ideas and opinions about the best way to fit the square peg into the round hole, only one person at a time can physically do it. But anyone who knows the frustration that comes along with performing a complicated task with someone looking over your shoulder also knows that those opinions and ideas are not always helpful. Of course, this poses the question of whether the role of implementers is to get the job done or to act out the ideas of others; that is, be effective and efficient or represent those who are not in the position to act but have an interest in the action. Ideally, these are not mutually exclusive goals, but sometimes they are in contradiction to each other (Meier & O'Toole, 2006; Peters, 2010). As implementers work toward the public interest as part of their role in public institutions, one has to think about whether their actions are a legitimate exercise of democratic authority.

In the previous chapter, I laid the foundation for understanding how ambiguity creates the core challenges of policy implementation; in this chapter, I turn to considering who are implementers and what role they play in democratic governance. The goal of this chapter is to conceptualize why implementation is foundational to democracy, and not just an afterthought of policymaking. To do so, I start with discussing where policy implementation fits into the causal pathway of democratic governance. Then, I consider the challenges of identifying policy implementers when there are many people who contribute to implementation but few whose focus is squarely on it. Of course, this has been exacerbated by the hollowing-out of government as public service delivery has been shifted away from public agencies and policies are now following a more complicated path from adoption to practice. I also examine how ambiguous policies force implementers to use their discretion, the pros and cons of appointed administrators being delegated authority over policies, and the roles and responsibilities of citizens in this process. The takeaway from this chapter is that policy implementers include a large, diverse group of people with the power to make choices about how policies work in practice, serving as key mechanisms for connecting the public interest, public institutions, and policy impacts on society in a system of democratic governance.

A Causal Pathway of Democratic Governance

Implementers' roles as agents of democracy in governance hinge on their ability to make choices during public service delivery. As democracy is a system based on rule by the people, the issue at hand is whether the what, when, where, and how of public service delivery reflect the will of the people, either directly or indirectly. By making choices that affect the quality and character of public services, implementers become as much of a part of the governance system's capacity to represent the needs and wants of citizens as the choices made by elected leaders. In other words, choices are key here, regardless of who makes them. However, accountability for implementers often follows a more complex pathway than that of elected officials, because they do not stand for election and citizens rarely, if ever, have the ability to directly judge the efficacy of their choices. In the previous chapter, I described how the multiple streams framework (MSF) accounts for the hows and whys of decision-making among both policymakers and policy implementers, and in the following chapters, I will add further theoretical depth to this. But, first, let us map out two pathways of democratic accountability, a direct path and an indirect path, that place implementers squarely within the system of democratic governance.

The core components of both pathways are the same: citizens have wants and needs that aggregate to form the public interest; policymakers formulate and adopt policy to see the public interest manifest in action by the government; and implementers put those policies into practice. Inherent in both pathways is also the assumption that when policymakers formulate and adopt policies, they clearly articulate the items in which there is consensus, but there are also instances where policymakers leave items ambiguous when they cannot find agreement (Zahariadis, 2007; O'Toole, 2000; deLeon & deLeon, 2002; Fowler, 2022). In turn, this requires implementers to use their discretion to make choices about how best to put into practice the theory behind the policy-in-writing. Where the two pathways diverge is how citizens, policymakers, and implementers are connected. If one follows the direct pathway, then democracy follows an ordered process from citizens to policymakers to implementers, where policymakers make policy to represent citizens and implementers execute those policies. By extension, implementation choices, then, hinge solely on what policymakers intended when formulating policy-in-theory, so that the actions that implementers take should serve to align policy-in-theory with policy-in-practice. This is simple, direct, ordered, and based on a conventional view of democracy (Wood & Waterman, 1991; Frederickson et al., 2015).

In contrast, if one follows the indirect pathway, then one must also recognize the inherent connection between citizens and implementers that does not require policymakers as an intermediary. Citizens and implementers often interact at the precipice of where policies are applied; this is particularly true for street-level bureaucrats who serve on the front lines of organizations and directly deliver public services. From this perspective, implementers must also account for the needs and wants of the specific citizens they are serving in the moment, and not just consider the abstract ideas that policymakers have pressed upon them. In other words, it is not simply a question of how policy-in-theory aligns with policy-in-practice as an aggregate set of behavioral norms, but also a question of how policy-in-theory aligns with behaviors in specific instances and whether those behaviors represent the intents of policymakers and/or the will of the people. Notably, rather than only responding to policymakers, implementers also must consider whether policymakers made a bad policy and how to correct for that during implementation (O'Toole, 2000; Hupe & Hill, 2007; Lipsky, 2010). On the one hand, this creates additional mechanisms by which citizens can find representation and strengthen democracy; on the other hand, it complicates the process of democratic accountability by opening the door to competing pressures on implementation choices that leaves implementers as the deciders of what is best (Hupe & Hill, 2007; Voorn, van Genugten, & Van Thiel, 2019).

Importantly, these pathways are not mutually exclusive and do not necessarily compete with each other. In fact, they can be mutually reinforcing, especially when the intents of policymakers are aligned with the public interests. Implementers only find themselves in a position to choose between competing pressures when policymakers are at odds with citizens. Unfortunately, this does happen more than one would hope, as policymakers must consider how to maintain public institutions in the long-term public interest in addition to dynamic public interest in the short term, while citizens are likely only concerned with the latter. In either case, how implementers are making choices becomes essential to the democratic character and quality of governance, particularly where policy-in-theory and policy-in-practice become disconnected. Of course, disconnects between the two can lead to both positives (e.g., better representation, better policy outcomes) and negatives (e.g., worse representation, worse policy outcomes). In either case, it is imperative to understand that how and why implementers are making decisions impacts democratic governance in big ways, for which MSF provides theoretical depth.

What's an Implementer? Who's an Implementer?

Now that we understand where implementers fit into democratic systems, let us further consider who they are as a group. One of the most pressing questions of examining policy implementation is: when someone says "policy implementer," who are they talking about? To this end, let us think about policy and administration as involving four major types of actors: policymakers, policy implementers, program managers, and policy entrepreneurs (Zahariadis, 2003; May & Winter, 2009). First, policy implementers are those whose primary job responsibilities involve putting policies, formulated and adopted by others, into practice. While almost every public servant essentially serves as a policy implementer to one degree or another, implementers most often take the form of street-level bureaucrats who are directly applying policy as they interact with target populations during public service delivery. Policymakers and policy implementers represent the key division between policy phases in that one group engages in collective choice and the other in collective action. Rarely do policymakers' and policy implementers' roles and responsibilities overlap, so that these are largely two distinct groups of actors. Notably, this means that implementers typically do not have direct knowledge of the agenda-setting or formulation stages of policymaking; instead, their knowledge of what choices have been made about the public interest is often secondhand (Nakamura, 1987; Fowler, 2019b).

Second, policymakers are those vested with authority to make choices representing the public interest and directing public institutions; typically, policymakers operate as part of a group decision-making body, such as a legislature. Third, program managers serve as intermediaries between policymakers and implementers. They do not typically interact with the public or directly provide services; rather, they supervise and organize a group of implementers working on a series of interrelated policies (i.e., a program). As such, they make decisions about how implementation should work when developing guidance for their subordinates, so they are involved in turning policy into practices by indirect means. Additionally, program managers are often called on to advise policymakers on the challenges that are likely to arise during implementation (Svara, 1998; Howlett, 2011). As organizations become more complex, there is an increase in the layers of management, placing a distance between those at the top (i.e., senior executives) and bottom (i.e., street-level bureaucrats) of agencies. This means that executives may sometimes be thought of as their own class of actor, particularly in large organizations. In general, program managers are neither implementers nor policymakers in a strict sense, which warrants separating them as a group distinct.

Fourth, policy entrepreneurs are those who do not have formal authority to make decisions about policy, but try to exert influence over those policymakers, policy implementers, or program managers that do. Of course, policymakers, program managers, or even policy implementers play entrepreneurial roles at times, but entrepreneurs are often those without a formal responsibility as it relates to a specific policy. For instance, program managers often use their authority over subordinates to guide how policies are interpreted, so entrepreneurship is inherent in their job responsibilities. However, those who are strictly entrepreneurs are actors who try to influence thinking from the outside. Most obviously, this would include lobbyists or public advocates, but citizens may also serve as entrepreneurs on a smaller scale as they plead their own case to implementers. When operating on a broad scale, entrepreneurs typically try to position themselves as power brokers in order to influence what decisions get made both when adopting policy and later when that policy is put into practice (Zahariadis, 2003; Herweg, Zahariadis, & Zohlnhöfer, 2018). Notably, these four categories are not mutually exclusive, and actors may shift back and forth depending on the specific tasks or responsibilities they are engaging in at the time. But separating actors into these four categories is a heuristic that aids in understanding the different groups that bring pressure on how implementers think about policy.

Of course, policy does not happen in a vacuum and, typically, any policy actor is involved with more than one at a time and countless over their careers, creating multiplexity in their roles. Most importantly, policy implementers are not tasked with just implementing a single policy at a time; they are often responsible for implementing multiple interrelated policies as part of a program. For example, a police officer who pulls over a driver for speeding may also check for other violations of the law (e.g., intoxication) as part of public safety programming. Additionally, it is not uncommon for an implementer to play a manager or entrepreneur role at the same time. For instance, a senior park ranger may serve as an implementer for wildlife management policies but have supervision of other rangers creating a managerial role too; she may try to influence how others outside her chain of command behave as well. Thus, implementation of a single policy is often just an aspect of any individual's larger responsibilities.

This means that almost all public employees implement policy as part of their job, even if few view policy implementation as their primary job function. For some, implementation is a means to an end; for others, it is an end unto itself. A key issue here is whether job functions are a product of policy or policy is a byproduct of a job function. For instance, an accountant implements numerous government policies on appropriate accounting practices in the process of serving their core job function of tracking financial transactions; in contrast, an environmental inspector's core job is seeing that private enterprises comply with environmental safety policies. Thus, there are two ways in which actors engage in implementation: 1) performing a function that exists independent of any policy but by which policy is implemented as a byproduct; and 2) performing a job that exists only because of a policy. Of course, this links back to the difference between implementation as administration versus implementation as policy. While one can lump both of these groups together when examining implementation, it is worth noting that many policy implementers likely do not view implementation as their primary job responsibility.

Policymaking and Administrative Discretion

Although the concept of an organized anarchy (see chapter 1), most readily applies to formal organizations, it also largely describes how policymaking works as an institutional process of decision-making, where policymakers function in an ambiguous world. Of course, this is the basis of MSF. From this perspective, it is assumed that policymaking institutions that include actors both inside and outside of government suffer from the same sources of ambiguity as more conventional organizations, so they too can be viewed as organized anarchies. Specifically, turnover in elected and appointed officials is high, policy alliances are shifting, and target populations are fluid; it is not always clear or understood who has authority over policies addressing problems that transect conventional jurisdictions or how policies can be turned into action; and policy actors do not always have a firm grasp over what they want or how proposed policies may fit their interests (Kingdon, 1995; Herweg, Zahariadis, & Zohlnhöfer, 2018). Complicating matters, policymaking requires a group of policy actors to come to a compromise in order to find enough consensus (e.g., majority rule) to adopt a policy.

While ambiguity can create disagreement on how to see things, it can also create agreement if actors are allowed to work through perspectives until they find one that rationalizes their support of a policy. In other words, if policymakers are forced to view everything the same way, there will be disagreement over which meaning among alternatives is optimal; but if they are allowed to find their own meanings among alternatives, they are more likely to find one that allows for compromise to be built. That is, policy can make strange bedfellows if people use their imaginations. Thus, in order to find consensus, policymakers often leave ambiguity in policies, rather than outright ascribe direct and clear meanings that can be used to guide implementation (Page, 1976; Zahariadis, 2003; Herweg, Zahariadis, & Zohlnhöfer, 2018). These policies are "incomplete" in that they have yet to fully address every issue that affects how the policies will function, leaving decision points for later. An incomplete policy, then, can be thought of as a building that is missing doors or windows or floors; it may have the structural components that make it look like a building from the outside, but from the inside, it is missing key pieces that make it a functional space.

By leaving ambiguity in policies, policymakers are fundamentally shifting the responsibility for dealing with it to implementers, where each point that can be interpreted in different ways requires a decision. Political institutions empower administrators with discretion to make these choices in lieu of policymakers, which creates the foundational problems of policy implementation (i.e., how and why implementers make choices) (West, 1984; Holzer & Yang, 2005). Ambiguity is inherent in organizations, but policy provides the decision points that allow it to influence behaviors. Hence, incomplete policies are a significant point of concern here, as the points of incompleteness shape the nature of implementation choices. While ambiguity can never be removed from organizations, policies that are complete minimize the number of decision points that implementers face. Although ambiguity cannot be removed from the equation, how many times it is added in can be reduced. Complete policies tend to: be written; rely on a logical and clear means–end pathway; include authorities that allow for optimal control over the problem parameters; be consistently applicable to a well-defined target population as a class; and rest on a clear purpose produced by consensus (DeHart-Davis, 2009a, 2017). Policies that lack one or more of these elements are incomplete insofar as decision points emerge related to the lacking elements, forcing implementers to deal with them later.

These decision points may be skipped over during the policymaking process in order to create the level of compromise necessary for the policy to be passed, or they may be unintentionally overlooked. Unsurprisingly, there are themes that appear in incomplete policies, such as those that are informal, do not create a categorical imperative, have internal or external conflicts, or have an ill-defined purpose (see table 2.1) (Empson, 1966;

Table 2.1. Common Types of Ambiguous Policies

Incompleteness	Example
Informal	Unwritten rules
No categorical imperative	Exceptions to the rule Rules made for the exceptions
Internal or external conflicts	One policy for more than one purpose More than one policy for one purpose
Purpose ill-defined	Purpose is hidden or obscured Purpose changes or becomes antiquated Self-fulfilling purpose

Source: Author.

DeHart-Davis, 2009a, 2017). A simple example is with informal policies where the policy in itself is never completely communicated to all parties responsible for acting on it. This leads to a rather complex game of "telephone" where implementers try to relay what they remember about the policy to the next person in line, which over time leads to distortion as the real meaning and intent of the policy is lost through the process of communication. Some informal policies also emerge through a series of unwritten rules because they are based on a rationalization that policymakers or administrative leaders are hesitant to put in writing, creating other ambiguities. For instance, many Jim Crow–era policies in the Southern US were left unwritten to give governments a legally defensible position in regards to racist intents of their implementation practices, leaving implementers to work through what the policy means in moral, conceptual, and/or practical terms (Berrey, 2015).

Additionally, unambiguous policies universally pertain to target populations as a class, so that implementers are left little discretion about when or where the policy applies; in contrast, policies made based on rare or exceptional circumstances (i.e., rules made for the exceptions) or that leave rare or exceptional circumstances unaccounted for create a decision point about how the policy applies (i.e., exceptions to the rule). For instance, while mask mandates in response to the COVID-19 pandemic seem straightforward, there can be some complications in understanding when and where masks are required (e.g., indoor vs. outdoor, public vs. private property, maintaining social distance), as opposed to creating a universal requirement that masks be worn at all times and places (e.g., Executive Office of the President, 2021). This produces a significant degree of conceptual and practical ambiguity, forcing implementers to decide when and where wearing a mask fits the intents of the policy and which cases are exceptional enough to be exempted. Of course, when target populations are adversely impacted, there are likely to be attempts to manipulate how implementers see the situation in order to affect enforcement (Schneider, Ingram, & deLeon, 2014).

Unambiguous policies are also free of internal or external conflicts that force implementers to make decisions about how to balance competing interests. Specifically, internal conflicts tend to emerge where one policy tries to serve more than one purpose; external conflicts, where more than one policy serves the same purpose. For instance, state policies to diversify electricity production sources are meant both to protect the environment and as a mechanism for economic planning, while both the environment and the economy are also regulated by other local, state, and federal policies (Fowler, 2015; Fowler & Johnson, 2017). So, what happens when these purposes or policies force implementers to prioritize one above the other(s)? These may be among the most ambiguous of policies. Both internal and external conflicts can lead to communicative ambiguity where implementers try to work through the policy language in search of any indication of which purpose or policy takes precedence; moral ambiguity as implementers consider which purpose carries a heavier moral importance; conceptual ambiguity as implementers try to figure out the logical framework that makes sense of the conflicts; or practical ambiguity as implementers try to reconcile the conflicts through practical mechanisms.

Similarly, unambiguous policies have well-defined and clear purposes that make it easy for implementers to understand what they are meant to do. In contrast, ambiguous policies tend to have hidden or obscured purposes, a purpose that has changed or become antiquated so that its original meaning is no longer applicable, or a self-fulfilling purpose. For instance, Southern states in the Jim Crow era often used poll taxes and literacy tests to disenfranchise minority voters in the guise of election integrity. Many of the same states also still have so-called blue laws (i.e., laws passed to restrict an activity for religious purposes, particularly to support a day of worship), such as dry counties or no Sunday alcohol sales, even though the original purposes have been lost as social mores have evolved (Lovenheim & Steefel, 2011; Wallenstein, 2005). Possibly the biggest sinner here are policies whose purpose is to do something just to do it, without a severable way to measure success or understand meaning. For instance, most education policy seems to be tied chiefly to producing an educated populace (i.e., educating to educate), so implementers are left to search for further meaning, impacting how they view it (e.g., educating citizens, educating economic actors). Consequently, implementers must unravel the moral, conceptual, and/or practical ambiguity as the search for purpose.

Regardless of which form they take, ambiguous policies require implementers to exercise discretion, which exists due to an implicit or explicit delegated authority to make choices about the execution of policy. This means that policies-in-practice hinge on how implementers use the discretion at their disposal; this is particularly important at the street level, as it is the primary vector from which citizens obtain access to public services. Thus, many would argue that administrative discretion is one of the most problematic issues of government, because it has seeped into almost all functions and there are few tools available for controlling how it is used (Epstein & O'Halloran, 1994; Holzer & Yang, 2005; West, 1984). Although organizations can take steps to structure choices to increase the likelihood they will follow designated pathways (West, 1984), "as decisions become more complex, it is more difficult to predict the manner in which discretion will be exercised" (Sowa and Selden, 2003, p. 702). This is further complicated by coping mechanisms used by administrators to deal with the stress and confusion that organized anarchies create. While they take on different forms, coping mechanisms serve as simple decision rules that provide a means for administrators to make choices without fully contemplating the gambit of communicative, conceptual, moral, or practical meanings that may impact their decisions (Lipsky, 2010).

For instance, a traffic officer may set an informal decision rule to stop any driver who exceeds the speed limit by 4 mph or a district attorney may offer a standard plea deal to any defendant charged with a specific crime, regardless of the confounding factors. In both cases, it saves the cop and the district attorney from having to go through the stressful process of considering ambiguous situations over and over again. Instead, it creates a shortcut that conserves cognitive resources by anchoring all of their future decisions (Lieder et al., 2018). Coping mechanisms then become an integral part of the policy-in-practice as they shape the normal behaviors surrounding implementation. Typically, coping mechanisms are informal and are constructed individually by implementers, although they may learn from each other about what works. Of course, the need for coping mechanisms increases as decisions become more complicated by volatile, complex, and/or uncertain circumstances that add dimensions to decision calculus. Thus, by leaving decision points in policies, policymakers are essentially opening the floodgate whereby crucial choices about public service delivery are made by implementers, rather than by legislators, and the more ambiguity, the less likely that implementers will behave as expected and/or the more likely they are to construct their own coping mechanisms.

Democratic Accountability

Now that there is a stated conceptualization of who implementers are and why they play a critical role in democratic government, let us further consider how they are held accountable for their choices; specifically, to whom are implementers accountable? By definition accountability suggests "a liability to reveal, to explain, and to justify what one does" (Scott, 2000, p. 40). Similar to other definitions (e.g., Mulgan, 2000), this implies that accountability involves a social exchange by which one party is asserting authority to impose obligations over another party who is responsible for carrying out those obligations. For example, one can think of elected officials as being brought to account for their policy decisions through routine elections by citizens, who ultimately wield the sovereign authority in a democracy. Of course, in a representative democracy, citizens delegate their authority to elected officials so that decisions can be made for them in the name of orderly and efficient government operations. In contrast, the pathway for accountability for implementers is more complicated, since most implementers are appointed and never stand to be directly judged by citizens for their decisions or job performance. Rather, implementers tend to be held to account by elected officials, or by program managers who answer to elected officials. Certainly, this obscures accountability for policy failures, where citizens hold elected officials accountable and elected officials hold implementers accountable.

Conventional thinking about bureaucracy tends to frame bureaucrats as agents of the political branches of government. For instance, legislatures, stocked with members elected to represent the interests of their constituencies, pass laws and bureaucrats execute those laws with deference to the elected officials who appointed them. This creates a simple, direct causal pathway of democracy, from citizens to elected officials to appointed officials, so that the preferences of citizens are distilled into cohesive ideas by legislators and then dutifully put into practice by bureaucrats. While this is was once a popular perspective in political science and public management, there is a significant body of work on political control of the bureaucracy that exposes how the integrity of this pathway begins to break down. Specifically, it assumes that the key decisions are made by legislators, bureaucracy is simply a "machine" that executes those decisions without need of higher-level thought, and elections and elected officials are the only mechanism for citizen representation (Cook & Wood, 1989; Wood & Waterman, 1991; Waterman & Meier, 1998; Frederickson et al., 2015). But since policies as adopted are often left incomplete, crucial decisions about public service delivery are left to bureaucrats, who in turn can also make decisions to represent citizens.

This places significant power in the hands of street-level bureaucrats, wielding discretionary power to make decisions on behalf of the government within confined situations. While bureaucrats see themselves as both professionals and public officials, they also have to find ways to manage their overwhelming workloads, creating competing incentives for their time and attention (Lipsky, 2010). This sets up what Hupe and Buffat (2014) term the public service gap, or "the differences between what is expected of public servants working at the street level (on the 'demand side') and what is given to them (on the 'supply side')" (p. 549). In other words, street-level bureaucrats are tasked with bridging the gap between citizen demands and government allocations (e.g., policies). Accountability in how those choices are made, then, occurs within the context of micro-networks that connect actors across administrative layers, and judgment of peers become an important issue as one's social or political capital within the organization is impacted by how others view one's choices and/or perfor-mance. This leads to different avenues and types of accountability across complex organizations that are clustered together and layered upon one another, so that street-level bureaucrats practice multiple accountability beyond the simple, direct relationships with citizens or their supervisor (Hupe & Hill, 2007; Hill & Hupe, 2014).

Of course, this also spurs some rethinking of the relationship between policymakers and policy implementers in order to place a bigger emphasis on the power and authority of administrators, particularly those at the street level, to make policy choices that affect both how government provides public services and how citizens interact with their government (e.g., Hjern, 1982; Lipsky, 2010). The key difference in this line of thinking is the assumption that implementers have a significant degree of discretionary power due to incomplete policies that create decision points. Further, it is also assumed that bureaucrats are capable of using their discretion to represent the public interest just as well as elected officials, and in many cases, this discretion is critical for adapting policies to the unique needs of communities (Krislov, 2012; Kennedy, 2014; Meier, 2019). As a causal pathway, then, legislatures pass laws and bureaucrats execute, but decisions are made along the way by various elected and appointed officials about how that policy should work. Of course, critics point to normative concerns of vesting authority to determine the whats, whens, and hows of public services in unelected officials, who have no direct accountability to the citizens they serve, as opposed to elected officials, who are routinely held to account via the ballot box (O'Toole, 2000; deLeon & deLeon, 2002).

Despite those concerns, advocates of representative bureaucracy generally argue that the scale and scope of bureaucracy tend to make it a better microcosm of society than legislative bodies, so public servants are more likely than elected officials to share sociopolitical and demographic backgrounds with their communities, as well as to have social networks with more breadth and diversity as a whole. This passive form of representation, in which it is assumed that people sharing values and interest would make similar choices, is also complemented by an active form, in which bureaucrats actively take steps to see that administrative processes reflect community preferences, particularly those of traditionally disenfranchised target populations (Krislov, 2012; Kennedy, 2014). Of course, there are organizational and individual factors that increase the likelihood that representation occurs and produces positive outcomes. For instance, bureaucrats that are highly productive, have job security, and view representing citizens as low risk are more likely to actively represent citizens; and client-citizens are more likely to be represented when they actively participate in public service delivery (i.e., co-production), share goals with the agency providing services, and have similar identities (i.e., intersectionality of gender, race, socioeconomic factors, etc.) to the bureaucrats that are serving them. Unsurprisingly, street-level bureaucrats are also more likely to feel the need to represent citizens where there is hierarchical segregation along racial or gender lines (e.g., glass ceiling for women or minorities) (Meier, 2019).

The wont of representation in implementation sets up a difficult conflict, particularly when one considers the competing pressures both to be responsive to the dynamic nature of the public interest and to maintain efficient, effective public institutions. To the latter point, when bureaucratic legitimacy is attacked by political pundits, it is most often on charges of wastefulness, laziness, and self-interested behavior, rather than ignoring the needs of the community. Of course, this stems from the view that bureaucracies should focus on dutifully executing laws, and leave representing the public interest to those elected to do so. On the other hand, what harms the image of bureaucrats most often in communities is the impression that they are uncaring or unaware of the plight of those they are supposed to serve, and are more beholden to paperwork and systems than to citizens. Thus, implementers are caught between a proverbial rock and a hard place, where they are expected to be both efficient and democratic. While those two value constructs are not mutually exclusive, they are diametrically opposed to one another insofar as democracy is an intensive process that takes up resources (including time) where efficiency is achieved by consuming as few resources as possible (Meier, 1997; Meier & O'Toole, 2006; Peters, 2010).

Consequently, when implementation systems are designed to streamline processes, they are often efficient, but they also deliver standardized services that are unlikely to adapt to the unique needs of individual citizens. In contrast, when systems are designed around citizens, services are often delivered to meet unique needs for even the most vulnerable in communities, and those services can adapt as needs change. But it is often difficult to achieve economies of scale or scope that facilitate efficiency when citizens are treated as individuals. Thus, there is a cruel irony here: efficient implementation is often unresponsive and responsive implementation is often inefficient. By extension, if one follows the conventional view of democratic accountability in which implementers are charged first with efficient execution of the law, then where implementation is representative of and responsive to communities, it will likely be seen as a failure by the elected officials and program managers who hold implementers to account. On the other hand, if one believes that implementers are also accountable to citizens, then building one-size-fits-all implementation systems will also be seen as a failure by citizens, regardless of how efficient the outputs. While implementers are agents of democracy, the tension created by competing groups seeking to hold them accountable leads to conflict in which values matter most when making choices about how to put policies into practice.

Hollowed-Out Government

While those implementing public policies are most often working directly for the government and therefore have a responsibility to democracy, there is also a significant portion of public service delivery that now occurs via collaboration, partnership, or contract with NGOs (Hill & Hupe, 2014). In many ways, policy implementers working for private or nonprofit firms experience the same challenges in converting policies into practices as those working directly for government; however, how they fit into public institutions is much different. Arrangements for joint or shared public service delivery take on a range of forms that tend to differ based on who is in control and how integrated organizations become. For instance, a partnership may involve two organizations integrating operations with oversight performed by a joint council representing both, while a contract would more likely involve a conventional principal–agent relationship where one party pays the other for performing a service (Teisman & Klijn, 2002; Feiock & Sholtz, 2009). Collaborative arrangements commonly arise where public agencies find they lack the capacity to effectively deliver public services. These capacities may be tangible (e.g., technology, manpower) or intangible (e.g., expertise, political clout), so collaboration tends to involve complex resource exchanges and dependencies (Provan & Huang, 2012; Fowler, 2019a). In any case, this results in policy following a more complex pathway from policymaker to implementer.

Private firms are often favored for partnerships or contracts because of their organizational flexibility, capacity to develop new innovative ways of performing tasks, and ability to quickly identify and abandon failed experiments. In general, this tends to result in more efficient processes that reduce costs. In contrast, nonprofit organizations tend to be better at serving target populations caught in market cleavages that exist where there is little political advantage for policymakers to invest resources and/ or private firms are unlikely to find ways to profit. As such, nonprofits are often able to provide high-quality, specialized services to unique populations (e.g., homeless) more effectively than public or private organizations. The drawback to working with NGOs, though, is risk of goal conflicts and information asymmetries (i.e., one party having more or better information than the other) that can result in the public interest taking a backseat to organizational agendas (e.g., sacrificing service quality for profits). Specifically, when policy implementation responsibilities are shifted to NGOs, they often know more about what is happening than policymakers or program managers overseeing their work. This provides NGOs the opportunity to take advantage and find ways to operationalize policies that serve their narrow organizational mission, which may be in conflict with the public interest (Andrews & Entwistle, 2010; Fowler, 2019a).

Furthermore, collaborative governance is an increasingly important means of delivering public services, whereby a collection of public, private, and nonprofit organizations work together through networks to address shared problems or to achieve a shared mission. Functionally, collaborative governance relies on networks, as opposed to hierarchies or markets, as a means of organization. Public agencies and NGOs work interdependently, where one does not have the power or authority to control others but the actions of one impact the work of others. The key organization imperative is the idea of shared problems or goals, so that participants collaborate in order to find synergies and enhance their own capacities where it makes operational sense (e.g., O'Toole, 1997, 2015; Ansell & Gash, 2008; Emerson, Nabatchi, & Balogh, 2012). In some scenarios, organizations may work in the same functional space, but have few formal ties. In other scenarios, organizations may invest in coordinating actions and mutually support efforts of others. Of course, this looks and operates differently than traditional mechanisms of policy implementation, whereby government agencies are siloed and NGOs operate on the fringes. Notably, the advent and diffusion of these types of arrangements have been principally driven by an operational imperative, as traditional approaches often underperform in comparison (O'Toole, 1997; Andrews & Entwistle, 2010; Fowler, 2020c).

Importantly, those working for NGOs often self-select into organizations based on their preferences for incentive structures, so that the public workforce is generally motivated by a different combination of intrinsic (e.g., helping people) and extrinsic (e.g., money) factors. Given that most public services are provided by the government, public employees generally display a degree of public service motivation, which motivates people to seek out employment that allows them to serve the public. Consequently, public service often becomes more of a life's work than just a job. In contrast, employees at private firms are more likely than public employees to prefer extrinsic rewards. While employees working for nonprofits tend to prefer intrinsic rewards, public employees are often attracted to a mixture of extrinsic and intrinsic rewards, so their motivations are more balanced than their counterparts working for NGOs (Wright, 2001; Fowler & Birdsall, 2020). However, in recent years, public servants have become more mobile in their careers, so they are likely to switch between public agencies and NGOs as opportunities present themselves (Light, 1999a). Of course, this is easier when NGOs are performing functions similar to those of government agencies.

This may or may not impact mechanisms of representative bureaucracy. On the one hand, it can largely be assumed that passive representation functions the same for NGOs providing public services as it does in public agencies. Interestingly, passive representation seems to come into play when making partnership and/or contracting decisions, insofar as program managers are likely to select organizations led by people that share their demographic characteristics (Leland & Read, 2013; Brunjes & Kellough, 2018). This would largely indicate that, at least at managerial levels, NGOs are demographically similar to the public agencies that would otherwise be implementing the policies. On the other hand, there has been little examination of active representation in this context. In general, previous work indicates that active representation is more likely to occur where administrators are intrinsically motivated or where they are extrinsically motivated and representation improves organizational performance. Based on differences in incentive structures across types of organizations, this would suggest that active representation is more likely to occur in nonprofits and public agencies than in private firms, unless doing so links to performance, and then the difference may be marginal (Krislov, 2012; Kennedy, 2014; Meier, 2019). Essentially, implementers working for NGOs may be agents of democracy similarly to those working for public agencies, unless representation and performance are contradictory with each other.

Naturally, this raises the question of how policy implementers are distributed between public agencies and NGOs. While there is no specifically reported data on this, Paul C. Light's work on the true size of government (1999b, 2020) gives us an indication. Since 1985, federal civilian (full-time equivalent) employees have ranged from 1.8 to 2.2 million (not including the military or postal service), compared to contract and grant employees (that is, non-federal civilian workers working on federal projects through NGOs), ranging from 3.8 to 7.1 million. During this period, the average ratio of contract/grant employees to federal civilian employees was approximately 2.5 to 1, indicating that non-federal workers account for a significant portion of federal government operations. This is part of a long-term trend since the 1950s in which federal civilian employment has remained around 2 million; thus, any expansion in the scope or scale of federal operations has been accomplished through contracts, grants, or partnerships with NGOs, or through devolving program authority to state and/or local governments (Light, 1999b, 2020). Although this does not tell us specifically how many employees are program managers versus implementers or how employees divide their time between implementation and other administrative tasks, it generally indicates that the number of implementers working outside of government likely outnumbers those working inside of government.

This would suggest that not only is implementing policy not the sole responsibility of public employees, but that the norms of policy-in-practice are constructed by an indiscrete group of workers employed across a range of organizations that are generally dynamic and difficult to define. While the key role of policy implementers working for NGOs is similar to that of those working for public agencies, they face a different organizational environment, which may at times impact how and why they make choices when turning policies into practices. That is, organizational environments and the types of employees they attract likely affect how implementers use the discretion at their disposal. Furthermore, as administrative structures become more complex and convoluted, policy is filtered through more organizational layers that put distance between those making decisions about the public interest and those turning those decisions into actions. This may give public employees some advantages as policy implementers, but non-public employees still have as much power to shape how policies are implemented. Thus, it is imperative that one think broadly about who implementers are when trying to understand how implementation works.

Citizens and Implementation

While I have discussed the roles of administrators, contractors, elected officials, and policymakers in the context of implementation, the role of citizens should also be considered here, given that they are the most important democratic actors. In recent decades, there has been a significant push to enhance citizen participation in administrative processes through formalized methods to collect public feedback and requirements that it be taken into consideration when formulating implementation strategies (Moffitt, 2014; Schafer, 2019). For example, many state and local governments have experimented with participatory budgeting processes that allow citizens to make choices about funding priorities (Rossmann & Shanahan,

2012). In general, these types of innovations create more opportunities for citizens to provide feedback to administrators making decisions about how to implement policies, at least at organizational or managerial levels. Even where these processes are manipulated by organized interests, such as industry lobbyists, they still allow citizens to engage with governments beyond elections. On the other hand, citizen feedback at the street level is most likely to come from person-to-person interactions, which more often than not happen when citizens are disappointed in their experiences (Hupe & Hill, 2007). Unsurprisingly, this means that how citizens interact with implementers and whether those interactions influence implementer behaviors varies drastically.

Of course, the capacities of citizens to effectively understand, interact with, and extract services from governments are crucial intervening factors here. While it is a foundational responsibility of democratic governments to educate their citizens well enough to constructively participate in the governance process, many governments fall significantly short on this metric (Dahl, 1998). This is particularly notable in the last few years as fake news, conspiracy theories, media bias, and incivility in public discourse have become a prominent issue in politics. Although family, schools, and media still serve as the primary vectors for socializing citizens into political life, this is separate from socializing citizens into bureaucracies (Jennings, 2007). That is, the former is about democratic norms and the responsibilities of citizenship, and the latter is about administrative processes. Engaging with bureaucracy remains the most effective way for citizens to learn how to navigate the complexities of rules, procedures, and hierarchies (i.e., learning by doing) (Oberfield, 2014). For instance, students attending institutions of higher education may be exposed to bureaucratic machinations so that they learn how to "fill out the paperwork" in order to graduate, while how to do so likely remains a mystery to those who forgo a college education; in turn, this experience can also be drawn on to understand how to apply for social services or a mortgage.

For better or worse, those who have been socialized into a bureaucracy through work, school, or seeking out public services often understand the logic behind rules and processes that allow them to influence how policies are implemented, either through person-to-person interactions with street-level bureaucrats or through other participatory processes. Unfortunately, this means that those who regularly interact with the government are also those most likely to have the knowledge and skill to influence government choices, while those who run into barriers to access, such as a lack of knowledge or fear of being denied services, are often left on the outside looking in. Additionally, those who engage government at different levels are also more likely to trust government, as they begin to understand how and why things happen (Wang & Wart, 2007; Lee & Schachter, 2019). Taken as a whole, this tends to cause a bifurcation of citizens, with one group engaging with and advocating for policies and practices that improve their communities and the other group often avoiding government even when they are dissatisfied with the quality of services.

In addition to the normative reasons implementers should engage citizens in a democracy, there are also practical reasons. Put simply, when target populations support policies, they are more likely to comply, which increases the likelihood of policy success (Wallner, 2008; Jackson et al., 2012). For instance, local governments around the US struggled with how to effectively implement mask mandates in response to COVID-19. While many citizens voluntarily complied due to concern for their own health, some citizens, who denied the veracity of the pandemic, were resistant to wearing masks, and local leaders were left with few practical options on how to enforce without escalating the political stakes of the situation. Certainly, this is why Idaho Governor Brad Little called a statewide mandate "problematic if the community doesn't believe in it" (Dawson, 2020). Thus, implementers must convince target populations to buy in to their implementation choices; otherwise, they face an uphill battle. Reed (2014) refers to this operational localism: "the construction and maintenance of political coalitions that endorse policies . . . and legitimate administrative decisions" (p. xiv). The need to create buy-in is in large part due to the co-production properties of most public services in which citizens must actively participate in production, rather than act as passive consumers (Durose & Richardson, 2016).

Others discuss this in terms of social capital, the network of relationships based on shared values and mutual benefit that allows societies to organize collective action. Social capital is possibly the most vital resource available to implementers. When implementers are able to leverage a community's social capital, it increases the likelihood of compliance to desired behavioral norms by playing on existing ties between citizens (Brewer, 2003; Andrews, 2012). Given that in most cases the causal pathway of policy ends with citizens, their willingness to go along with prescribed behavioral changes is a vital factor in predicting success. That is, if the causal pathway assumes that implementers change how they interact with citizens so that citizens change their behaviors in response, citizens must both interact with implementers and be affected by them for this to work. However, if citizens are disengaged from policy implementers and unconcerned about what policies say, then their behaviors are unlikely to change, leading to policy failure. In essence, citizens are unlikely to adapt behaviors to policies that they do not believe in or understand, so implementers often have to design practices around community norms in order to gain compliance.

Of course, this is all complicated by the assertions spelled out earlier in this chapter—namely, that implementers are an indiscrete group that is often fluid and dynamic, as many implement policies in some way but few focus on it. This means there are a myriad of decisions being made by a complex group of people that all contribute to what becomes behavioral norms, but those decisions are not always focused on how to best translate policy-in-theory into policy-in-practice. Adding a layer of complexity is a complicated causal pathway of democratic accountability that connects citizens, policymakers, and policy implementers, as policymakers shift responsibility for dealing with ambiguous situations to implementers. Of course, the hollowing-out of government has transferred public service delivery from governments to NGOs, so that it is not only public employees implementing policies. Citizens are not bystanders here, as they also play a key role in figuring out what it means for a policy to work in practice. While implementers do not always face the same circumstances, they are ultimately faced with the same challenge over and over again: how does the square peg fit into the round hole? With that said, the next step is understanding the parameters of implementation decisions. Therefore, in the next chapter, I will turn our attention to how people make decisions, with a particular focus on the mechanisms that are hardwired into our brains and bias how information is interpreted.

3

Decision-Making under Ambiguous Circumstances

While the focus of policy implementation is often on policies or institutions, its roots are in the decisions made concerning how to operationalize policies. These decisions are often made in the face of ambiguous circumstances (see chapter 1), so that who is paying attention to what is crucial for how they ascribe meaning to the situation and come to conclusions about what should be done. Importantly, implementation decisions are not made once; they are made every time policy is applied. For instance, a teacher applies policy every time she walks into a classroom or engages with a student, not just when writing a syllabus. Underlying this is a complex cognitive process by which attention, search, and selection of information is biased, where individuals do not always find or use relevant information and/or use irrelevant information instead (Zahariadis, 2014). A key component here is whether implementers rely on their intuitive judgments that create a bias toward repeating behaviors, or engage in more deliberative thinking that lends itself to new and innovative ways of understanding how policies are meant to work. Although Herbert Simon argued over a half century ago that the key unit of analysis for administration was the decision, there is now a greater understanding of how micro-level information processing and decision-making underpin patterns observed in meso- or macro-level institutions, which provides significant insight into these questions (e.g., Simon, 1997; Stoker, Hay, & Barr, 2016; Bhanot & Linos, 2020).

In this chapter, I apply the logic of the multiple streams framework (MSF) to cognitive processes in order to understand how policy norms are constructed and deconstructed at the micro level. The goal of this chapter is to examine how cognitive processes cause patterns of policies-in-practice. To do so, I first discuss two types of thinking: system 1 that relies on intuitive judgments, and system 2 that relies on more deliberative judgment. I also discuss the role of cognitive biases in decision-making, and examine a few key types that likely affect implementers. Then I present a survey experiment that asks respondents about their preferences for how to implement policies in order to illustrate how variations in conditions impact implementation tactics. Finally, I discuss why what policy implementers are paying attention to is such an important factor during policy implementation. The key takeaway from this chapter is that there are inherent biases in how people process information that often favor repeating existing behavioral patterns, so that implementers rely chiefly on their intuition in applying policies to the real world, unless jolted into more deliberative thinking.

Intuitive versus Deliberative Judgment

Ideally, when faced with a decision about how a policy or policies apply to a real-world situation, implementers analyze the circumstances, factor in relevant information about the problem, target population, and stakeholders, and consider the policy-in-theory as well as existing policy norms in order to develop a strategic approach that fits the specific situation. From that strategy, they then determine an appropriate set of behavioral steps (e.g., submit form, issue a formal citation) that serve to operationalize the policy based on its meaning within that specific context. This is as complicated and taxing as it sounds, so it does not always happen due to both the time constraints placed on decisions and the intensive process that it requires. In other words, this type of deliberative thinking is not always practical, particularly when it is likely to yield the same results over and over again. More often than not, after applying the same policy to similar situations multiple times, implementers develop behavioral patterns that allow them to skip to the end and just repeat the steps to operationalize the policy without (or with little) thinking. This approach is naturally simpler and less demanding, so it should be no surprise that is relied upon whenever possible (Kahneman, 2011).

Kahneman (2011) brought popular attention to dual cognitive processes in his book *Thinking, Fast and Slow*, but cognitive scientists had become aware of such a model as early as the 1980s (e.g., Chaiken, 1980; Petty & Cacioppo, 1986). In general, this model describes two systems of thinking: system 1, or intuitive, quick judgments; and system 2, or deliberative, deep examination of information (Epstein, 1994; Hammond, 1996; Kahneman, 2011). System 1 operates automatically and involuntarily, so that only the final product is consciously registered. It is thought of as a universal form of cognition that is shared between humans and animals that evolved to provide continual basic assessment of one's surroundings and make quick decisions about how to survive. Although humans in modern societies are not constantly faced with survival threats, the same mechanisms still work today at a cognitive level. Specifically, humans often operate off of learned memory, innate instincts, or heuristics to associate new information with existing behavioral patterns, rather than creating or identifying new patterns based on new experiences. This may manifest as looking for decision cues that allow for inferences to be made without fully examining the situation or substituting simple questions for more complex ones and drawing conclusions accordingly. While some portions of system 1 are universal aspects of human experiences, others are reinforced through socialization and experiences, so that system 1 judgments may differ between individuals (Kahneman, 2011).

On the other hand, system 2 thinking is analytical, intensive, and voluntarily controlled by the individual, so that both the final product and the process of determining that product are consciously registered. Scholars theorize that system 2 thinking evolved in later humans as a general-purpose reasoning system that coexists alongside system 1, as opposed to replacing it. Some scholars point to the archaeological record as evidence of a change in human cognitive abilities around 50,000 years ago that gave humans an advantage over animals and allowed for the development of more complex societies. While it is not clear why system 2 thinking evolved, it provides humans a capacity to analyze information at a deeper, more advanced level than system 1 thinking (Evans, 2003). System 2 is less innate and emotional than system 1, and is often developed through formal learning processes and critical reflection (Thaler & Sunstein, 2008). Additionally, system 2 is controlled and self-aware, so humans are fully cognizant of the logical process that leads to decisions and can alter that process if necessary. However, the trade-off is that system 2 thinking is cognitively demanding, so humans are often constrained by the time and energy it takes to engage in it (Kahneman, 2011).

This leads to an ordering of decision mechanisms whereby system 1 is the default, but system 2 thinking may be invoked under circumstances that warrant it. Specifically, system 2 thinking is mobilized when system 1 thinking fails to come up with an acceptable solution to a problem, when an event violates the mental model of the world that system 1 operates in accordance with, or when it detects an error is about to be made. Thus, under the most likely circumstances, humans will make an intuitive judgment based on system 1 thinking, which will then be tacitly endorsed by system 2 if there are no cues that deeper thinking is required. If situational features cause system 2 thinking to be triggered, the intuitive judgment provided by system 1 thinking will serve as an anchor and be adjusted based on deliberative analysis. On the other hand, if it is determined that the intuitive judgment provided by system 1 thinking is incorrect, it will be discarded and system 2 thinking will be used to come to a new decision. If no intuitive judgment is available from system 1 due to a lack of experience or knowledge, then system 2 thinking will be used to come to a decision (Alter et al., 2007; Kahneman, 2011).

Essentially, this means that the human mind is hardwired to uphold status quos by extending the same intuitive judgments to new experiences, as long as those new experiences do not greatly differ from previous experiences and continue to be met with relatively positive feedback (Kahneman, 2011). In terms of policy implementation, intuitive judgments are tied directly to policy-in-practice so implementers are primed to undertake the same behavioral steps in response to each new implementation scenario. If new experiences do differ enough to trigger system 2 thinking or it appears relying on intuition is likely to result in an error, humans will then engage in more deliberative thinking. For instance, a police officer is likely to follow the same basic routine every time she pulls over a driver for a traffic violation. Her intuitive judgments about whether to stop a driver or not, how to approach the vehicle, or even what to say are learned over time, reinforced by departmental standard operating procedures and/or feedback from other officers or citizens, so that they occur almost unconsciously. However, if there is suspicious activity that causes the officer to become alarmed, she is likely to engage in a more deliberative analysis of the situation to determine the best course of action.

The psycho-emotional implications of operating in ambiguous contexts are also important for understanding the impacts of cognitive processes here. In general, decision-making under ambiguous conditions places significant stress on individuals, particularly where they are faced with cognitive dissonance (i.e., incompatible thoughts) and/or where they cannot get closure (it is emotionally draining to invest oneself in a decision and then not know the outcome) (Shaffer & Hendrick, 1974; Van Hiel & Mervielde, 2002; Kahneman, 2011). This dovetails with recent work that connects ambiguity with emotional labor and burnout among public servants (e.g., Davis & Stazyk, 2022), suggesting that the taxing process of dealing with ambiguity becomes too overwhelming for some. Tolerance of ambiguity (i.e., degree of comfort with an ambiguous situation) is often an important mitigating variable in predicting both the type of decision process used and the level of psycho-emotional distress caused by ambiguity (Furnham & Ribchester, 1995; Furnham & Marks, 2013). Research also shows that even where two people come to the same decision on an ambiguous issue, the person with a higher tolerance for ambiguity experiences less neurological distress than a person with a lower tolerance (Hargreaves et al., 2011).

Additionally, research indicates that people who are "certain about the future" tend to have poorer information-seeking behaviors and/or antisocial tendencies. Specifically, when someone believes they know what will happen in the future, they tend to stop seeking out new information when making decisions, and when others challenge their conclusions, they often respond with passive aggression or open hostility (Okten, Gollwitzer, & Oettingen, 2022). Of course, the paradox here is that these behaviors then insulate one from information or knowledge that challenges their existing ideas (Gollwitzer & Oettingen, 2019). Alarmingly, in a series of experiments incorporating the 2020 presidential election and COVID-19 pandemic, Okten, Gollwitzer, and Oettingen (2022) found that respondents who were more certain about the future were also less likely to listen to technical experts, perform well on a general knowledge quiz, and/or comply with public health guidance, and more likely to believe in conspiracy theories and/or endorse violence. On the one hand, this often means that most people avoid ambiguity and retreat toward safe spaces where there is a degree of certainty around what is known in order to protect themselves from the strain of dealing with ambiguous choices. On the other hand, it also means that those who are certain about the future are most often unequipped to deal with an uncertain future and, in turn, lash out in antisocial ways when faced with events that they did not predict.

This not only inevitably favors the status quo for existing policies, but it also means that when new policies are adopted, implementers are likely to default to intuitive judgments based on existing norms in order to avoid the unpleasant psycho-emotional consequences of ambiguity. In order for new policies to result in changing behavioral patterns, implementers must at least partially engage in deliberative thinking and analyze how behaviors should change to meet new policy demands. Fortunately, there are inherent mechanisms in place to break away from the status quo. Specifically, policy implementers who are facing drastically different circumstances than before or who receive negative feedback are likely to be jolted into a more deliberative approach to decision-making (Quattrone & Tversky, 1988). Over time, this new approach then becomes part of their intuitive judgments via learning processes, so that as implementers fall back to relying on intuition, it results in different behavioral patterns. Of course, whether new policies are a continuation of existing patterns or not is a matter of interpretation, especially in the context of organized anarchies. Thinking in terms of MSF, it should be expected that if new policies are presented as business-as-usual by coupling existing politics and problems, then implementers are more likely to rely on intuitive judgments, as opposed to when new policies are presented alongside changing political and problem conditions that can be framed as a significant departure from the past.

Cognitive Biases in Search and Selection

Inherent in intuitive judgments are cognitive biases or "systematic deviations from the norm whereby individual subjective social reality directs responses to stimuli as opposed to objective standards" (Battaglio et al., 2019, p. 306). Cognitive biases are essentially shortcuts used in information processing that reduce the intellectual energy needed to analyze a situation but, as a consequence, create patterns of bias in decision-making that often lead to errors in judgment. Of course, this causes decisions to appear illogical at times, especially as humans may not be able to consciously identify the logical pathway. Rather than design flaws, cognitive biases may be more like design features of cognitive processes, evolved to solve specific problems and facilitate quick judgments (Haselton, Nettle, & Murray, 2015). On the one hand, cognitive biases have been tied to coping mechanisms used to navigate complex job tasks (e.g., Das & Teng, 1999; Lipsky, 2010) and are likely to buttress status quos by leading people to quick judgments. On the other hand, cognitive biases also affect how individuals search for information and select between alternatives when moving beyond intuitive judgments, which opens the door for manipulation in how implementers interpret and ascribe meaning to policy.

While scholars have identified dozens of cognitive biases, there is no comprehensive list (Haselton, Nettle, & Murray, 2015). For the purposes here, one can think of cognitive biases as either buttressing status quos or manipulating deliberative thinking by affecting how relevant and irrelevant information is used. Of course, distinguishing between relevant (i.e., closely related, applicable, and pertinent to decision-making) and irrelevant information is not always easy, so individuals are likely to rely on intuitive judgments about what information is useful for decisions. Consequently, cognitive biases may cause relevant information to be overlooked or irrelevant information to be given more credence than it should be. Information pools that are limited by missing relevant information often serve to rationalize the status quo, because information included tends to support pre-existing beliefs or behavioral patterns (Zaller, 1992; Chong & Druckman, 2007; Scheufele & Tewksbury, 2007; Baekgaard & Serritzlew, 2016). In contrast, information pools overloaded with irrelevant information often serve to bias how deliberative thinking proceeds as the applicability of information becomes muddled and entrepreneurs have an opening to manipulate how it is interpreted. Essentially, when cognitive biases support initial intuitive judgments, implementers tend to stick with the status quo, but when implementers engage in deliberative thinking, they are subject to manipulation.

Confirmation and/or disconfirmation bias may be among the most common examples of cognitive biases that favor the status quo. Specifically, confirmation bias occurs where people choose to expose themselves to information that supports pre-existing beliefs, while disconfirmation bias occurs where people seek out information that denigrates arguments that counter their beliefs. In both cases, the effect is the same: information is only used as part of motivated reasoning (i.e., reasoning to justify a pre-existing position) (Klayman, 1995; Edwards & Smith, 1996; Nickerson, 1998). For example, in one experiment, Taber and Lodge (2006) provided participants information on gun control and affirmative action; participants were critical of arguments that they interpreted as opposed to their beliefs and were accepting of arguments that they interpreted as supporting their beliefs. In effect, they were misinterpreting and/or seeking out reasons to validate or invalidate arguments, rather than fully considering the implications of the information on their belief system. By implication, implementers are likely to seek out information that confirms that their behavioral norms and/or coping mechanisms are producing positive impacts, and ignore any negative feedback that may trigger the need for more deliberative thinking (Quattrone & Tversky, 1988). Other cognitive biases, such as anchoring or halo biases, can be thought of as working in a similar manner, even though they move beyond simple intuition.

Specifically, anchoring occurs where people's estimation of a value is biased by an initial value. For instance, in one experiment, participants' estimations of the number of African countries were biased when they were provided with a random number at the beginning of the experiment (Tversky & Kahneman, 1974). Typically, people make iterative adjustments to the initial anchor based on situational features, but it is not necessary that an anchor be externally provided (Epley & Gilovich, 2004; Lieder, et al., 2018). In contrast, haloing occurs where people exaggerate consistency in judgments in order to retain simple cohesive narratives, so that people tend to like everything or nothing, including things that have not been observed (Nisbett & Wilson, 1977; Belle, Cantarelli, & Belardinelli, 2017). For example, in an experiment using personnel evaluations, Belle, Cantarelli, and Belardinelli (2017) found that public managers were more likely to rate employees higher if exposed to a higher anchor and consistently across performance dimensions, so that employees thought of as "good employees" were marked as such on evaluations regardless of the evidence. Thus, even when situational features cause individuals to move beyond initial intuitions, status quos are often adjusted, rather than reconsidered entirely. To this end, one could infer that implementers are likely to assume that one good area of performance means that all areas of performance are good, and negative feedback is just an outliner, providing reason to stick with existing ways of doing things.

Ultimately, these and similar cognitive biases cause decisions to be made based on a pool of relevant but limited information that often supports continuation of existing behavioral patterns. Therefore, in most cases, implementers will not consider new information that draws into question the accuracy of their intuitive judgment, so they do not move into higher-level thinking processes; this then results in repetitive behaviors that uphold status quos. In essence, behavioral norms in policy implementation are constructed first at the micro level once implementers begin to internalize those status quos as the basis of their intuitive judgments. However, this does not preclude implementers from using system 2 thinking; it just makes it less likely, as implementers must first be signaled that their intuitive judgments are flawed. If they do move beyond intuitive judgments, other cognitive biases allow the information considered in more deliberative thinking to be biased toward one set of alternatives, rather than all potential possibilities. For instance, policy entrepreneurs can manipulate how implementers come to decisions when formulating new policy norms. Thus, moving away from the status quo may solve one decision-making problem, but it also triggers a new one.

Two examples of these types of cognitive biases are framing and narratives; both are functions of how information is presented. Framing occurs where a communicator uses a subset of information to construct the essence of an issue, and in doing so, emphasizes certain aspects over others in order to draw attention to information that aligns with the communicator's preferred interpretation of the issue (Kahneman & Tversky, 1979; Kahneman, 1981; Slothuus & de Vreese, 2010). For example, Nelson and Oxley (1999) framed the same facts around land development and welfare reform in alternative ways; their results indicated that participants' opinions were affected by which frame they were exposed to even if the facts remained unchanged. In contrast, narrative fallacies occur due to the tendency to connect events and create linear plots when presented with information, which often leads one to accept a cause-and-effect relationship and/or to discard information that does not fit a preferred storyline (Kahneman, 2011; Crow & Jones, 2018). For instance, Jones and Song (2014) found that when participants were exposed to cogent stories about climate change, they were more likely to organize their own thoughts in a similar pattern, as opposed to being exposed to data in bullet points supporting the same position. In other words, telling a better story is often more important than possessing better facts. While there may be other cognitive biases with similar implications, these illustrate how system 2 thinking can also suffer from systematic errors.

Of course, the effects of framing and narratives are not lost on MSF scholars, who have long pointed to how selection of policy alternatives are biased by these mechanisms. While coupling strategies are a relatively underdeveloped part of the MSF scholarship, previous research points to both narrative and framing as tools for connecting streams (Herweg, Zahariadis, & Zohlnhöfer, 2018). For instance, Blum (2018) presents a typology of argumentative lenses to understand how "policy claims" connect information and are supported by evidence. Arguments tend to take one of three forms: consequential, which follows a problem-solving logic and justifies policy claims based on the impact of solutions on problems; doctrinal, which places the emphasis on how solutions fit within pre-existing doctrinal schemes; or political, which focuses more on how decisions are used to satisfy political pressures. Depending on the argumentative form, entrepreneurs may offer different claims for how choices should be valued and how evidence supports this valuation, so that the judgment of decision-makers is biased when selecting between alternatives. Entrepreneurs may also use these policy claims to over- or under-emphasize the dynamics of one stream in order to lead implementers to believe that conditions are normal or abnormal (Zahariadis, 2003; Herweg, Zahariadis, & Zohlnhöfer, 2018). For instance, one entrepreneur could argue that a new policy constitutes a dramatic shift, while another could claim that it is just a slight tweak to existing policies and requires no further attention.

While much of the MSF scholarship on coupling strategies has focused on the institutional level (Herweg, Zahariadis, & Zohlnhöfer, 2018), research on cognition shows that administration is not just a social process (e.g., Battaglio et al., 2019). It is also hardwired into cognitive processes, so that this is really about manipulation of how people think. In other words, the construction and deconstruction of status quos begins at the micro level. The most likely avenue for decision-making (system 1) is designed to repeat behaviors, and the second most likely avenue results in intuitive judgments being adjusted based on situation features; both inevitably result in maintaining status quos so that implementation behaviors do not change. Thus, one should expect status quos to dominate under most "normal" conditions. To invoke system 2 thinking, there has to be a triggering event to cue individuals that their intuitive judgments are insufficient to base decisions (Kahneman, 2011). This is certainly where MSF provides insight into how implementers are jolted (i.e., via stream coupling) into deliberative thinking so they consider new ideas about what to do and how to do it. It also suggests that a key strategy for biasing deliberative thinking processes is through the manipulation of information about politics, policies, and problems.

Implementation Preferences under Varying Circumstances: A Survey Experiment

While there is a significant body of research on cognitive biases and the behavioral aspects of public policy and administration, there is relatively little consideration of these issues within the context of MSF, even though previous works make inferences about how people consume and process information as an underpinning to patterns that manifest at organizational or institutional levels (e.g., Grimmelikhuijsen et al., 2017; Bhanot & Linos, 2020). To this end, MSF can be adapted to understand why individuals move from more intuitive to more deliberative decision-making when formulating implementation behaviors. Specifically, under normal circumstances, implementers will use intuitive judgments that repeat established behavioral norms when identifying and choosing preferable mechanisms to implement policies. This means that the preferable course of action for implementers is likely the same in a predominant number of scenarios. But, under abnormal circumstances, implementers will engage in deliberative thinking that results in conclusions that substantially differ from established behavioral norms. Here, abnormal circumstances are likely to be perceived to occur where the politics, problems, and policy streams come together to trigger implementers' reinterpretation of the situation; for instance, a new policy could be framed as more of the same or as a paradigm shift in light of the political and problem parameters.

Of course, what constitutes normal and abnormal circumstances is subjective and depends on both how the situation is framed and how implementers perceive it, so that other factors likely also affect whether implementers are triggered to engage in deliberative thinking. For instance, unless the magnitude and direction of change signal a consistent path, it will be difficult to create a cogent narrative about what is occurring (i.e., coupling streams) or challenge an existing way of thinking (i.e., decoupling). Even if implementers initially engage in deliberative thinking, they are likely to abandon it when competing information creates cognitive dissonance (i.e., stress caused by inconsistent thoughts or beliefs related to behavioral decisions) (Festinger, 1957). In other words, a worsening problem can be offset by attention shifting away and policies remaining unchanged as it becomes more difficult to present a cogent narrative that has an impetus for new behaviors. That is, implementers may think about what to do but decide not to change their course of action or become overwhelmed in trying to decipher the situation and fall back on their intuition. Additionally, coupling of the streams relies in part on the problematic preferences of implementers (see chapter 1), so that those with more rigid belief systems are more likely to stick with their instincts and be less willing to consider new information (Moynihan & Lavertu, 2012).

In order to illustrate these dynamics, I use data from a survey experiment (see "Methods Memo for Chapter 3" in the Appendix for more details of survey methodology and data analysis). Participants were asked to role-play as a city employee responsible for the implementation of an ordinance limiting the amount of time vehicles may idle. Experimental text read:

> Imagine you are a city's environmental manager. In response to recent concern about regional air quality, the city council has passed an anti-idling law which limits motor vehicles idling to three minutes while the vehicle is parked or stopped. The law allows violators to be fined up to $500. This is a civil, rather than a criminal, penalty—citizens can be fined for violations, but cannot be arrested. This law is scheduled to go into effect January 1, 2021. How to enforce the new law and the specific fine schedule is left to your discretion.
>
> A recent poll shows that public concern about air quality has [**increased/decreased/ remained the same**] since the previous poll, conducted last year, and new data shows air quality has [**improved/worsened/remained the same**] over the past year.

Respondents were, then, asked to rate their preferences for a set of potential implementation tools from strongly support (7) to strongly oppose (1). Tools include a mixture of activities that may occur at the street level or in office settings:

1. Instruct police to not enforce the law, unless there are flagrant violations

2. Instruct police to enforce this law in all areas of the city, including private property

3. Increase police patrols in areas of the city where idling is common to write tickets for violations

4. Do nothing for the first 90 days, and wait to see if idling improves on its own

5. Develop a media campaign [e.g., website, flyers] to inform the public about the new law and how to comply

6. Install signs in areas of the city where idling is common to notify citizens of the law

7. Create a tip line for citizens and businesses to call in and report violations

8. Hire a private company to monitor and enforce this policy, including patrolling high traffic areas, issuing tickets, and collecting fines.

9. Create a tax incentive for "good" behavior in which people with no violations receive a discount on their car registration

10. Create a committee of public officials, business owners, and citizens to develop an action plan

Treatment groups receive varying information about the political and problem conditions; specifically, that public concern and the relative problem (e.g., air pollution) is either increasing, decreasing, or remaining the same. The control group is provided no additional information about political or problem conditions.

I consciously chose to survey a general population here, as opposed to a specific population of public administrators operating within the context of their jobs. While people respond to the world around them, I am actually testing whether the conditional effects observed at institutional levels in previous MSF scholarship also occur on the micro level; specifically, whether these micro-level effects exist in the absence of the confounding factors that occur when people are operating in organized anarchies. In other words, I am looking to see if respondents' perceptions of implementation mechanisms shift in response to the information provided absent the type of real-world repercussions or social interactions that would normally create pressures to be responsive. This allows me to identify if this is a phenomenon that is inherent in the way people process information, or one that is structured by their environment—nature versus nurture, so to speak. But, in order to do this, I have to find some way to separate people from that environment, hence the use of a general population survey. However, the experience and expertise of public servants should not be discounted as important aspects of their decision processes. This is important given that social-level processes, real-world consequences, and/or learned behaviors often reinforce cognitive biases.

To this end, the experiment here is more concerned with whether the availability of information impacts choices, as opposed to the quality or implications of those choices. Asking people who have little exposure to the issues at hand should result in findings that are more indicative of how people process information and make decisions in general, as compared to a sample that includes people who may be swayed by their lived experience. This can, then, be extended to understand whether conditional effects of policy, political, and problems streams result at least partially from cognitive processing, in addition to the types of social interactions and institutional pressures that also influence choices in organized anarchies. Notably, research on decision-making (e.g., Kahneman, 2011) suggests that it tends to be similar across a host of individuals, so there is no reason to expect that one's job would influence how one responds to the specific information provided. If anything, this design would be likely to *overestimate* the effects of information, as laypersons have less information about the topics and would likely be more receptive to new information or likely lack intuition reinforced by previous experiences (Zaller, 1992; Baum & Jamison, 2006). Additionally, while this experiment does not principally examine ambiguity in the same sense that it is used in other places in this book, the varying levels of information and types of decision-making processes provide an illustration of the implications of decision processes occurring under ambiguous circumstances.

I use ordinal logistic regression to make comparisons between control and treatment groups, which indicates whether and under which circumstances exposing respondents to additional information affects preferences for specific implementation mechanisms. In the interest of brevity, tables 3.1 and 3.2 provides a summary of statistically significant results by

Table 3.1. Summary of Results Comparing Treatment and Experimental Groups

	Install signs	Enforce only flagrant	Enforce all violations	Increase patrols	Tax incentive/ grant program
Increase/increase					
Same/increase	–				
Same/decrease		–			–
Decrease/increase					
Decrease/decrease		–			

Note: + =positive coefficient; – = negative coefficient.
Source: Author.

Table 3.2. Summary of Comparison, by Problematic Preference Sub-groups

	Install signs	Enforce flagrant	Enforce all	Increase patrols	Private contractor	Planning committee	Do nothing
Increase/ improve				+h	+h	+h	+l
Increase/ same			+h	+h	+h		
Same/ improve				+h	+h	+h	
Same/ same					+m	+l	
Same/ decrease					+h		
Decrease/ improve	+h		+h	+h	+h	+h	
Decrease/ same					+h +l	+h	
Decrease/ decrease		−m				+l	

Note: h = high sub-group; m = moderate sub-group; l = low sub-group; + = positive coefficient; − = negative coefficient.
Source: Author.

treatment group and implementation tools, while full results are available in the "Methods Memo" (see tables A3.2 and A3.3). Experimental results indicate that in the vast majority of cases providing additional information about political and problem conditions had no effect on respondent preferences, so one can surmise that in most cases, respondents used quick intuitive judgments in formulating preferences that were not responsive to circumstantial changes (see table 3.1). In practical terms, this likely suggests that respondents quickly scanned the text, overlooking the pertinent parts concerning political and problem conditions, and then rated their preferences so that patterns were essentially the same regardless of what information was provided.

Even where respondents may have thoughtfully considered the information and their responses, their preferences were likely anchored by initial intuitive judgments, so that differences from the control group were marginal at best. This largely suggests that the likelihood of an implementer choosing to implement an idling ordinance via media campaign, creating a tip line, hiring a private contractor, organizing a planning committee, or doing nothing is roughly the same regardless of what information they have about the political or problem conditions. In general, this supports the contention that intuitive judgments dominate when deciding how to implement a policy. However, there are some cases in which differences between control and treatment groups do emerge. But it also appears that how respondents react depends on the implementation tool, so there is a targeted shift in preferences as opposed to a general shift across all tools. This indicates that the likelihood of an implementer choosing to implement an idling ordinance by installing signs, enforcing only flagrant violations, or giving a tax incentive depends on what information they have about conditions. This, then, supports the contention that under the right political and problem conditions, implementers are triggered to think more deliberately about how to make policies work, and in turn, come to different conclusions about the best way to turn policies into practices.

These trends are more interesting when problematic preferences are taken into consideration as well. To this end, I use the variance across a set of questions concerning respondents' beliefs about the environment to gauge how rigid and/or formulated their beliefs about specific policy issues are:

1. Where would you place yourself on this scale from (1) regulate business to protect the environment to (7) no regulation because it will not work and will cost jobs?

2. Do you think the federal government should be doing more about rising temperatures (7), should be doing less (1), or is it currently doing the right amount (4)? [recoded]

3. How much of an environmentalist do you consider yourself on a scale from (1) I care very much about the environment and actively play a role as an environmentalist to (7) I care very little about the environment and take no action to protect the environment.

Respondents in the low-variance sub-group have a relatively consistent set of beliefs (i.e., they know what they want) and those in the high-variance sub-group have relatively inconsistent beliefs (i.e., they don't know what they want). Here, the base comparison group is the control group with no information on political and problem conditions that has moderately consistent beliefs. Results indicate that there are relatively few differences that emerge for the moderate and low sub-groups, indicating that preferences for implementation tools for respondents with rigid beliefs are often not dependent on what information they have about political or problem conditions (see table 3.2). In contrast, six of nine treatment groups for the high sub-group were responsive to political or problem conditions for at least one implementation tool. This would indicate that preferences for respondents with inconsistent beliefs about the environment are likely to fluctuate based on the circumstances. In other words, when respondents are more likely to be unsure of what they want or how they feel about the environment, they are more likely to look for circumstantial information when calculating their preferences.

Furthermore, statistically significant coefficients for the high sub-group are exclusively positive, suggesting that when preferences are malleable, respondents are more likely to support implementation tools in general. That is, respondents who do not know what they want are more likely to consider the circumstances and support doing something, instead of being opposed to doing something. The most likely explanation here is that respondents with consistent, rigid beliefs were more prone to ignoring the circumstantial information provided, having confidence in their intuition so that additional information did not trigger higher-order thinking. In contrast, respondents with inconsistent beliefs were more likely to pay attention to the information and consider it when deciding whether an implementation tool should be used. Even if sub-groups were engaging in the same level of intuitive versus deliberative thinking, the high sub-group is coming to different conclusions about the preferability of implementation tools than other sub-groups, suggesting at minimum that their cognitive processes are operating differently. From this, one can infer that implementers with rigid ideas about policies will be far more likely to fall back on status quos, while those with problematic preferences will not only be more deliberative but will also be prone to doing something differently.

Despite some limitations (see "Methods Memo"), the experimental findings here largely indicate that under most conditions, individuals make choices based on quick judgments that do not fully account for all relevant information, but if triggered, they will engage in more deliberative thinking that results in different preferences. In general, this causes there to be quite a bit of agreement across respondents with different information on the political and problem conditions (e.g., media campaigns and installing signs were popular choices). One could likely infer that when the intuitive judgment on what to do is common across respondents with different information, there is a "normal" way of thinking about how that policy should be implemented. In the real world, this would likely become the status quo across a large indiscrete group of implementers making individual choices. However, it is the mechanisms that lead certain treatment groups to break away from that intuition and develop alternative preferences that represent what it takes to start rethinking how policies work in practice, and why inconsistent behavioral norms emerge across implementation sites. Specifically, when the political and problem conditions suggest that a policy means something different, implementers are likely to prefer using new and different implementation tools.

Who Is Paying Attention to What?

Policy implementation is ultimately about choices. Choices made about how to turn policy into action. Choices made more complex by ambiguity in the face of policy, politics, and problems that are hard to understand, and even harder to map causal relationships onto. Choices made not once, but hundreds of times. Fortunately, there are mechanisms hardwired into the human brain that facilitate choice even where there is insufficient time or information (Kahneman, 2011). But, before choices can be made, implementers must make sense out of a world that is only partially comprehensible. They do this by ascribing meaning to ambiguous situations, which can easily be biased by what information they are paying attention to (Zahariadis, 2014). For instance, if one focuses on drug control laws, then drug use is a criminal action that should be met with citation or arrest; but, if one focuses on the well-being of the individual, then drug use is a mental health issue that should be met with treatment. Certainly, either perspective can be justified if one pays attention to the right information. Just as importantly, mistaking relevant information for irrelevant information or vice versa can fundamentally shift how implementers understand what is going on and the causal impact of their actions. This opens the door for implementers to be manipulated into perceiving the world in such a way that their actions further the agenda of those doing the manipulation (Zahariadis, 2003; Zahariadis & Exadaktylos, 2016).

Central to what information implementers are paying attention to is whether that information indicates that intuitive judgments are built on flawed mental models, which in turn trigger system 2 thinking. This is where stream coupling comes into play, so that entrepreneurs who manage to supply and frame information that connects policy, problems, and politics can challenge intuition and convince implementers to rethink how policies become actions. Specifically, if one can present a cogent argument for why a policy means something different in the context of problems and political conditions than what an implementer originally assumed, then they would likely begin reformulating their mental model of the world. If entrepreneurs do it well, implementers find meanings in policies that drive behaviors in a specified direction; if they fail, implementers are likely to fall back on established behaviors in absence of better alternatives. Of course, these same dynamics also offer the opportunity for those who wish to ward off change by disrupting how implementers make sense of the situation, which naturally causes implementers to stick with their intuition and repeat the same behavioral patterns even when dealing with new policies (Zahariadis & Exadaktylos, 2016).

To be clear, the goal is not to replace intuitive judgment with deliberative judgment, especially where they are likely to result in the same conclusions. Rather, the goal is to understand which roles each plays in shaping how implementers ascribe meaning to ambiguous circumstances, and use each system of thinking appropriately. Intuition is imperative to establishing behavioral norms for policy-in-practice, particularly as it reinforces an established view of the world that aligns with preferred policy interpretations. For instance, in situations where one wants to build consensus around policy meanings so that routine practices across sites provide citizens with consistent experiences, implementers should be using their intuition to repeat behaviors. In contrast, deliberative thinking is imperative to deconstructing those policy norms. In situations where it is clear that problems are complex, uncertain, and/or volatile, managers need to trust implementers to do more than just repeat behaviors in order to see that policies actually solve problems as they exist in the real world. The challenge is often that implementers use intuition at times when they should be thinking deliberatively, so their choices appear to serve bureaucratic interest more than the public interest. Conversely, when implementers overthink the simple decisions, implementation is needlessly complicated and burdensome. In either case, policies-in-practice fail to live up to expectations.

To this end, the key takeaway from this chapter is that there are inherent biases in how people process information so that what people are paying attention to is crucial to how they make decisions; specifically, whether they continue to do the same thing over and over again or think through what policies mean and how that should drive actions. Ambiguity tends to be a key barrier to deliberative thinking, as ascribing meaning is cognitively intense, while adopting the status quo is the path of least resistance. But micro-level cognitive processes are only the first part of this story, as decisions made by the collective body of implementers aggregate together to create patterns of policy practices at the organizational and institutional levels. Implementers are not completely autonomous, as they are often boxed in by organizations that shape what information is available, how that information is used, and how individuals understand their roles and responsibilities; of course, entrepreneurs are at work trying to manipulate this as implementers navigate organized anarchies. While this chapter has examined how implementers make choices, in the next chapter, I will shift focus to examining how organizations and managers set out to bias implementation decisions in both targeted and systematic ways.

4

Organizations, Managers, and Entrepreneurs

While implementation is rooted in the decisions made about how to operationalize policies (see chapter 3), those decisions are not made in a vacuum, as they are subject to influence from organizations. Of course, this is why so many scholars focus on organizations when examining implementation, since one can often make inferences about implementer behavior from how organizations operate (e.g., Montjoy & O'Toole, 1979). Organizations are essentially devices to superimpose logic onto anarchy in order to create order and rationale for decision-making where it otherwise does not exist (the "organized" part or organized anarchy). Specifically, managers use formal (e.g., administrative procedures) and informal (e.g., culture) mechanisms to structure how implementers make decisions. Managers also often operate as entrepreneurs using their power over subordinates to influence how they think about their roles and responsibilities within both the organization and the policy process. To this end, managers largely serve as mitigating factors on the decision processes used by implementers, where implementers are nudged in a direction preferred by organizational leaders, who often think in terms of the long-term viability of institutions rather than short-term service to the public interest.

Meier and O'Toole (2007) describe the managerial role as having three parts: "contribution to organizational stability through additions to hierarchy/structure as well as regular operations"; "management's efforts to exploit the environment of the organization"; and "management's effort to buffer the unit from environmental shocks" (p. 504). In other words, managers are simultaneously working to further the imposition of logic onto anarchy while also utilizing ambiguity to manipulate how people operationalize that logic and moderating how their subordinates view the dynamics of the policy, problems, and/or politics streams. Managers are, then, both fighting against ambiguity and using it to their advantage at the same time, which requires a balance between management and leadership. This largely sums up the complicated role and importance that managers have in organizations, particularly if one focuses on how implementers come to ascribe meaning to policies and try to chart a course through an ambiguous environment that is often complex, uncertain, and volatile. Of course, "good" managers know how to use both formal and informal tools at their disposal to further these goals by shaping perceptions of organizational preferences, who participates in decision-making processes, and how technology is understood to work.

In this chapter, I examine how organizations and managers shape thinking about policies. The goal of this chapter is to contextualize the pressures that implementers face to conform to the preferences of program managers who are attempting to organize anarchies. To do so, I discuss how administrative procedures, managerial tools, and culture shape the search for and analyses of information when figuring out how policies apply to real-world situations, and how implementers are socialized into bureaucracies. Additionally, I discuss authority as a formal mechanism tied to organizations as opposed to power as an informal capacity to influence others, and how managers leverage both to coerce and/or nudge implementers in a desired direction. I delve into this deeper by interviewing program managers and policy implementers to illustrate how this looks from the perspective of those making policies work in practice. Finally, I discuss why management matters in policy implementation, and the complex role managers play in rectifying the dual pressures to maintain public institutions and execute the public interest. The key takeaway from this chapter is that organizations are designed to guide what information implementers look for and how it is used, during the continual competition between perspectives concerning how they see their responsibilities and goals.

Imposing Organization on Anarchy

Organization matters in numerous ways for how bureaucracies operate, as it imparts both a social construction and an economics to how decisions are made. In the context of organized anarchies, organization is used to superimpose logic so that rational, predictable choices can be made within ambiguous environments based on a shared understanding of the world (Cohen, March, & Olsen, 1972). Organizations, and the decision logics that they propagate, are naturally oriented around maintaining public institutions as organizations are chiefly a manifestation of those institutions (see the Introduction). Of course, this causes conflict with executing the public interest, at times, as organizations favor status quos and are naturally averse to the risks that come with change. In large part, this is because different ways of thinking not only create ambiguity and uncertainty, but also create de facto challenges to the efficacy of organizations. For instance, adopting a new way of thinking implies that the previous way was wrong. By extension, if organizations are wrong, does this mean that the political institutions that they represent are wrong? Thus, introducing new ways of thinking is often disruptive and inherently questions the legitimacy of previous decisions, so program managers use structure to absorb new policies and responsibilities without recalculating organizational logic.

From a social constructivist perspective, imposing structure is about laying the foundation for a collective perception to be built, so that organizational actors can ground their decisions and logics in the same world. While social construction is very much based in a subjective reality, achieving a shared perspective is one step closer to an objective reality from which rational choices can be made (Farmer, 1994; Herman & Renz, 1997; Frederickson et al., 2015). For instance, organizational identities arise from a collective perception of characteristics that define the vision, mission, and norms of an organization, and who organizational actors are as an extension of it. Since organizational actors develop their perceptions independently and those perceptions evolve over time through interactions with other actors, managers make claims about this identity through both formal and informal mechanisms in order to encourage actors to see the organization through a similar lens (Ran & Golden, 2011). Otherwise, internal conflict arises over what the organization's purpose is, and for the individual, what it means to be a part of it (van der Velde & Class, 1995). Of course, if actors accept the claims of managers, then the number of ways of thinking about these questions is reduced, and with it, ambiguity.

Imposing structure can also alter how people perceive the costs and benefits of choices by removing or creating transaction costs, which managers can use to buttress their claims about the organization. In other words, if organizational rules make it more difficult to do one thing and less difficult to do another, actors will inevitably choose the latter. Additionally, as uncertainty leads to risks that require steps to mitigate potential threats, people will inevitably choose the option that presents more certainty. This means that managers can use structure to negate the marginal utility of thinking in new ways, and, more importantly, to boost the marginal utility of conforming to their preferences—again, reducing ambiguity as a result (Williamson, 1997, 2015). While program managers do not have absolute control over the sources of ambiguity, they can make organizational preferences less problematic, technology clearer, and/or participation less fluid by structuring how decisions are made. To this end, program managers have numerous instruments at their disposal for imposing structure onto anarchy in order to address the underlying causes of ambiguity.

Possibly one of the most common forms of such instruments are administrative procedures, or rules that constrain what, when, where, who, and how tasks can be performed or decisions made. Specifically, administrative procedures reduce "uncertainty about how agencies perform their policy activities, how future political coalitions might influence the agencies performance, and how to solve complex policy problems" (Potoski, 1999, p. 623) by structuring and constraining the mechanisms of decision-making. In doing so, procedures increase the clarity in organizational technology by identifying constraints on what can be done and reducing the fluidity in decision participation by ordering when and who gets input. For example, universities use administrative procedures for promotion and tenure to define who gets input in evaluating applicants and the criteria that they should consider in order to provide structure to an otherwise amorphous decision proposition surrounding what constitutes sufficient merit through research, teaching, and service. But administrative procedures also create barriers that are time and energy intensive to surmount, so that following the path of least resistance equates to rule compliance (Balla, 1998; Potoski, 1999, 2002). In other words, administrative procedures constrain both how one can manipulate the use of information and the marginal utility in doing so, so that the ways of thinking preferred by managers (or policymakers) become difficult to dislodge.

In contrast, performance management tools are essentially mechanisms used to guide employees toward behaviors that align with the overall goals of organizations. Essentially, performance management defines expectations, so employees that conform are rewarded (Moynihan, 2008).

While these tools are not counterproductive to the short-term public interest, managers most often use performance management to encourage their subordinates to make choices that are likely to protect the long-term viability of organizations. For instance, a manager may adopt a merit-based pay system in order to spur increased productivity from her team with the broader goal of improving organizational efficiency, even if it means that quality in service or outputs declines. Of course, bureaucrats have a natural tendency to only work toward metrics that are measured and monitored, particularly when incentives or disincentives are involved, so that performance management tools often create de facto boundaries to job responsibilities (i.e., if it isn't measured, it doesn't count) (Brehm & Gates, 1999; Hvidman & Andersen, 2014; Gerrish, 2016). Thus, program managers are signaling to their subordinates what is valued, so that implementers focus on tasks that further the organizational agenda. In contrast to administrative procedures that constraint how implementers think, performance management tools reduce the problematic nature of organizational preferences by sending signals about what organizations value and rewarding behavior accordingly.

Alternatively, information management tools create de facto organization around information processing and workflows, which structures who has access to what information (Mohr, 1971; Aldrich, 1972). In a simple way, creating a form reduces transaction costs in performing a task by clarifying what information implementers should look for, but the workflow surrounding that form also dictates who becomes part of the decision process. In recent years, information technology has also led to a shift from street-level to system-level bureaucracies as public services are delivered in digital form, removing windows for manipulation and opportunities for actors to insert themselves into decision-making (Bovens & Zouridis, 2002; Danzinger & Andersen, 2002). For instance, if one applies for social services online, there is little opportunity to tell a compelling narrative or frame problems to bias how a social worker evaluates the case at hand. To this end, information management tools reduce the prospects of innovation by mitigating fluidity in decision participation and the problematic nature of organizational preferences via transaction costs surrounding preferred behaviors (Jaskyte, 2011). For example, if teachers have to complete mountains of paperwork to go on a field trip, then schools are signaling their preferences about teachers taking students off campus by making it more difficult to accomplish. In essence, information management tools organize information to reduce the fluidity in participation and to further signal organizational preferences via transaction costs.

Likely the most important instrument in dealing with ambiguity, though, is organizational culture, or the informal patterns of attitudes and behaviors that manifest through day-to-day activities and interactions that result from operating within the confines of a specific organization. Culture tends to be driven by what is perceived as appropriate or acceptable ways of responding to ambiguity surrounding decision windows, so it is tacitly reinforced through routine interactions between organizational actors at different levels. While conformity is met with social rewards, nonconformity is often met with backlash (Bozeman & Kingsley, 1998; Wagenaar, 2004; Schein, 2017). For instance, water cooler talk between colleagues can be a signal of how managers have placed value on workers being present in office (as opposed to telework or remote work) or whether there is generally trust between co-workers. Additionally, informal chats can also be a mechanism for communicating experiences, so that colleagues learn from one another what works. By extension, those who conform to expectations get to participate and learn from their colleagues, while those who do not conform are treated as part of an out-group and are left on the outside looking in (Mahler, 1997; Taylor, 2014; Schein, 2017). To this end, culture provides informal signals on who should be involved in decisions, what organizational preferences are, or how to use technology, reducing ambiguity in multiple ways (Robertson & Swan, 2003).

For culture to be an effective tool in dealing with ambiguity, actors must be socialized so that they effectively understand the signals about participation, preferences, and technology; otherwise, they are left to their own devices when figuring out how organizational structures bound their world. Managers seeking to reduce ambiguity tend to rely on socialization tactics that focus on institutionalizing "newcomers to think and behave according to preestablished rules, thus encouraging them to follow very structured processes" (Moyson et al., 2018, p. 611), as opposed to allowing socialization to occur more by default than design, which gives newcomers room to innovate when defining their organizational roles. Socialization tactics include a range of things such as onboarding practices or orientation sessions, training, mentorship, network building, or meetings or interactions with other organizational members (Antonacopoulou & Guttel, 2010). For instance, a training session may explicitly spell out how the organization interprets policies related to job tasks, or new employees may be introduced to existing employees who can answer questions as they come up. These tactics are used to identify and introduce organizational newcomers to both people and information that address the unwritten rules related to their responsibilities, particularly in terms of how they should go about making sense of ambiguous policies and situations (Ashford & Black, 1996; Chappell & Lanza-Kaduce, 2010).

The ultimate goal of socialization processes, though, is indoctrinating actors into a shared set of beliefs and attitudes; specifically, for implementation, a set of shared beliefs and attitudes about how policy is interpreted and what it means in practice. This indoctrination tends to psychologically bind individual organizational members to the broader goals and purpose of the organization, so they are more likely to conform to managerial claims about how to best serve. Of course, this is also likely to cause group-think (Ziller, 1964; Wanous, Reichers, & Mailk, 1984; Ashforth & Mael, 1989). A key factor in successful socialization is often person–organization fit, or the "congruence between newcomers' expectations, values, or behaviors and those of their organization, team, or network" (Moyson et al., 2018, p. 614). Many scholars assume there is a degree of self-selection at work, where employees choose organizations that fit their pre-existing values or preferences for structures and incentives, which eases the socialization process (Rainey, 1983; Bright, 2009, 2018). This likely extends to preferences for policy interpretations or mechanisms for ascribing meaning, so that implementers end up in organizations in which they easily conform to established norms. In sum, managers reduce ambiguity by using both formal (e.g., administrative procedures) and informal (e.g., culture) instruments to impose structure on anarchy via social construction of shared understandings and/or manipulation of cost-benefit perceptions (Stazyk & Goerdel, 2011)

Power, Authority, and the Art of Manipulation

In addition to reducing the sources of ambiguity, organization also creates a framework for the exertion of power over organizational actors. In this context, organization provides structure for how power, as the capacity to influence the decisions and behaviors or others, can be used and by who. Specifically, it is not the ability to give commands that defines one's power; rather, it is whether others accept and act on those commands (Barnard, 1968). Of course, organizational structures are designed so actors accept the commands of those in charge, which serves to facilitate the manipulation of implementers by those whom the organization has vested with power (Fairholm, 2009). Power tends to be based on one's capacity for three things: 1) the ability to punish (i.e., coerce) or reward another party so that their behaviors adapt based on the perception of costs and benefits; 2) the acquisition and application of knowledge and skill (e.g., charisma or expertise) so that others are persuaded to adopt the preferences of a competent person; and/or 3) the holding of a position of authority so that others respond out of a sense of social responsibility (e.g., to obey chain of command) or vested interest in the institution (French & Raven, 2015). Of course, these are not mutually exclusive and one may use multiple sources simultaneously in order to obtain a desired outcome.

Authority is a special type of power here because it grants someone the ability to speak for the organization, as organizations cannot speak for themselves, within the narrow confines of their job description. That is, a police chief wields the power vested in the city government within the confines of his jurisdiction, while a police sergeant is granted authority over a smaller administrative unit of that jurisdiction. Both represent their perceptions of the organization and how it imposes logic onto anarchy to their subordinates below and superiors above in the course of their job responsibilities. For instance, the police sergeant conveys her interpretation of messages sent from the police chief about how officers should do their jobs, on the one hand, and to the chief about how doing things a certain way affects the job performance of her subordinates, on the other hand. This means that managers are often the key mechanism for representing the organization's interest to implementers, so managerial claims about organizational preferences are seen as a legitimate expression of the organization itself (Westley, 1990; Morgan et al., 2006; Huy, 2001; Valentino, 2004; Chen, Berman, & Wang, 2017). In this way, they serve as linchpins in cultivating and communicating the organization's preferences, designing and training others on technology, and serving as gatekeepers for participation. Therefore, managers have significant control over where ambiguity emerges and how it is dealt with.

With the authority of the organization, managers are also often able to use organizational resources and structures to coerce and reward, and have opportunities to display their expertise or build trust with other organizational actors (e.g., Gioia & Sims, 1983, Kahn & Kram, 1994). For example, a police sergeant can gain power to influence the officers under her command by providing good guidance and support, or by controlling shift assignments and overtime pay. Of course, when managers do a poor job of speaking for the organization (e.g., saying things that are contradicted later) or unfairly apply coercion, they likely undermine the legitimacy of their position as subordinates question their competence and/or whose interest they are acting in. On the one hand, this sets managers up as key figures in influencing how implementers think about ambiguous situations; for instance, a powerful manager can simply say what a policy means and the implementers under her will dutifully accept that interpretation, while a weak manager will be unable to exert influence over her subordinates' thinking. On the other hand, it also means that those positioned outside one's chain of command often do not have the same capacity to wield authority, apply coercion, or provide rewards in ways that comply with ethical standards, so they have limited opportunities to influence how policies are interpreted.

But there are also limitations to power based in one's position, particularly in modern democratic societies, as no public servant nor elected official has absolute authority. For one, even in strictly hierarchical organizations, authority is often fragmented so that subordinates answer to more than one manager for different tasks and tend to have opportunities to "go around" managers with whom they disagree, so competing and/or contradictory signals that increase rather than reduce ambiguity are common (Crank & Langworthy, 1996; Sveningsson & Alvesson, 2003; Marchington et al., 2005). Furthermore, even in the event that an employee outright refuses to respond to legitimate authority, there is a cost associated with dismissing or disciplining subordinates. While bad employees may have a negative impact on culture, turnover leads to losses in institutional knowledge and workforce capacity, and to new transaction costs in hiring and training. Additionally, new employees also tend to be a question mark, and it is hard to predict how well they will fit the organization (Meier & Hicklin, 2008; Bradbury, Sowa, & Kellough, 2013; An, 2019). Thus, where subordinates will not respond to positional authority, it may be better to leverage other sources of power to manipulate their way of thinking in order to elicit desired behaviors, rather than engage in open conflict over their adherence to social norms surrounding one's authority.

In the absence of direct hierarchical authority over implementers, entrepreneurs positioned outside the organization trying to influence how policies are interpreted must rely on other sources of power (Nicholson-Crotty & Nicholson-Crotty, 2004). For instance, a citizen trying to argue his way out of a speeding ticket may try to claim knowledge of the law (i.e., expertise), make threats of filing a complaint (i.e., coercion), or tell a sob story in an effort to get the officer to rethink writing a traffic citation. Of course, the citizen in this case has no legitimate authority to tell the officer how to do her job, so the citizen must focus on manipulating how the officer sees the situation. However, for policymakers or entrepreneurs with political clout (e.g., lobbyists), the most cost-effective route is likely to focus their efforts on managers, who can then leverage their own positions and power to further the entrepreneurs' cause. For instance, a legislator may signal to an agency director how she believes a policy should be interpreted either using formal tools like legislative hearings or through more informal ways like private conversations. In either case, the ultimate goal is still to manipulate which policy interpretations proliferate by leveraging power over others.

Thinking about the exertion of power as manipulation is unique in that it assumes the underlying dynamics here are about how the world in general, and policy in specific, are interpreted, as opposed to purely rational or socially constructivist perspectives (Zahariadis, 2014). If one assumes that implementers are utility maximizers, then altering their behaviors is about the application of coercion or divvying out rewards; that is, changing how people see the costs and benefits of their choices. If one assumes that implementers just need to come to a shared understanding of the world, then altering their behaviors is about persuading them to think differently through the use of expertise or reference. But if we assume that ambiguity stands as a barrier to both, then altering behaviors is an exercise in manipulating how implementers think about the world so that their concepts of rational choice and collective perceptions align with those preferred by management. In essence, managers must leverage different forms of power in order to reduce ambiguity surrounding both how implementers see their own self-interest and the organization's interest so that they come to a desirable conclusion about what a policy means and how it should be applied. This may entail threats of punishment or debate over details, but if successful, implementers are indoctrinated into a way of thinking and are not just complying for the time being.

As discussed previously (see chapters 1 and 3), coupling ideas to problems and politics is a key mechanism for exercising power over how people think, as it connects means to ends and to the external environment (e.g., Zahariadis, 2005). The challenging part is that some organizational actors are more self-interested and others more altruistic, so that entrepreneurs have to understand which types of power to leverage (Fowler &

Birdsall, 2020). Manipulating the self-interested type likely requires leaning on assumptions of rational choice, and focusing tactics on how ideas solve problems that impact the individual and whether those solutions are palatable to authorities in direct proximity. For instance, one may present thinking in a certain way as a means for an employee to gain rewards and prominence in an organization. In contrast, manipulating the altruistic type likely requires leaning on assumptions of social constructivism, and focusing tactics on how ideas solve broader organizational or social problems and the perceptions of those ideas in the larger community. For example, one may present a certain behavior as serving the greater good for society. In reality, no one is wholly self-interested nor altruistic, so it is best to think of people as sitting on a sliding scale. In turn, manipulation involves calibrating how one leverages power and frames ideas, so entrepreneurs often must couple streams at both individual and organizational levels simultaneously (e.g., doing X is a means to serve both the self-interest and the greater good).

Manipulation relies heavily on cognitive biases and the dynamic way that people process information (see chapter 3). Specifically, it is imperative that cogent narratives be presented, so that implementers have a clear understanding of the logical pathways they should follow when making choices (Jones & Song, 2014). Initially, this is likely to focus on triggering deliberative thinking so that entrepreneurs can dislodge intuitions that are counterproductive to their preferences, but over time, it becomes more about reinforcing status quos that are seen as desirable. Doing so requires entrepreneurs to frame and reframe narratives to focus on different elements of the story as a means to test which is the most effective for the given target (Kahneman, 2011). For instance, one may initially start out by presenting a narrative about how a policy interpretation improves quality of services for a disenfranchised community, but realize based on feedback from the target that it is having little impact on their way of thinking. If so, the entrepreneur may then shift the narrative to focus on how improving services will likely positively impact the organizational reputation or the personal reputation of the implementer. Over time, entrepreneurs repeatedly interacting with the same targets are likely to learn how to frame narratives to be effective. In sum, organizations create a framework for how power is exerted over implementers, but skill and effort are still necessary to alter how people think about the world.

Organizational and Managerial Influences:
Interviews with Managers and Implementers

While one can think about these dynamics in sophisticated theoretical terms, in practice, they are much more banal as they tend to follow existing behavioral patterns and occur instinctively as a part of social interactions, for most people. In other words, leadership and managerial skill are often engrained in one's daily life, particularly for those who are experienced in public service organizations, so it is not as labored or explicit as it may seem from a theoretical perspective. In order to illustrate how managers and implementers operate within this context, I conducted semi-structured interviews with 10 employees of federal, state, and local environmental and public health agencies across four Western states to gather data on the perceptions of public servants. I use open-ended questions to probe how rules shape policy interpretations and decisions processes, and how organizational socialization plays into all of this (see the "Methods Memo for Chapter 4" for more information on recruitment strategy, interview questions, and data analysis). Although interviewees had a diversity of experiences and backgrounds, several themes emerged that generally indicate that organizations set parameters on how individuals operate and that managers play a key role in guiding how their subordinates understand those parameters to exist.

Interestingly, most interviewees lamented that their job was not to make decisions, even though all described making key decisions in how policies were implemented throughout interviews. This suggests that decision-making in implementation is not always explicit, transparent, or well understood by those who are doing it. However, common across interviewees was a perception that their role was chiefly as a problem-solver or doer, as opposed to a rule-follower, and by extension, policies, as well as organizational rules or procedures, tend to serve as mechanisms to create boundaries on what they can do, as opposed to directing what to do. Managers in particular tended to see themselves as responsible for facilitating problem-solving for their subordinates, namely as questions emerge regarding how to achieve mission-based goals while complying with organizational rules. When speaking about experiences with a more direct implementation role, the perception seemed to focus on performing a job that was defined by objective measures, technical merits, and/or professional responsibilities; that is, doing something that was independent and severable from policy. For instance, one interviewee said "a lot of my job is very practical. It doesn't seem very much like policy. That's more the environmental side. It's when I feel like my supervisor, or supervisors above him, are looking at what I do. That's when I really focus on the rules that I am implementing. That's when I'll really look to make sure the paperwork is in order."

The same interviewee further expressed that she initially thought that her role as an environmental inspector seemed universal, but she had learned over the years that her counterparts in other jurisdictions were doing the same job differently. Of course, the technical components were consistent, but the strategy of regulatory enforcement and administrative procedures varied enough that she was unsure how much of her job was grounded in policy and how much in environmental science. Another interviewee, serving in a more managerial role, explained this as follows: "Statute and legislative mandates are still broad in nature, and that is probably appropriately so. Then, that still leaves room to operationalize within the cultural norms or organizational norms how that is actually problem-solved or implemented." However, that discretionary space tends to decrease as one moves down the chain of the command. As she put it, "as you're closer to the work, parameters are more specific, in terms of timelines and procedures. It is important to give staff clear direction on what has to be done." It is unclear whether this is because actionable items become easier to specify as one gets closer to the street level or whether there is less trust in the use of discretion as one moves down the organizational hierarchy.

Overall, there was a sense among the interviewees that their positions were mission driven, rather than policy driven, in that they had a practical job to accomplish that was broader than any single policy or rule. Multiple interviewees stated that when faced with conflicting signals on what to do or beliefs that policy is contradictory to organizational goals, they tended to fall back on the agency mission as a guide toward the appropriate pathway. As one interviewee put it, when discussing environmental permitting rules, "If I follow the established rules, there's not a chance in hell that we'll get the backlog handled. I have to figure out where do we push, where do we shortcut, where do we make assumptions, what battles do we fight. . . . Rules get you to that ninety percent level, but from a management perspective, it is figuring out how to operate in, above, below, through the rules." During one back-and-forth, the same interviewee described these dynamics using a maritime analogy where policies or rules worked like buoys and he was charged with navigating

between those buoys to get to his destination, which was defined by organizational goals. Of course, in some cases, there is significant space that
allows one leeway on both tactics or strategies which is where managerial
skills come into the equation in the same way that seamanship skills are
used in getting from one port to another.

Notably, interviewees with managerial experience specifically mentioned that they routinely referred back to the "letter of the law" when
trying to interpret policy, and several also indicated that they reference
notes or staff reports from legislative hearings or consult directly with
policymakers when they are unsure about what a policy means. This
group clearly connected these efforts to understanding the intent of the
policy, and framed a key part of their job as communicating that intent
to their subordinates. Most interviewees referred to policy intent at least
once during interviews. However, they still argued that implementation
was a "trial by fire," and decisions often needed to be made with imper-
fect data. As one interviewee put it, "If everything was that clear cut,
everyone would know exactly what to do. But, that's where you end up
with a Soviet system where 'You didn't check this box. This form doesn't
ask for that information. So, you're rejected.' The problem is that we're
not actually thinking about why we're doing what we're doing." Moreover,
another interviewee without managerial experience contended that she
rarely looks at specific policies or rules, and instead relies on her managers
to explain what a policy means—in her words, "interpreting that policy
through my supervisor."

Several interviewees also described an iterative nature to figuring
out this navigable space as policymakers or senior managers pushed back
against certain interpretations. For instance, one interviewee remarked,

> When these policies are getting made, a lot of the time policy-
> makers do not understand what the actual day-to-day impact
> is going to be. When you share that with them, and ask: is
> this what you meant? This is the outcome on the ground. Is
> this your intention? A lot of times, they will say that we didn't
> think about that. So directly asking and explaining the impact.
> Like, your policy says this, it is going to make me do this, is
> this what you meant to do?

Another interviewee described it as

Here is what we're supposed to be doing. Here is the box that we're stuck in, and if this box remains, this is the result. If that is fine, then we can move forward with that, but we all need to do that knowingly. Because I'm not going to go into this situation and be handcuffed, and then be attacked because I was handcuffed. . . . A lot of times, we have to make the best of it in a kind of crappy situation.

Interestingly, managers also seemed to have a certain degree of political awareness. Most indicated that they were cognizant of how policies-in-practice were perceived outside the organization, but suggested that it was the job of agency executives to deal with the politics. Nonetheless, one interviewee spoke to the importance of using messaging, saying, "What is it that [policy] actually says and this is how we would implement what it says, but this is what people are saying about it. So how would we bridge that gap. We could be implementing policy the best we can, but if you are not telling people why we are doing what we are doing, then you'll get your knees cut out from you, because there will always be people who don't like what you are doing." Another discussed how turnover among policymakers had led her organization to considering certain new ideas, that would not have previously been considered, out of anticipation that new policymakers would push in that direction. Most intriguing was one interviewee who regularly considered how political interests may push back against rule interpretations, as certain lobby groups "have considerably more political clout than [his agency] with the legislature." However, interviewees without managerial responsibilities largely implied that they wore blinders, and only became aware of political interests when they exerted pressure that trickled down the hierarchy. These discussions largely suggest that political pressures become less acute as one gets closer to the street level.

Within this context, most interviewees indicated that their focus when a new policy is adopted is to first contemplate how it affects day-to-day operations, but also indicated an iterative nature. One interviewee succinctly explained the decision-making process in his office:

I had my initial opinion. We're looking at. We started making decisions on. I don't like necessarily to go back and change decisions. I like moving forward. . . . But I kind of learned from those decisions. Almost like a funnel approach, I start

wide and keep narrowing the internal voice, the internal
questions to get down to what I think is something that will
work. . . . Now that I have more experience [working with
this policy], I have kind of come to a conclusion that the most
important factors [are different than what I thought initially].
It ties back to what is the intent of [this policy]. I have sort of
changed not my focus, but the measures that I am looking at
[in evaluating decisions]. I keep building on it. . . . Just keep
learning more about it and make future decisions based upon
that. . . . Make [a decision] twice, it's a precedent. Look back
after making the same decision six times, of course it's going
to be different. We don't have to adhere to that first decision,
because we are learning.

Interviewees also generally spoke about how decision processes and ways
of interpreting rules or their roles were shaped by organizational cultures
or norms; that is, there is a "way things are done" within their organizations. For instance, one interviewee stated, "There's definitely been an
established inspection protocol that has been passed down from generation to generation. It does get rehashed a little bit, but definitely a status
quo. . . . [Training on it] was almost exclusively verbal. Just through my
fellow inspectors. I didn't look through an SOP for like four years. Didn't
even know we had them. It was two years before I read the [program]
rules." She also stated that consistency within these interpretations had
been a problem in the past, but "over several years, we've done a really
good job of getting consistent within the program to see that we're interpreting the same things the same way even if it's a little different from the
rules." When questioned about the source of these norms, interviewees
indicated that they were largely built on institutional memory and/or
drawn from organizational missions. For example, one interviewee said a
supervisor made a call on how to enforcement a certain ordinance, and
that norm has continued since, even though some disagreed with that
interpretation. In contrast, another said that it was normal in her office
to routinely review the law, because of past experiences where someone
had "stepped out of bounds."

Interviewees also indicated that organizational norms tended to
align with professional standards and were driven, to a certain extent, by
interactions with colleagues in other agencies or through networks tied
to professional trade associations. This includes participation in national

training courses designed to create standardization and consistency across the industry. For instance, one interviewee said that she had a large network and when she was unsure, she reached out to colleagues and asked. Other interviewees talked about forms of horizontal communication both within and across agencies, where front-line operators or managers in similar positions would compare notes to "get on the same page." In some cases, this manifested as workshops; in other cases, it was less formal or coordinated. Furthermore, some interviewees also argued that reliance on professional networks was more important when their agency was dominated by people without technical training (e.g., lawyers, career bureaucrats). In general, the implication is that when faced with open questions, managers or implementers will seek guidance from others who have experience with similar issues in order to obtain information on what works and what does not.

The majority of managers interviewed also discussed efforts to teach or mentor their subordinates to buttress these norms. Most reflective of this was one interviewee who remarked, "I try to mentor my staff that report to me to think about the why of what we're doing. It's a fundamental tenet of management that you can tell people what to do, but if you aren't telling them why, then you are not going to get exactly what you're looking for." This would largely suggest that he is keenly aware that shaping their thinking was key to getting the behaviors that he wanted. In general, interviewees expressed that much of this learning occurred informally through "water cooler talk" or through informal interactions with colleagues. Notably, many also indicated that learning occurred as much through their peers as through managers. For instance, one said "I think a lot of it's mentoring from people that were there before. I see people go a lot to the people who have been here the longest, and asking: Am I reading this right? Is this the way we do this?"

In most cases, this occurs through training, which may include both formal and informal mechanisms, depending on the agency. For example, one interviewee discussed initiatives within his agency both to create "continuity desk reference" materials (e.g., guidebook to specific job positions) and to organize meetings for programmatic staff across the state to discuss policy or administrative rules. During these meetings, staff work through case studies together to encourage consistency in how implementers/managers interpret situations. In other cases, managers discussed their role in "messaging" around new policy initiatives; specifically, one interviewee described her role as sending messages to her subordinates about what those policies entailed. In doing so, she also noted her position as an intermediary between those above and below in the organizational hierarchy and how she both received messages from her superiors and refined those messages for her subordinates. Other interviewees talked about standard operating procedures (SOPs) and best management practices (BMPs) as key sources of information on how to do their jobs, but also noted that many of the most important lessons were learned from interacting with other experienced colleagues, as opposed to reading a manual.

An additional trend from discussions of organizational norms was the role of hiring and employee selection. Multiple interviewees indicated that there was a split in their organization that they attributed to work experiences. Specifically, they believed that those who were newer to the organization were more willing to question the existing status quos than those who had spent longer parts of their careers in the same organization. Interviewees were unsure if this was due to "coming into the situation with fresh eyes" or from having more perspective as a result of working for different types of organizations over the years, in contrast to employees who carried institutional memories forward. Interestingly, it was also suggested that experiences in public versus private sectors was a factor here, which may suggest that people self-select into organizations based on how they think about policies, with different types ending up in different sectors. One interviewee also stated that hiring managers in her organization often asked questions indicative of "soft skills" during interviews in order to identify applicants with "philosophies" that fit the organization. This would suggest that at least some managers are aware that certain personality types or ways of thinking are more malleable to the prevailing organizational logic.

Management Matters

By no means is it lost on scholars of public policy and administration that management matters for how bureaucratic agencies function in general and how programs perform in particular (e.g., Meier & O'Toole, 2007; Howlett & Walker, 2012). Managers' unique position within both organizations and the policy process provides opportunity and power to impact how policies work in practice, more so than other policy actors. Specifically, managers serve as the linchpins between the often competing and conflicting interests of maintaining the legitimacy and long-term viability of public institutions and serving the dynamic and evolving public interest. For example, when states pass laws that limit what material can be taught in college classrooms (e.g., critical race theory), it is often deans and department chairs that find solutions that respond to the demands from elected officials to temper their curriculums, under threat of budget cuts, without damaging the image of the university as a place where reason trumps politics. Of course, it is the faculty as implementers who will ultimately decide how such a policy works every time they enter their classrooms, but managers have tools to shape how instructors interpret the intent and implications of these laws for both the individual and organization.

Managers also serve as a key variable in connecting the top-down and bottom-up forces at work during policy implementation. On the one hand, leaders at the top of organizational hierarchies often treat implementers as cogs in the machine, and believe implementation can be structured through a series of rules and procedures. On the other hand, implementers often create coping mechanisms to sort through the complex rules governing their behavior while trying to respond to the ambiguous environments at the street level. Unfortunately, these two approaches have long been treated as mutually exclusive by scholars, resulting in a debate that has become stale and antiquated (O'Toole, 2000; Hill & Hupe, 2014). However, these two can be reconciled by managers, who are often positioned between the pressures from organizational leaders above and the realities that implementers face below. Managers do this by shaping how implementers think about the rules imposed by organizations, so that those coping mechanisms align, rather than conflict, with the organizational rules. For instance, if implementers use their intuition to make choices when delivering public services but that intuition is grounded in how managers have trained implementers to think, then bottom-up and top-down processes are not at conflict and may actually be mutually reinforcing.

However, much of this hinges on the quality or qualities of individual managers and their capacities to act on these imperatives. There are long lists of what people consider "good" qualities in managers (e.g., leadership, public speaking) and the types of things on resumes that are likely to demonstrate those qualities (e.g., education, training, prior work experience). Scholars have grappled with how to adequately measure it in a way that effectively explains which qualities lead to better program performance, employee job satisfaction, etc. (Meier & O'Toole, 2002; Johansen, 2013; Rainey, 2014). Nevertheless, implicit within the amorphous construct of managerial quality is a set of undefined skills in knowing how to balance the conservatorship of institutions by protecting that which cannot be easily reestablished if lost (e.g., culture) with entrepreneurial activities in reforming and improving organizations—that is, balancing stability with change (Terry, 2003; Moon, 1999; Meier & O'Toole, 2002). There is also a balance between using organizational tools to manage and using power to lead. Consequently, managerial quality is far more grounded in the ability to influence behaviors and decode organized anarchies than it is in technical skills. In essence, managerial impact on policy implementation largely hinges on the power of individual managers to affect how implementers ascribe meaning to policies in the face of ambiguous conditions that often cause one to question one's own intuition.

The key takeaway from this chapter is that organizations are designed to structure the search for and analysis of information, and managers are well positioned to use their power to influence how implementers interpret policies. Of course, a natural response to anarchy is to impose logic and order; this is how anarchies become organized. While managers wield formal tools to build structure, socialization into the cultural norms of the organization is one of the most powerful mechanisms for setting boundaries on how implementers should think and behave. Essentially, the real goal of organizations is to influence how people ascribe meaning to their roles and responsibilities within society by structuring perceptions of preference, participation, and technology. This adds further depth to understanding the context in which implementers use both their intuitive and deliberative judgment processes in applying policies, as organizations often want implementers to build their intuitive judgments on the guidance of management. Consequently, managers are among the most essential policy actors in implementation. In the next chapter, as an extension of this, I look more specifically at how policy functionality and organizational processes are aligned as implementers experiment with different ways of interpreting policies and managers design processes to create consistency in those interpretations.

5

Functionality and Formalization

Moving beyond how implementers make decisions (chapter 3) under ambiguous circumstances (chapter 1) and how organizations shape those decisions (chapter 4), I now shift focus to the specific ways in which these interact to create two intertwined constructs that emerge when turning policy into practices. In the first, implementers figure out what works by experimenting with different ways of doing things and responding to feedback from stakeholders. This is the function construct, where implementers determine how a policy should be implemented by field-testing policy interpretations. Functions are where implementers learn to cope with ambiguity and determine what fits the problem and political parameters best. Behavioral norms that constitute policies-in-practice have their roots here. In the second, organizations build formal processes around successful experiments in functionality. This is the process construct, where program managers use formal organizational tools to structure how a policy will be implemented. Processes are used to reduce the uncertainty, complexity, and volatility of implementation decisions by creating rigid, rule-based decision metrics, so that implementers become more predictable. Behavioral norms become established here. Although building good processes is essential to policy success, processes do not always flow from functionality as they should, as program managers misinterpret what makes policies functional (Fowler, 2021). But the relationship between functions and processes is crucial to connecting policy-in-theory to policy-in-practice.

In this chapter, I examine how implementers and organizations cope with ambiguity and uncertainty by experimenting with policy functionality and building processes to make implementer decisions more predictable.

The goal of this chapter is to connect the dots between where implementers figure things out and where organizations use structures to formalize decision-making tools. To do so, I first discuss the purpose and logic behind both functions and processes as two separate constructs in policy implementation, and I consider their complicated relationship and why neither can be relied upon alone to make policy work. Then I use program evaluation data from state implementation of a federal environmental policy to illustrate what functions and processes look like in practice and how they impact policy success. Finally, I discuss how to move past red tape and get to "green tape" by building processes that encourage policy functionality and success, rather than inhibit it. The key takeaway from this chapter is that policy functionality is a result of experimenting with different ways of doing things in ambiguous circumstances and processes result from formalizing successful experiments in order to reduce the unpredictability of implementer behaviors.

Making Policy Functional

A functional policy is practical and useful for both implementers executing policy and target populations trying to extract benefits from public organizations, and results in a policy-in-practice that is consistent with its intended purpose. In other words, a functional policy solves the problem that policymakers intended it to while also not creating roadblocks to public service delivery (Stazyk and Goerdel, 2011; Zahariadis, 2014; Davis and Stazyk, 2015). Functions are, then, the informal activities that occur during policy implementation that are frequently undefined but serve as a key mechanism in adapting policies to the circumstances that affect the meaning of policy in ambiguous situations (Fowler, 2021). While some policies may have more functionality than others by design, functional policies allow for these informal activities to develop, while dysfunctional policies tend to have limited utility for key stakeholders as a result of impractical components that block behaviors from evolving to meet dynamic problem and political conditions. To this end, functions tend to emerge through a combination of "satisficing" behaviors (i.e., what will satisfy and suffice) and the politics of what is possible given practical limitations on resources and time (Simon, 1997; Jones, 2003), as well as normative political concerns (i.e., pathways from elected officials to implementers; see chapter 2). This means that functions fluctuate based on policy interpretations, so that they may not be fully transferable between implementation sites where the problem and political circumstances significantly vary.

The key question of functions is: how *should* a policy be implemented? The answer to that question will always depend on what meanings are ascribed to policy, as the same policy interpreted in alternative ways dictates diverging pathways for how to make policy work (Fowler, 2021). For instance, if one interprets the meaning of speed limits as a mechanism of "broken window" policing (i.e., creating an atmosphere of law and order), then traffic enforcement should produce an impression of strict law enforcement by routinely stopping vehicles; officers should then target vehicles in high-profile areas that will be widely seen. In contrast, if one interprets speed limits as a mechanism to protect public safety, then officers should target unsafe drivers in all areas, while placing less emphasis on minor violations in order to concentrate resources on more serious violations. Based on the policy interpretation, officers will develop strategies to guide their individual behaviors. The purpose of functions is then to adapt policy-in-theory to the ambiguous conditions that make it difficult to prescribe appropriate action beforehand, by interpreting policy in such a way that actions gain the buy-in from policy communities that legitimize implementation decisions (i.e., operational localism) (Reed, 2014). Making a policy functional hinges on finding policy interpretations that appropriately operationalize policies based on the prevailing political mood and problem conditions, so that practices do not create resistance to compliance or undermine legitimacy of policies.

Functions are grounded in bottom-up approaches to implementation, so one can think of functions in similar terms as coping mechanisms used by street-level bureaucrats to craft simplified decision rules in order to deal with complex job roles (O'Toole, 2000; deLeon & deLeon, 2002; Lipsky, 2010). Often, these decision rules are used expressly to reduce ambiguity through heuristics or other mechanisms that reinforce intuitive judgments, so that implementing policies becomes less onerous and more practical in the face of constraints on time and analytical capacity (i.e., bounded rationality) (Simon, 1997; Kahneman, 2011). Logically, this relies on a "backward mapping" approach by focusing on the last step of the implementation process and then working backward through proceeding steps when designing a course of action (Elmore, 1979, 1985; Fiorino, 1997). For instance, a traffic officer may initially think through the situation in which they believe writing a speeding ticket best serves the purpose of the policy, and then work backward to understand how to target those cases. The benefit of backward mapping is that it allows implementers to prioritize decisions about how policy works for those consuming it at its end stages (i.e., target populations), so that practices at the point of delivery are purposely designed, rather than just an end result.

From this perspective, one can think of implementation as a natural experiment, and innovation scholarship argues experiments are motivated by the potential to profit and conditions of uncertainty (Nelson, 1959). The latter condition often spins out of ambiguity, but the former condition is important insofar as experimenting with different ways of implementing policies must present some kind of benefit for implementers (e.g., reduced workload, less conflict). Of course, absent the potential for benefit, implementers are unlikely to experiment, and instead follow the status quo. Furthermore, the development and deployment of human knowledge (or know-how) is often hampered by the strength of understanding the underlying dynamics of a phenomenon. For instance, if a scientist has a strong understanding of the physical processes underlying her scientific experiments, then it is much more likely that she can develop and test alternative treatments and effectively evaluate their impacts. In contrast, where those dynamics are not understood, experimenting becomes much less effective in advancing human know-how, as impacts cannot be successfully replicated under varying conditions (e.g., Nelson, 2003). To this end, rational choices about which innovations to adopt are most likely to occur where there is sharp, persuasive feedback. Absent that, though, innovation choices are likely to be driven by socially constructed perceptions of what works (Nelson, Peterhansl, & Sampat, 2004).

Thus, policy functionality largely rests on implementers' ability to experiment, or to learn from their experiences and analyze whether practices are working or not (May, 1992; Moynihan & Soss, 2014). When done well, policies become functional. However, when implementers struggle to find positive feedback or adjust behaviors based on negative feedback, they will either move on to another interpretation and develop new ideas about what is functional, or settle on the path of least resistance and use whatever practices are easiest (Lipsky, 2010; Fowler, 2021). Of course, this can lead stakeholders to question policy efficacy and/or pushback against implementation choices. To separate the functional from dysfunctional, implementers experiment with different ways of interpreting policies and executing tasks, the goal of which is to figure out what works best in practice (i.e., political and technical feasibility) (Damanpour & Schneider, 2009; Lipsky, 2010; Osborne & Brown, 2011; Fowler, 2021). The casual observer may label this as common sense, "common" being reflective of the socially constructed understanding of policy meanings and "sense" being reflective of rational choice in that context. To this end, functional policies tend to be seen as common sense as they seem rational to the average person. In contrast, dysfunctional policies often leave people questioning the purpose of doing it that way.

Nevertheless, implementers rarely systematically identify and test a series of alternatives so that not all potential alternatives are considered. Rather, functions heavily rely on implementers' intuition and experience to guide initial ideas about what is likely to work. Then implementers follow an anchoring approach by making iterative adjustments based on feedback from stakeholders who include program managers, policymakers, policy entrepreneurs, target populations, and other implementers. Deliberative thinking may also be used where intuitive judgments are met with such opposition that it causes implementers to reformulate their mental models of policy (Kahneman, 2011). Since stakeholders may have alternative perceptions of what works best, feedback can be conflicting and send mixed signals on what adjustments are needed. Thus, functionality is not about what is optimal, but rather about quickly finding an alternative that satisfices. In practice, this often appears as one using common sense, as stakeholders in direct proximity agree that choices seem reasonable and rational. But it is notable that not everyone has common sense or the ability to decode social situations and make rational choices, contributing to perceptions of dysfunctional government.

While organizations integrate formal feedback mechanisms into processes, implementers often learn what works through informal feedback gained from repeated interactions with target populations, or through communicating with other implementers (Lipsky, 2010; Moynihan & Soss, 2014; Hendriks & Lees-Marshment, 2019). Feedback from these sources tends to be more narrowly focused on individual experiences, so program managers play key roles in connecting functional choices to indirect impacts or aggregate patterns in order to provide implementers with a fuller view of whether their practices are working (e.g., performance metrics). Given the informal nature of how functions are used, implementers are often left to their own judgment when compiling feedback and determining how to respond to it. Unfortunately, this means that implementers are at risk of coming to different conclusions about what works, and it is often difficult to understand the causal relationship between functions and policy performance. As a consequence, functions "tend to result in a lack of consistency across implementers, making it difficult to identify or replicate specific practices that lead to improved policy outcomes" (Fowler, 2021, p. 583).

Building Processes

Processes are used by organizations to establish uniformity and consistency in policy practices, so that implementer decisions become more predictable. In essence, processes formalize policy interpretations by constraining what information is relevant and how that information is used when making decisions. While functions are driven by practical concerns of public service delivery, processes are driven by organizational concerns over risks created when implementers are allowed to experiment with different policy interpretations (Scott, 1997; Potoski, 1999; Wood and Bohte, 2004; DeHart-Davis, Chen, & Little, 2013). Processes, then, "manifest as a set of organizational systems and procedures, which create rather rigid guidelines for decision-making and formalize acceptable behavior" (Fowler, 2021, p. 584) and serve as the mechanism for galvanizing how implementers perceive policy interpretations. This means that where processes work, implementers should have a consistent understanding of what a policy means and how to put it into practice, regardless of the problem or political circumstances. Processes tend to emerge through organizational imperatives to create objectivity in decision-making, so that the quality or character of policy-in-practice is not a function of how implementers read a situation. To this end, organizations with high capacity for processes are capable of building rules and procedures around functionality that lead to policies working as intended and needed at the street level, while organizations with low capacity struggle to promulgate rules and induce compliance so that implementers are left to rely on their own ingenuity when making choices (Fowler, 2021).

The key question of processes is: how *will* a policy be implemented? In contrast to functions, this is less about what works and more about creating predictability in an unpredictable world by installing mechanisms that focus implementer perceptions and decisions. For instance, an application for food stamps requests specific information about applicants and by doing so, this form essentially bounds both the criteria considered by and the information available to whomever is reviewing the form. Where functions are used to cope with ambiguity, processes are used to cope with uncertainty where implementers make sense of circumstances and managers try to predict their decisions (Fowler, 2021). This is achieved through compliance with rules, regulations, and procedures that reduce the impact of dynamic external circumstances. Specifically, where complex, volatile, and uncertain conditions make it more likely that problem and political parameters affect policy interpretations, processes focus implementers on an objective set of guidelines that direct how to think about the situation. Ideally, this leads to consistent interpretations of policy and following a set of desirable behaviors (Potoski, 1999, 2002). Furthermore, with efficient workflows, implementers are less likely to become distracted about their roles and responsibilities, and are able to focus on the task at hand (Gajduschek, 2003; Jung, 2014).

Processes are grounded in top-down approaches to implementation, so one can think of processes as being driven by the concerns of program managers interested in preserving the long-term viability of their organizations over the more narrowed interests of how a single policy works at the street level (O'Toole, 2000; deLeon & deLeon, 2002). While functional coping mechanisms are an extension of intuitive judgments made by implementers, processes are designed to replace the intuition of the implementer with that of the organization, so that quick judgments are aligned with managerial preferences (Kahneman, 2011). Logically, processes tend to follow a "forward mapping" approach by focusing on the first step of implementation and then moving sequentially forward with defined expectations established along the way (Elmore, 1979, 1985; Fiorino, 1997). For instance, a social worker will begin by finding the appropriate form to fill out for a person seeking public assistance, then, on the basis of that form, come to a decision about whether they qualify. The result is that those who qualify meet the same objective standards (e.g., employment status), regardless of who the implementer is. As this assumes that those at the top of organizations can define and direct what implementers do at the street level, it follows a logical pathway that is not subject to dynamic conditions or implementer whims.

One person interviewed for this book described his agency's approach to developing and improving processes as an iterative, intensive process involving a large group of stakeholders. Specifically, within his agency, a group of managers and implementers would regularly get together to map out decision trees and create flow charts. Then, from those flow charts, they would identify bottlenecks or redundancies that reduce the efficiency of the process or create inconsistencies. In his words, the goal here is to come up with the most streamlined, most easily repeatable process. . . . [Their approach] breaks down the process completely, so everyone is dealing with the process from a shared pool of knowledge. Then, you sort of rebuild the process to get it as streamlined and efficient as possible, and something that can be consistently utilized over and over and over again. Of course, that's not a one and done. As new things come up, we store them and we see how we integrate those into the processes. . . . We are constantly updating our processes to ensure that they make sense and to ensure that things are touched as few times as possible and this creates an opportunity to consistently deliver quality work.

Ideally, processes derive from successful experiments in functionality, so that the behavioral norms mandated by organizations are based on practices that are proven to make policy work for both implementers and target populations (Fowler, 2021). For instance, if a police officer figures out that giving a warning and providing counseling reduces the likelihood of recidivism among youth offenders, other officers are likely to follow a similar strategy until program managers recognize the utility of doing so and it becomes an official part of department standard operating procedures. However, there are two challenges to this. First, program managers who design rules do not always understand why an experiment is successful or not, so they may misinterpret what to formalize. This often happens when program managers are distanced from the action so that personal experiences are unlikely to change their thinking, or where managers are influenced by entrepreneurs looking to institutionalize their preferred policy interpretations. Unfortunately, this means that managers are predisposed to focus chiefly on information that supports certain narratives about how policies work or are supposed to work (Moynihan & Lavertu, 2012). Second, installing new processes tends to create conflicts between different organizational components, so that a process that improves one person's job may make another's harder. In balancing these competing interests, program managers often prioritize risk to the organization over policy functionality, so that processes produce as little disruption as possible (Bozeman & Kingsley, 1998).

Of course, this creates a thin line between processes that work and those that amount to red tape. Bureaucracies are notorious for the dysfunction, inefficiency, and/or counterproductivity that often occurs when implementers over-rely on black-and-white rule interpretations that neither further intended policy goals nor serve the interests of implementers or target populations. While red tape occurs for many reasons, common causes are program managers misinterpreting what makes a policy functional or miscalculating organizational risk from disruption of status quos compared to ineffective policy, or unintended consequences when the impacts of processes are not fully considered (Bozeman, 1993; DeHart-Davis, 2009a). But processes can also lend themselves to normal bureaucratic function and stakeholder rule compliance. Believe it or not, this can be common in organizations that are capable of creating rules, regulations, and procedures that focus on policy goals and that are easily complied with. While good processes can both advance functionality and produce greater consistency, this is not a given, and bad processes can be counterproductive to both (Pandey & Kingsley, 2000; DeHart-Davis, 2009a, 2009b, 2017). It cannot be understated here how important processes are for creating shared norms for policies-in-practice, so where red tape proliferates, the status quo for policy-in-practice is tantamount to policy failure.

Connecting Functions and Processes

Now let's think about how functions and processes help us understand the story of how policies turn into practices. A new policy gets adopted. Program managers pass along information and guidance to implementers on what they need to know about how policies fit into existing organizational schemes. Implementers grapple with what this means for how they do their job—specifically, what, if any, changes they need to make to their routine. They use their intuition to come up with initial ideas. If their initial ideas are met with positive feedback, they become the way things are unofficially done. If they are met with negative feedback, adjustments are made until implementers settle on something that they feel satisfies the competing interests. The more negative feedback received, though, the more likely implementers will start thinking deliberately about what is working and what is not. While it is not necessary to affect change, entrepreneurs are prone to target implementers with negative feedback (e.g., complaints) in order to get them to rethink what they are doing. As entrepreneurs frame and reframe information by coupling problems, politics, and policy to create a cogent narrative about what the policy means, implementers may be convinced that certain courses of action are warranted. In some cases, entrepreneurs may also follow up with positive feedback to encourage implementers to settle on this understanding of policy, so streams are not decoupled.

If implementing the new policy easily fits within existing ways of doing things, there is no need to adjust organizational processes, and implementers should be able to rely on their intuitive judgments on how to extend behavioral patterns to new situations. But if implementers start running into negative feedback when following existing processes, they will start experimenting with functionality, creating anomalies that challenge the structures imposed by program managers. Program managers, then, must make sense of what is broken and how to fix it in order to promulgate new rules and procedures to stamp down the uncertainty that these anomalies create. These processes serve to divert implementers' search for alternatives in directions preferred by management. As implementers begin deferring to these processes, policy interpretations converge, so there is a general shared understanding of what policies mean among implementers. In turn, implementers start following similar behaviors, so that a common set of practices emerge as well. As practices normalize, policies-in-practice stabilize across implementation sites, so implementers are likely to do the same things over and over again. As a result, target populations are exposed to the similar experiences with policy, regardless of who is providing it.

Over time, target populations respond to these norms and social conditions change as a result. In effect, these processes are socializing target populations by creating consistent experiences that are transferable between implementation sites, so that knowledge travels with the population affected by the policy (Tyler, Fagan, & Geller, 2014; Schneider, Ingram, & deLeon, 2018). This contributes to target populations learning how bureaucracies work, enabling them to have a better understanding of how to comply with processes, cooperate with implementers, and participate in democratic governance. Notably, social capital from target communities is one of the most effective resources available for implementation, as it mitigates the struggles of co-production where public services require active participation to be effective (see chapter 2) (Brudney, 1985; Smylie & Evans, 2006; Brandsen & Honingh, 2016). In contrast, where bureaucratic regulations are unclear and lead to red tape, target populations are less likely to understand what is being asked of them or to learn how to navigate the system, creating a barrier to compliance and cooperation. Given this, if functions and processes are reflective of the intents of policymakers that originally designed the policy, then the changes that emerge in social conditions through new behavioral norms should equate to successful policy.

Can processes work without functions or functions without processes? In organized anarchies, functions and processes occur as a natural result of program managers trying to impose logic so implementers can make enough sense of the world to chart a course of action. Ideally, there is a cyclical relationship between the two, where functions arise when implementers find flaws in processes and processes adapt from experiments in functionality. Under these conditions, one can imagine that not only will implementers figure out how to make policies work in practice but organizations will produce processes that institutionalize these practices; subsequently, policies will be successful or, at least, policy implementation will not be the cause of failure. But, in reality, functions often become disconnected from processes and vice versa, as unworkable processes cause implementers to give up on functionality or program managers misunderstand what makes a policy functional when designing processes. Unfortunately, when functions and processes become disconnected, implementers struggle to cope with ambiguity, and organizations with uncertainty. Policies, then, never quite make sense to implementers, causing them to flounder as they try to apply the policy to situations faced at the street level.

Although many implementation practices fit neatly into the function or process boxes, there are also some activities that seem to straddle the line in between. While I have described functions and processes as two distinct "ideal" types of implementation activities, it may be better to think of this as a continuum (Fowler, 2021). On one end are activities driven by implementers trying to cope with ambiguity, and on the other end, activities driven by program managers trying to cope with uncertainty; in between is a sliding scale of activities that combine elements of both in different ways. Additionally, functions and processes are highly interrelated, or at least they should be, so they are difficult to fully separate even if they can be described as distinct theoretical concepts. For instance, an implementer engaging with a client to understand what a policy or policies mean for her circumstances is predominantly function based, while filling out the corresponding forms to collect objective information used to make determinations on what benefits a client is eligible for is predominantly process based. In practice, these two are happening simultaneously and may be difficult to understand as two separate activities, particularly where they become intertwined in the minds of implementers. But, theoretically, they serve discrete purposes in understanding how policy is made to fit into the chaotic situations occurring in the real world.

Best Practices for Environmental Policy: A Natural Experiment

While functions and processes are not always easy to identify in the real world, particularly as functions tend to be informal and unspoken norms, federal monitoring and evaluation of state environmental policy provides data from a natural experiment in policy implementation. Specifically, most federal environmental policies in the US, such as the Clean Air Act (CAA) of 1963, as amended in 1970, 1977, and 1990, operate based on a system of partial preemption, whereby the US Environmental Protection Agency (EPA) delegates primary implementation authority (known as primacy) but sets minimum thresholds for performance. As a result, states with primacy over the CAA have significant discretion to design and operationalize programs to meet the unique needs of their jurisdictions, while working within a set of federal guidelines and performance requirements (Woods, 2006; Fowler, 2020b). EPA monitors states for compliance, and since 2004, uses the State Review Framework for Compliance and Enforcement Performance (SRF) to evaluate state programs across a series of objective metrics for the CAA, along with programs related to the Clean Water Act (CWA) and Resource Conservation and Recovery Act (RCRA) (US EPA, 2005). Fortunately, this provides an in-depth perspective of how functions and processes manifest across 50 state experiments in applying the same policies to varying real-world circumstances.

SRF evaluations focus on program elements (see table 5.1) that cover data management, compliance inspection, violation identification, compliance enforcement, and penalty assessment. In general, program elements are measured using a series of quantitative metrics based on a review of state and federal data systems, while evaluators also provide qualitative comments to add context and explanation. For the purposes here, I am particularly interested in two types of data: 1) during the 2009 to 2013 evaluation cycle, a "good practices" designation was used to identify practices that were implemented exceptionally well; and 2) for each program element, state programs are awarded a rating of area for improvement, area for attention, and meets expectations (US EPA, 2021a). Notably, EPA evaluators are the ultimate judge of whether a practice is good or not, so there is far more emphasis on perceptions of how federal guidelines have been implemented and complied with, as opposed to direct impacts

Table 5.1. Program Element Definitions

Data
• *Data completeness:* Degree to which the minimum data requirements are complete.
• *Data accuracy:* Degree to which the minimum data requirements are accurate (e.g., correct codes are used, dates are correct).
• *Timeliness of data entry:* Degree to which the minimum data requirements are timely.
Inspections
• *Completion of commitments:* Degree to which all enforcement/compliance commitments in relevant agreements (e.g., PPAs, PPGs, categorical grants, CMS plans, authorization agreements) are met and any products or projects are completed.
• *Inspection coverage:* Degree to which the state completed the universe of planned inspections/compliance evaluations (addressing core requirements and federal, state, and regional priorities).
• *Quality of inspection or compliance evaluation reports:* Degree to which inspection or compliance evaluation reports properly document observations are completed in a timely manner, and include accurate description of observations.
Violations
• *Identification of alleged violations:* Degree to which compliance determinations are accurately made and promptly reported in the national database based on compliance monitoring report observations and other compliance monitoring information (e.g., facility-reported information).
• *Identification of SNC and HPV:* Degree to which the state accurately identifies significant noncompliance/high-priority violations and enter information into the national system in a timely manner.
Enforcement
• *Enforcement actions promote return to compliance:* Degree to which state enforcement actions include required corrective action (i.e., injunctive relief or other complying actions) that will return facilities to compliance in a specific time frame.
• *Timely and appropriate action:* Degree to which the state takes timely and appropriate enforcement actions in accordance with policy relating to specific media.
Penalties
• *Penalty calculation method:* Degree to which the state documents in its files that initial penalty calculation includes both gravity and economic benefit calculations, appropriately using the BEN model or other method that produces results consistent with national policy.
• *Final penalty assessment and collection:* Degree to which differences between initial and final penalty are documented in the file along with a demonstration in the file that the final penalty was collected.

Source: US EPA (2021a).

of management practices on environmental quality. While this provides a mechanism to make comparisons about implementation practices that are largely independent of policy design, it also means that ratings are more likely a manifestation of what it means for a policy to work in practice from EPA's perspective, than from other stakeholders (Fowler, 2020a, 2021).

With this data, I employ a two-stage analytical strategy. First, I use qualitative analysis of the individual good practices to identify specific examples of functions and processes and to determine how functions and processes manifest under each program element. Second, I use the qualitative analysis from stage 1 to construct a theoretical model of how program elements correspond to functions and processes, and then I use a structural equation model (SEM) to test both whether these exist as latent constructs within the evaluation data and whether there is a causal relationship with program outcomes (see "Methods Memo for Chapter 5" in the Appendix for more details of methodology and analysis strategy). Program elements are coded as: (0) area for state improvement; (1) area for state attention; and (2) meets expectations. The dataset includes 93 program evaluations from the 2009 to 2013 and the 2015 to 2019 SRF cycles, representing 88 percent of potential evaluations (i.e., 53 state/ territorial CAA programs × 2 evaluation cycles = 106 potential reports). Due to incomplete data within some reports, observations for individual program elements range from 49 to 93 (see table A5.1 in the "Methods Memo"); in total, this provides 981 observations of individual elements, representing 77 percent of potential observations (i.e., 106 state programs × 12 elements = 1,272 potential element observations).

To connect functions and processes to CAA program outcomes, I use airborne toxic chemical releases reported to EPA's Toxic Release Inventory (TRI) database. The TRI database tracks self-reported data from regulated facilities in the manufacturing, mining, utilities, waste management, or wholesale trade industries that produce more than 25,000 pounds of toxic chemical releases a year (US EPA, 2021b, 2021c). Since airborne toxic releases are affected by other factors as well, I also control for economic outputs from industries required to report toxic releases (in per capita 2009 dollars), state environmental expenditures (in per capita 2009 dollars), and partisan control of the state legislature. Unsurprisingly, findings show that states that spend more on the environment and that do not have Republican-controlled legislatures also tend to have fewer airborne toxic chemical releases, which is consistent with previous research (e.g., Fowler & Kettler, 2021). Findings for industry are not statistically significant. I obtained data from the US Bureau of Economic Analysis (2021), the US Census Bureau (2021), and the National Conference of State Legislatures (2021).

Table 5.2 provides a summary and examples of good practices from CAA programs. Given that by their nature process-based practices are easier to identify and delineate than function-based practices, process-based practices are more commonly mentioned in SRF reports, the predominant group of which includes checklists, templates, or forms that ensure policy compliance, and documentation that supports findings. In general, this group of practices includes organizational tools developed so that implementers "fill in the blank" when conducting inspections or other

Table 5.2. Best Practices for CAA Implementation

Functions	Processes
• Liaison officer (*Virginia*) • Completed planned inspections/ grant obligations (*Massachusetts, Wyoming*) • Developed alternative inspection strategy or exceeds inspection requirements (*Virginia, Wyoming*) • Inspector performance plans (*Virginia*) • Reports are well written, thorough, detailed, or beyond minimum requirements (*Maryland, New Hampshire, Virginia, West Virginia, Wyoming*) • LEAN process informs inspection strategy (*Connecticut*) • "Attentive to HPV policy" (*Wyoming*) • Prioritizes injunctive relief (*Maine, Rhode Island, Texas*)	• Workflow/information flow (*Virginia*) • Monthly quality checks (*Massachusetts*) • Quality control checkpoint (*Massachusetts*) • Checklists/templates/forms (*Alaska, Connecticut, Massachusetts, Rhode Island, Virginia, Wyoming*) • Documentation (*Connecticut*) • Pre/post inspection reports (*Massachusetts*) • Timely reports (*Maine*) • Checklist (*New Hampshire*) • Documentation of enforcement actions (*Maine, Rhode Island*) • Sends notification letters outlining necessary steps for compliance (*Texas*) • Penalty calculation template (*Pennsylvania, West Virginia*) • Documentation (*Maine, North Dakota, Rhode Island CAA*) • Penalty assessment template (*Pennsylvania*)

Source: Author.

tasks. Two other themes also emerge with processes: data management and workflow. Both of these fit a similar mold in that agencies have constructed mechanisms for consistency and efficiency that increase oversight of individual implementers. In most cases, these are relatively mundane in that they do not reflect an innovative way of thinking about how to implement the CAA; rather, they reflect a way to reduce how much critical thinking implementers must do in the course of their jobs. Additionally, many of these practices appear to be easily replicable in other settings; in some cases, sharing between agencies is even mentioned in reports.

Shifting attention to the SEM provides further context into how processes and functions manifest as different types of practices associated with CAA implementation (see tables 5.3 and 5.4). Specifically, functions are correlated with completion of commitments, inspection coverage, data completeness, enforcement promotes compliance, and quality of inspection reports. In general, these program elements are defined in more sophisticated terms than those for processes insofar as success is tied to complex tasks (e.g., completing projects) or defined across multiple dimensions (e.g., reports are timely, accurate, and provide documentation). Moreover, standards are far more ambiguous (e.g., quality) or tied to circumstances (e.g., commitments) that may vary. In contrast, processes are correlated with identification of alleged violations, identification of significant noncompliance (SNC) and high-priority violations (HPV), data accuracy, and timely and appropriate action. In large part, these program elements are

Table 5.3. Results from SEM of SRF Program Elements: Structural Model

Structural Model	
Processes	−.375 (.159)*
Functions	.390 (.178)*
Industry	.074 (.097)
Expenditures	−.283 (.095)†
Legislature	.350 (.091)‡
R^2	.265

Note: Standardized coefficients reported. Standard errors in parentheses. P-value = * < .05, † > .01, ‡ > .001. N = 93.
Source: Author.

Table 5.4. Results from SEM of SRF Program Elements: Measurement Model

Measurement Model	Function	Process	R²
Data completeness	.491 (.121)‡	.0002 (.0008)	.241
Data accuracy		.598 (.084)‡	.358
Completion of commitments	.836 (.104)‡		.699
Inspection coverage	.645 (.131)‡		.416
Quality of inspection reports	.411 (.181)*	.136 (.168)	.259
Identification of alleged violations	−.175 (.321)	1.0001 (.236)‡	.808
Identification of SNC & HPV	−.070 (.264)	.711 (.183)‡	.448
Enforcement promotes compliance	.443 (.224)*	.224 (.185)	.372
Timely and appropriate action	.248 (.182)	.317 (.158)*	.261
Covariance process-function	.635‡		

Note: Standardized coefficients reported. Standard errors in parentheses. P-value = * < .05, † > .01, ‡ > .001. N = 93.
Source: Author.

defined in terms of meeting black-and-white criteria, such as accurately making compliance determinations or reporting data to national databases. Additionally, there is more clarity surrounding what these program elements hope to achieve (e.g., accuracy, prompt action). Taken as a whole, this would support functions as being tied to ambiguous tasks with less specificity or rigidity, while processes are more closely tied to practices with rigid criteria and constraints.

The SEM also provides evidence to how processes and functions affect program outcomes—in this case, airborne toxic chemical releases (i.e., air pollution). Specifically, processes are negatively correlated with air pollution, while functions are positively correlated. This means that in states where agencies perform better at processes, there are fewer toxic chemicals released into the air when controlling for differences in industries, spending on the environment, and legislative partisanship. In contrast, where agencies perform better at functions, there tend to be more toxic chemicals released. This would generally suggest that creating processes ultimately leads to better program performance, where making policies functional likely does not have such a direct relationship. Although it may seem that producing quality reports is more important than accurately reporting to national databases for reducing pollution, this really reflects whether agencies are capable of establishing compliance with rules and procedures as compared to facilitating innovation. To this end, these results would suggest that innovations are more likely to be counterproductive to performance goals as a whole, even if individual experiments prove to be successful. In contrast, creating consistency and removing uncertainty in implementation practices is highly likely to advance program goals and improve outcomes.

Finally, it is also worth noting that the covariance between processes and functions is positive and statistically significant, meaning that both fluctuate in the same direction (i.e., where agencies score high on function-based program elements, they are also likely to score high on process-based elements). While this does not imply a causal relationship between the two, it does indicate that they are not unrelated. Of course, a causal relationship is difficult to isolate here, as theoretically, functions and processes should adjust iteratively in response to the other over time and SRF data reports only provide a snapshot. That snapshot may not be able to fully capture the complex dynamics, especially when SRF reports were never designed to do such. But, given that there is a strong correlation between the two, it would suggest that the association is not spurious. A possible analogy here is this relationship is similar to that between alcoholism and depression; certainly, they can exist independent of each other, but in many cases, they coexist and one tends to reinforce the other.

In general, these findings largely confirm the conceptualization of process and functions as two separate constructs within policy implementation: one to deal with ambiguity and one to deal with uncertainty. This likely explains why function-based practices and program elements are less defined and allow for a degree of subjectivity that can adjust to different ways of thinking, while process-based practices and elements create a more objective standard for how implementation will work in order to create certainty in the face of fluid and dynamic conditions. Findings also connect this to program outcomes, where consistency in practices is more important than functionality. Of course, processes that work to improve outcomes are likely tied to figuring out functionality, so the role of functions cannot be discounted as a factor here even if the relationship is not as direct. While this analysis would generally indicate that processes and functions help explain different types of practices used in policy implementation, the specific observations of how they are structured is limited to the CAA, so it may be difficult to extrapolate to other cases. For instance, although checklists and templates may be a universal aspect of processes in any public service organization, the same checklists used by air quality inspectors are unlikely to be applicable to other programs. In contrast, functions in general are likely to vary widely depending on the policy design and purpose, problem parameters, political atmosphere, and/or stakeholders.

Getting to Green Tape

"Red tape" may be one of the most common phrases associated with the pathologies of bureaucracy, particularly in the public sector, where managers tend to be concerned about its impact on their ability to do their job (Rainey, Pandey, & Bozeman, 1995; Bozeman & Feeney, 2011). It is often used to describe excessive or meaningless paperwork, overburdensome constraints, or unnecessary rules and procedures. Predictably, red tape has negative impacts on organizational performance, as well as employee morale and job satisfaction (Quratulain & Khan, 2015; Jacobsen & Jakobsen, 2018; Kaufmann, Taggart, & Bozeman, 2018; George et al., 2021). Of course, red tape is not strictly the result of incompetence; rather, it tends to emerge through attempts to ensure processes are representative and accountable and meet the demands of stakeholders. While less common, the terms "white tape" and "green tape" have both been used to describe processes that stand in contrast to red tape, in that they further organizational or policy goals, even if they create barriers and constraints as a by-product. In most cases, the purpose of white tape is to use processes to protect organizations by mitigating risks and balancing interests through formalization; of course, this creates a thin line between red and white, as a rule used to protect one interest can quickly become overburdensome as it relates to others (Bozeman, 1993; Kaufmann, 2015).

In contrast, the purpose of green tape is seeing that policies achieve their intended goals by formalizing thinking and behaviors that effectively operationalize ambiguous ideas into behaviors at the street level. While red tape can be differentiated from white and green tape by its inherent meaningless or unnecessary nature, the difference between green and white tape hinges on green tape as a mechanism to achieve intended policy objectives, as opposed to protecting organizations, and to encourage stakeholder cooperation, as opposed to balancing competing interests against each other (Bozeman, 1993; DeHart-Davis, 2009a, 2009b). In effect, one can think of white tape as resulting from processes designed to maintain public institutions, green tape from processes designed to serve the public interest, and red tape from processes that hinder both of those goals.

Harkening back to the challenges of balancing the long-term interests of institutions and the short-term interests of the public during democratic governance (see chapter 2), red, white, and green tape further illustrate the pitfalls of democratic policy implementation. On the one hand, designing processes with white tape may protect institutions, but it will also likely lead bureaucracy to being seen as disconnected and unyielding to the citizens that it is supposed to serve. On the other hand, designing processes with green tape may serve citizens, but it is also likely to lead to operational inefficiency and open administrative agencies to political attacks from elected officials campaigning against government waste.

This leads us to the question of whether implementation should be designed to be efficient with the impetus on citizens to learn to use the processes to extract the benefits they are entitled to or whether it should be designed to be democratic and focused on citizen needs with the impetus on bureaucracy to find efficiencies where possible. While we can be certain that red tape will always be the least favorable option, both white and green tape represent flawed approaches to serving the competing interests of democratic governance, and one can quickly veer into red territory if processes are not designed with these issues at top of mind. To this end, white tape is not necessarily a bad thing, but it does complicate policy implementation in that risks to the organization are prioritized above the intents of policy. Unsurprisingly, white tape does not always equal policy success, and at times can hinder implementers from making policies work. In contrast, green tape is ideal for furthering policy goals, and while it may not always protect organizations from difficult decisions, green tape is unlikely to cause organizations to fail. Consequently, the goal for implementation, in most cases, should be getting to green tape.

So, how does one wrap processes in green tape? First, implementers need to be allotted the discretion and flexibility to figure out the best ways to make policies work in practice for stakeholders with diverse perspectives and interests. While functionality in itself is unlikely to lead to desired policy outcomes, experiments in policy interpretations are essential to finding meanings that create consensus among stakeholders, so their cooperation can eventually be leveraged to obtain buy-in to implementation choices. Additionally, when implementers are figuring out how to make a policy work, it also serves as a testing ground for the technical parameters of policies-in-practice (i.e., is this policy enforceable in practice?). Second, program managers should use feedback mechanisms (both formal and informal) to evaluate what works and why it works, so processes are not based on the types of flawed logic that inevitably lead to red tape. It is imperative that processes be tied to mechanisms that make policies functional, so that success can be replicated. This often means that managers and implementers need to move beyond their preconceived narratives and motivated reasoning in order to consider functionality from different perspectives.

Third, formalization should be built around what works. Specifically, processes need to institutionalize policy interpretations that direct implementers to focus on certain sets of information and ways of thinking about it. Processes are not just about developing checklists. Processes are about developing checklists that encourage an implementer to interpret a policy in a specific way when faced with uncertain circumstances, so that the outcomes of her choices are predictable and consistent and align with policy goals. Fourth, implementers need to be socialized into processes so they understand how they are designed and what they hope to achieve. Checklists in themselves do not shape behaviors; how implementers understand those checklists do. Specifically, when implementers approach a checklist as an exercise in checking boxes, the underlying purpose of each item on that checklist is overlooked, essentially neutralizing its effectiveness. Thus, implementers must understand processes as more than just hoops to jump through. Finally, this cycle should be repeated and repeated, ad nauseam. Implementation is an ongoing exercise, so functions and processes must continually be adjusted to emerging ways of thinking about what a policy means and the dynamic circumstances that may confuse implementers about their goals. While there is no guarantee that this ends in green tape, these steps should get processes closer with each iteration.

The key takeaway from this chapter is that functionality comes from experimenting with ways of coping with ambiguous circumstances, and processes come from formalizing those experiments in order to reduce uncertainty. While much of this occurs naturally in response to organized anarchies, program managers play a key role in building processes, so that green tape facilitates implementers achieving policy goals through a collective effort. As an extension of previous chapters, this adds further depth to how intuitive judgments combined with organizational pressures buttress status quos and make it difficult to trigger change in the behavioral norms surrounding policies, especially where red tape creates barriers. Of course, implementers are still likely to rely on intuitive thinking when figuring out how to turn policy meanings into action as they navigate competing pressures from policies, organizational imperatives, and dynamic problem and political parameters that challenge established status quos. Certainly, trying to reconcile these contradictions is why experiments in functionality are pivotal to the ebb and flow of implementation. Furthermore, balancing functions and processes, as well as green and white tape, also connects back to some of the core issues that emerge with the role of policy implementation in democratic governance. In the next chapter, I extend this to the macro level and examine how these mechanisms manifest in patterns across institutions and amount to the large-scale changes in social or environmental conditions as intended by policymakers.

6

From Ideas to Action and Actions to Outcomes

While one can see how policies are implemented from the previous chapters, this still has not quite answered the question of why policies succeed or fail to impact society as intended. Policies may succeed or fail in isolated moments; indeed, some policy failure may even be "business-as-usual" (Peters, 2015). But one isolated failure or success is often not enough evidence to understand whether a policy has effected positive change in society, even if it does affect the lived experience of the individual. To understand policy success and failure, it is necessary to look more broadly at the patterns of policies-in-practice at the macro level, and ask whether policies have led to change in the status quo. While the core questions of policy implementation focus on how implementers make meaning when applying ambiguous policies to the real world, the impacts of these choices tend to be observed best at the institutional level where the collective effort of an amorphous group of implementers manifests as policies-in-practice. In other words, when one wants to understand how a policy has been implemented, analysts and policymakers often look at the broad trends, rather than the isolated case. For instance, a single student's experience in a classroom may not be an accurate representation of how a policy works, but the collective experience of every student in that classroom or across a school likely is, and is also telling about whether education policy is working.

Furthermore, how often is it that a new state education law or school district policy makes a difference to the experiences of students, either individually or as group? Certainly, the power to change the world is not in the hands of implementers alone. Thus, one must consider the effectiveness of policies in terms of fixing what's wrong with the system or why some policies worked and others failed to influence changes in the policies-in-practice. To this end, policymakers and implementers share governance responsibility as they both wield power to shape solutions, which aids depth to the complexities surrounding how change comes about inside organized anarchies with institutionalized status quos (see chapter 1). Of course, how implementers make choices (chapter 3), how organizations shape those choices (chapter 4), and how processes and functions are used to cope with ambiguity (chapter 5) are key to understanding the causal relationships that underlie the institutional patterns and how this affects democratic governance (chapter 2). But equally important is understanding how collective choice (i.e., policymaking) is intertwined with collective action (i.e., implementation), so one can also understand the causal pathway from good ideas to a better world.

In this chapter, I examine where policy implementation fits into a broader policy process and how it is interdependent with policymaking. The goal here is to examine how implementation exists on an institutional level that represents the cumulative efforts of both policymakers and implementers as part of a governance system. To do so, I first present a model of the whole policy process, based on the multiple streams framework (MSF) and centering on ambiguity as a key factor plaguing policy, that explains both how policy choices are made and how those choices are implemented. I also provide empirical evidence to support this model, using a dataset of state implementation of federal environmental policy that extends the data from the previous chapter to understand how policies-in-practice manifest across states and over time. Finally, I discuss the broader implications for how collective choice becomes collective action, and what this means for understanding democratic governance. The key takeaway from this chapter is that there is a causal pathway that goes from collective choice (i.e., policymaking) to collective action (i.e., policy implementation) to social conditions.

Implementation in the Bigger Picture

As one can easily surmise, policy implementation is not isolated from policymaking. In fact, many would argue that implementation should start with a thorough reading of the letter of the law, but as has been discussed at length in this volume, the letter of the law is often too ambiguous to clearly instruct implementers on what to do. This perspective also implies a sequential ordering to key events so that policy plays out in distinct stages with implementation naturally predicated on policymaking (Nakamura, 1987; Smith & Larimer, 2016); by extension, this also assumes a sequential ordering to how ambiguity is reduced systematically by a process that flows from policymakers to implementers. But implementation is not simply what happens after policies are adopted. Implementation is more intertwined with policymaking than that. Specifically, how policies are implemented is largely responsive to the same dynamics that drive how policies are adopted (i.e., making choices under ambiguous circumstances), and which policies are adopted is often influenced by how previous policies were implemented. Thus, the "textbook" model of policy stages is often misaligned with the practical reality of policy, where policymakers and implementers use different sets of tools to advance toward the same goal. To this end, policy should be thought of as playing out through an iterative process where policymaking influences implementation and implementation influences policymaking as ideas and actions are tweaked until problems are solved.

Fowler (2022) introduces a model of the entire policy process, or more accurately policy cycle because there is an inherent recurrent nature to its elements, based on MSF logic that serves just this purpose. Here, the five structural elements are laid out to capture the interrelated aspects of both the policymaking and implementation phases as part of a larger process with the goal of illustrating how policy moves from proposed ideas to actions to impacts on the world (see figure 6.1) with the key assumption that ambiguity is an implicit factor throughout. To start, there are actually three outputs that mark important choke points in the policy cycle, or points by which one can monitor progress and isolate cause-and-effect relationships. Policymaking outputs, or new policies adopted to address non-ideal conditions, mark the end of the choice phase and the beginning of the action phase. Implementation outputs, or behavioral norms resulting from the implementation of policies, represent a predetermined endpoint to evaluate what has occurred in the process of putting a policy into action. This is a predetermined endpoint because implementation never really stops until policies are terminated. Policy process outputs, or the changes in non-ideal conditions that policy is designed to address, are the cumulative impacts of policymaking and implementation on social or environmental conditions, and mark the end of one policy cycle and the beginning of the next.

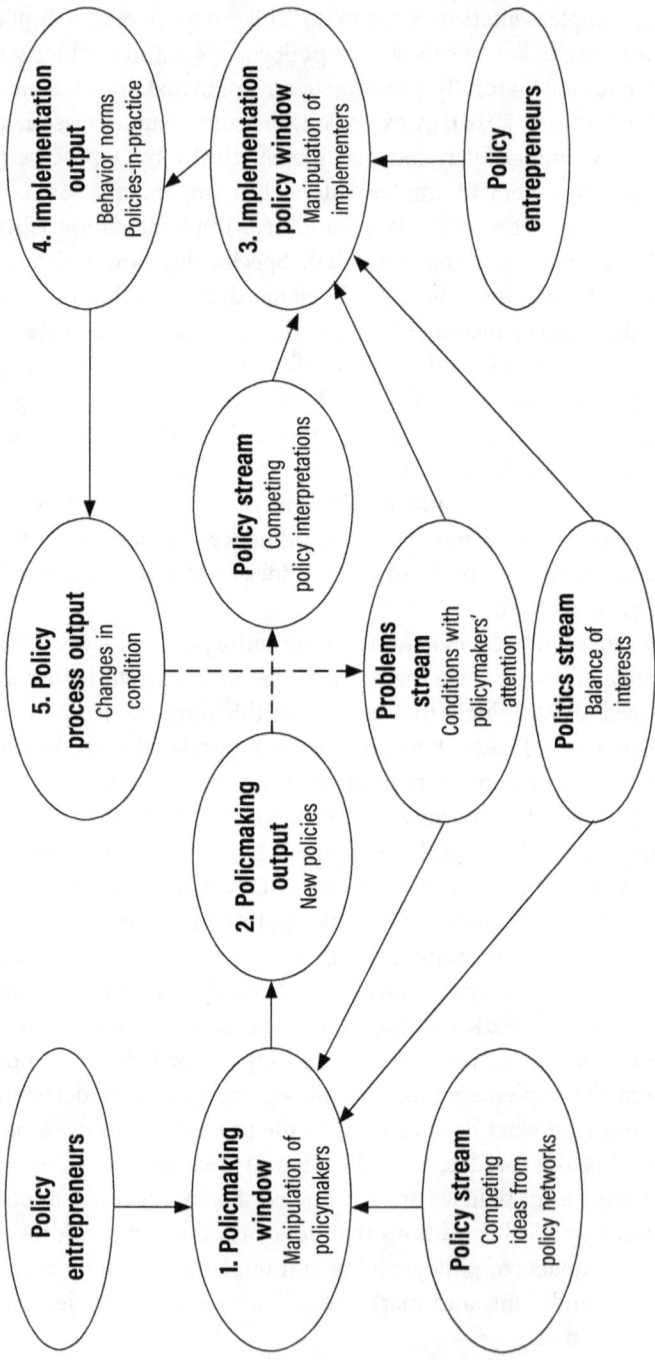

Figure 6.1. Diagram of MSF Structural Elements in Policy Cycle. Numbers denote order sequence of windows and outputs. *Source:* Fowler (2022).

While there is a sequence by which policy windows open (i.e., policymaking windows come before implementation windows), much of what happens in the policy cycle happens concurrently, as opposed to serially, so policy implementers are largely reacting to the same issues as policymakers in real time. This typically means that implementers often "wait and see" if or how policymakers will respond to changing dynamics before taking up an issue. This enables implementers to determine if choices from policymakers reduce ambiguity, which may simplify their decisions. Additionally, implementers are likely hesitant to drastically reinterpret existing policies without a trigger from policymakers, particularly if they believe policymakers are going to update or replace existing policies in the near future. Of course, policymakers may also use this to their advantage by purposely deflecting certain issues to implementers. For instance, if policymakers are concerned that an issue is too toxic or creates too much electoral risk, they may shift the spotlight to administrative agencies instead. This often does not trigger an implementation window where status quos are reformulated; rather, it is more likely that slight adjustments occur in hopes of dissipating political interest or tamping down a problem without a complete overhaul.

The policy and problem streams are the most dynamic here and serve as the key conduits by which the cycle is tied together. For policymaking, the policy stream consists of policy proposals arising through policy communities or networks. If a proposal is adopted, it feeds into the implementation process as the new policy stream, where competing interpretations jockey for attention from implementers. This means that implementation begins with policy adoption, even though administrators may be working to solve problems before policies are adopted. Of course, if administrators take the initiative to work on an issue before a policy can be adopted, it is likely to affect how they interpret policies later on. Thus, the serial versus concurrent assumptions are important here, as the process prescribes sequence but reality allows, and often dictates, people working out of order. It also means that policymakers and implementers are working with two different dynamics in the policy streams. Specifically, the policy stream encountered by policymakers is stocked with a series of competing ideas about how to solve problems that policymakers must sort through and examine, while the policy stream for implementers has largely been pared down to a specific idea, but one that may not be clearly or objectively articulated. Policymakers thus play a key role in shaping implementation decisions via the policies they produce.

While the problems stream remains consistent for both policy-makers and implementers insofar as it consists of non-ideal conditions, the important part is that the problems stream is fed by policy process outputs. Specifically, the impact of policymaking and implementation on these conditions affects how problems manifest in future policy cycles. To this end, if policy processes are successful in fixing problems, then future policy processes are not driven by the same problems; but if they are unsuccessful, then policy processes restart with a focus on solving the same problem, even if problem parameters have changed. This, of course, accounts for the cyclical nature of policy. The politics stream remains relatively consistent in how it affects both policymaking and implementation, in that it consists of how competing interests are balanced. Of course, political actors are dynamic, so the prevailing dialectics shift when there is turnover in elected officials or administrators, interest group campaigns, or the general public mood. This often means that a politically acceptable solution to a problem one day could be unacceptable the next day. In any case, it is assumed that both policymakers and implementers are responsive to political changes occurring around them, even if those political circumstances may be more nuanced or focused for implementers who have a more confined jurisdiction and set of authorities.

Finally, there are two windows, one for policymaking and one for implementation. During the policymaking window, streams are coupled by entrepreneurs attempting to manipulate decisions from policymaking bodies so that they enact preferred policies. During the implementation window, streams are coupled by entrepreneurs attempting to manipulate decisions from implementers who are interpreting and enacting policies. When these windows work together, they lead to the iterative reduction of ambiguity, so that assumptions about how to align with the way the world is with how it ought to be become clearer. Policy entrepreneurs are not necessarily dedicated to one phase or the other, but they do tend to specialize as they develop networks and a skillset catered to distinct audiences. Notably, there is a sequence for windows opening, starting with agenda-setting windows triggered by changes in the political or problems streams. Once a new proposal makes it to on the agenda, a policymaking window opens; and once a new policy is adopted, an implementation window opens. Of course, this does not mean that implementers cannot adjust their behaviors in response to changing political or problem dynamics without a new policy adoption; it simply means that it is unlikely that implementation behaviors drastically shift to the point that old status quos have given way to new status quos without a new policy. In all cases, windows are fleeting opportunities, so entrepreneurs must be ready to carry the momentum of opening windows forward to the next stage.

From Policy to Governance

Up to this point, the focus here has largely been on how implementers deal with individual policies. However, implementers are often working with more than one policy at a time, creating a layering of responsibilities, incentives, and barriers to actions (see chapter 2). The issue is not simply that many implement policies but few focus on implementation, it is also that many implement many policies at once while few focus on a single policy at a time. To this end, policies do not exist in a vacuum; rather, they exist as part of a broader system that governs the actions of policy actors oriented toward solving public problems. It is imperative that one consider how this multitude of policies come together to impact social or environmental problems through complex causal pathways. This broader perspective is often referred to as governance, which "emphasizes the full set of relationships that constitute systems for policy choice and action" (Meier, O'Toole, & Nicholson-Crotty, 2004). Governance systems are most frequently organized based on shared goals or problems and as a rebuke to traditional bureaucracies that reflect the politics of the time and may not be consistent with either democracy or effective administration (Peters & Pierre, 1998; Wood & Bohte, 2004).

Furthermore, where traditional bureaucracies are organized by hierarchical authority or market mechanisms, governance systems tend to be driven by connections built by policy actors who have become more strategic in developing interdependent relationships with other actors (O'Toole, 1997; Agranoff & McGuire, 2001; Provan & Kenis, 2008). This creates tension to a certain extent for those who work within traditional bureaucracies but also participate in governance, as they are caught between conventional institutions and fluid systems that include an array of policy actors with both the capacity to influence choices and the responsibility to contribute to outcomes (Meier & O'Toole, 2006). Within a governance system, individual policies are still the building blocks. Policies tend to be designed around narrow purposes that are often more specialized than the overarching shared goals of governance systems, and are limited by the authority of those who adopted them. Collective choice is, then, reflected as the overarching goals and principles uniting a group of policy actors, who articulate that vision in narrow messages as a policy; and collective action is, then, how that group of policy actors establish a communal set of norms dictated by a compilation of policies deriving from different sources (Ostrom & Ostrom, 2014). To this end, one could argue that policymaking and implementation, as bureaucratic ideas, are replaced with the notions of collective choice and collective action.

For instance, while the Affordable Care Act (ACA) of 2010 was a significant overhaul of healthcare regulation, it is not the only healthcare policy that governs how doctors or nurses provide care to patients, as they are also governed by other federal, state, and local laws, as well as the rules and ethical guidelines of professional associations, such as the American Medical Association. Here, one may think of the ACA as representing a narrow approach to enacting what is a broader collective choice concerning how healthcare access should work. Thus, implementing the ACA can at times create synergies between overlapping and complementary laws, and at other times create conflicts where institutional norms or rules are contradictory (Thompson, 2015; Beland, Rocco, & Waddan, 2016). The ACA, then, is both a standalone policy with its own requirements and metrics of success, and a part of a broader system hemmed in by numerous other policies propagated by governments and NGOs. Thus, a story that begins with the implementation of a simple law often gets more complicated as interrelated policies and actors work to craft a system for governance.

In essence, this means that while implementation of an individual policy is a stepping stone on the pathway to better communities, single policies are often too narrow and too limited to affect the larger social or economic conditions that societies view as problems, regardless of how successful their implementation is. Even if a single policy finds success, it is often not sufficient to counteract systematic governance failure; in contrast, where governance systematically works, the failure of a single policy is also not enough to disrupt the entire system (Peters, 2015). Thus, the questions here are not only about making a single policy work through implementation, but also about how to make policy implementation work systematically in order to solve large scale social or environmental problems. In other words, making the ACA or the CAA work in practice is imperative to improving healthcare or protecting air quality in the US, but to achieve those goals, governments at all levels and NGOs must work collectively to adopt and implement policies that address the nuanced issues that emerge within their jurisdictions. In essence, solving the big problems of government and democratic governance often requires thinking small, particularly on the issues that challenge how ideas are turned into actions.

An Empirical Model of US Environmental Policy Governance

Environmental governance in the US further demonstrates these dynamics. Federal laws, such as the CAA, CWA, and RCRA, are designed to reduce the emission of pollutants in air, water, and land, respectively. While EPA is responsible for overseeing its implementation, state agencies have been delegated authority over day-to-day operations of these policies and been allotted discretion to organize their management systems based on the unique sociopolitical or economic conditions local to their jurisdictions. Some states even further delegate this authority to local governments. But this is not the only way that the federal government influences air, water, or land pollution. Energy laws, like the Energy Policy Act of 2005, fund renewable energy that reduces emissions by replacing fossil fuel production, and federal funding of public transportation reduces emissions from automobiles. Of course, states, as well as many local governments, also have laws dealing with environmental quality in addition to related issues like transportation and energy. There is also an array of actions from NGOs that are relevant here, such as Amazon's policies on shipping logistics or the American Lung Association's advocacy work (Fowler, 2020b). In other words, policy tells only part of the story, and improving environmental quality requires more than effectively implementing a single federal law, even ones as complex as the CAA, CWA, and RCRA.

Despite the notoriety of and focus on federal environmental law, states tend to serve as the action arena for environmental policy governance in the US (Schlager & Cox, 2018). While they are responsible for implementing most federal environmental policies, states also adopt and implement their own environmental policies, so that state-level implementers are often working with several overlapping sets of regulations simultaneously. Although states are hemmed in by federal guidelines, they enjoy a considerable amount of discretion in funding, organizing, and operating environmental protection schemes, so that policies-in-practice may not be consistent across states (Fowler, 2020b). Additionally, where local governments or NGOs are involved, state agencies tend to influence their involvement in one way or another. Thus, on one side, state policymakers set budgets and regulate how state agencies operate, and on the other side, state agencies implement federal and state policies in the process of protecting the environment (Fowler, 2022). Therefore, by examining states here, I can move beyond a narrow focus on a single policy in order to understand how a myriad of actors work together in a complex system to both make collective choices about environmental governance and then execute those choices. This provides an opportunity to understand how policymaking and implementation 1) are impacted by the dynamic nature of politics, policies, and problems; and, 2) function as interdependent phases of a larger governance process.

Subsequently, I aim to test two MSF hypotheses here: 1) the *coupling hypotheses*: that the effects of any stream on both policymaking and implementation outputs are conditional on the other streams; and 2) the *interdependent process hypothesis*: that the effects of streams on policymaking are not independent of their effects on implementation (Fowler, 2022). In terms of the first, one can assume that given the character of environmental federalism in the US, states largely follow a similar set of approaches to environmental governance, so that status quos effectively take shape in a context of national and temporal consistency. Thus, I assume that both environmental policymakers and implementers follow a set of similar behavioral norms, unless the political, policy, and/or problem conditions of specific states trigger alternative behaviors. Despite state quasi-independence, one should expect policymaking and implementation to be quite similar, except where a unique set of circumstances arises (e.g., Fowler, 2020b). In terms of the second, one can also assume that the factors that drive how legislatures make policy and the factors that drive how implementers make that policy work are not independent of each other. Therefore, it is difficult to get an accurate understanding of one without accounting for the dynamics of the other (Fowler, 2019b, 2022).

In order to test these hypotheses, I use a pooled dataset of state-level variables that captures the institutional-level factors at play here (see "Methods Memo for Chapter 6" in the Appendix for more details on methodology). The full dataset includes 50 state-level observations across 14 years, from 2005 to 2018; due to missing data, the analytical dataset was reduced to 460 observations. Data was collected from publicly available databases managed by the US EPA (2021b), US BEA (2021), US Census Bureau (2021), and the League of Conservation Voters (LCV) (2021), as well as some variables drawn from previously published materials as cited. I use two dependent variables: one representing policymaking outputs, change in environmental expenditures; and the other representing implementation outputs, change in toxic releases. I label these as (t_2-t_1) to denote they represent change from the initial year (t_1) of observation to the following year (t_2). The dependent variables are designed to capture whether there are non-incremental changes (i.e., changes to the status quo) correlated with interactions between policy, politics, and problem streams.

The primary predictor variables represent the politics stream, state averages for LCV scorecards; the policy stream, state environmental expenditures; and the problems stream, toxic releases.[1] Stream variables are measured in change from one year to the next in order to capture their dynamic nature, specifically whether non-incremental changes occur. I label these as (t_1-t_0) to denote they represent the change in the initial year of observation (t_1) from the prior year (t_0). Thus, the models test whether changes from one year to the next in the stream variables affect changes in policymaking or implementation to the following year. Given the findings from the previous chapter on the importance of processes and functions, I also include these as co-variates. Specifically, I re-ran the SEMs using data from SRF evaluations for the CAA, CWA, and RCRA, and estimated values for both processes and functions for each state in order to account for capacity of state agencies to cope with ambiguity and uncertainty (see chapter 5). Additionally, I use control variables for state expenditures and toxic releases in the initial years of observation to set a baseline, the bureaucratic structure of state environmental agencies (i.e., mini-EPA), and state authority over the CAA, CWA, and RCRA.

I assume concurrent processing where policymaking and implementation occur simultaneously. This is in keeping with the practical reality that environmental policy governance is an ongoing endeavor where both policy choices and execution are constantly occurring. Since the core interest here is changes in status quos, the modeling strategy relies on a difference-in-difference approach in order to account for how changes in predictor variables correlate with changes in dependent variables. Additionally, while previous scholarship (e.g., Fowler, 2022) assumes serial processing (i.e., implementation follows policymaking), concurrent processing is assumed here. Serial processing is often characterized as the "textbook" approach to policy processes, and makes for a "cleaner" approach to modeling a multi-step process by creating a temporal sep-

---

1. Environmental expenditures are measured as per capita in real 2009 dollars, and toxic releases as pounds of toxic chemical releases per capita. LCV scores were calculated as the average of each state's Congressional delegation.

aration between steps and reduces the risk of autocorrelation. However, many have criticized serial processing assumptions as disconnected from reality, where administrators are often working on policy problems before policymakers have finalized their decisions (Nakamura, 1987; Baumgartner, Jones, & Mortensen, 2018). This is even more true in governance systems where efforts have been ongoing for some time, and policymaking and implementation have become intertwined. Given the trade-offs, I elected to model this as concurrent processing that assumes the process of determining funding for environmental programs largely occurs simultaneously with the process of managing those environmental programs.

Finally, I use an innovative statistical analysis technique called seemingly unrelated regression (SUR), which allows one to jointly estimate two equations through a single iterative procedure. Specifically, SUR estimates separate equations and then makes iterative adjustments to each so that they have the same variance and are uncorrelated, essentially adjusting one equation based on the other (Martin & Smith, 2005; Fowler, 2022). This is particularly useful here where I assume that policymaking and implementation are separate but interdependent. Additionally, since interaction terms can lead to inflated standard errors, I cluster standard errors at the state levels, which assumes errors are correlated within states over time but not across states. This also provides an extra safeguard against potential serial correlation issues that exist in pooled cross-sectional datasets (Beck & Katz, 1995, 1996; Primo, Jacobsmeier, & Milyo, 2007). I present two models: 1) a base model that focuses on an interaction between streams (model 1); and 2) a model that incorporates how that interaction affects implementation in states with high as compared to low process capacity (model 2).

First, findings in both models indicate that effects of politics on policymaking are conditional on existing policies and problems (see table 6.1). Specifically, the statistically significant interaction between stream variables denotes that the effects of any one stream are conditional on the values of the other streams. That is, the impact of politics, $LCV(t_1-t_0)$, on change in environmental expenditures, $Expenditures(t_2-t_1)$, is conditional on the values of policies, $Expenditures(t_1-t_0)$, and problems, $Toxic releases(t_1-t_0)$, so that political changes do not have a consistent impact on budgeting for state environmental protection. As illustrated in figure 6.2 (upper right corner),[2] where changes in prior expenditures or toxic releases are at mean levels,

2. Graphs are based on findings from model 2. The mean and maximum observation in the dataset are used to represent the average case and the most extreme case when graphing the results.

Table 6.1. SUR Results

	Model 1	Model 2	
Dependent variable: Expenditures (t_2-t_1)			
LCV (t_1-t_0)	.052 (.082)	.052 (.082)	
Expenditures (t_1-t_0)	−.304 (.044)‡	−305 (.044)‡	
Toxic releases (t_1-t_0)	−.002 (.015)	−.002 (.015)	
Expend. (t_1-t_0) × Toxic rel. (t_1-t_0)	.0008 (.0004)+	.0008 (.0004)+	
LCV (t_1-t_0) × Expend. (t_1-t_0)	.005 (.005)	.005 (.005)	
LCV (t_1-t_0) × Toxic rel. (t_1-t_0)	−.007 (.001)‡	−.007 (.001)‡	
LCV (t_1-t_0) × Expend. (t_1-t_0) × Toxic rel. (t_1-t_0)	.0003 (.00005)‡	.0003 (.00004)‡	
Expenditures(t_1)	.465 (10.387)	1.885 (10.401)	
Program authority	.270 (2.627)	.321 (2.627)	
Constant	−.575	−.747	
R^2	0.162	0.1622	
Chi-squared	89.100	89.13	
Dependent variable: Toxic releases (t_2-t_1)			
		Low process capacity	*High process capacity*
LCV (t_1-t_0)	−.185 (.221)	−.828 (.266)†	−.158 (.218)
Expenditures (t_1-t_0)	1.334 (.115)‡	1.665 (.110)‡	−.100 (.178)
Toxic releases (t_1-t_0)	−.711 (.040)‡	−.699 (.034)‡	−.471 (.137)‡
Expend. (t_2-t_1) × Toxic rel. (t_1-t_0)	−.019 (.001)‡	−.025 (.001)‡	.022 (.003)‡
LCV (t_1-t_0) × Expend. (t_1-t_0)	−.088 (.014)‡	−.150 (.013)‡	.008 (.020)
LCV (t_1-t_0) × Toxic rel. (t_1-t_0)	−.055 (.004)‡	−.699 (.034)‡	.081 (.016)‡
LCV (t_1-t_0) × Expend. (t_1-t_0) × Toxic rel. (t_1-t_0)	.001 (.0002)‡	.002 (.0002)‡	−.010 (.002)‡
Process	37.855 (31.448)		
Functions	−33.032 (23.304)	−4.700 (5.976)	
Mini-EPA	3.181 (4.783)	7.273 (3.627)*	
Program authority	−9.388 (7.546)	−5.368 (5.692)	
Toxic releases (t_1)	.103 (.023)‡	.282 (.027)‡	
Constant	5.745	−1.855	
R^2	0.737	0.851	
Chi-squared	1286.000	2621.33	
N	460	460	
BIC	8972.444	8749.109	
Correlation of residuals	.099	.078	
Breusch-Pagan Test of Independence	4.490*	2.773+	

Note: Standard errors in parentheses. P-value = * < .05. † > .01, ‡ > .001. N = 93.
Source: Author.

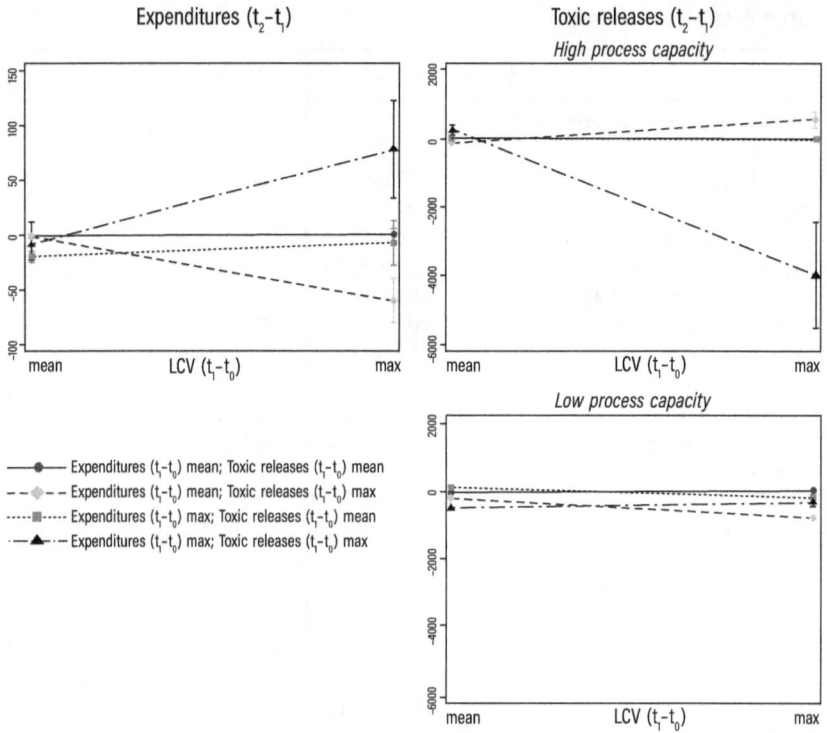

Figure 6.2. Graph of Interaction Terms from SUR (Model 2). *Source:* Author-created image.

increases in environmentally oriented voting by policymakers have only a marginal impact on changes in expenditures, or where prior expenditures already increased by maximum levels, may actually lead to decreases. However, where both changes in prior expenditures and toxic releases are at maximum levels, increases in LCV scores are positively correlated with changing in spending, so that one can predict that the largest increases in spending will go hand-in-hand with the largest increases in environmentally oriented voting. In other words, non-incremental changes in policymaking are most likely to occur where there is an interaction between extreme conditions in politics, policies, and problems.

Second, findings in both models also indicate that effects of politics on implementation are conditional on existing policies and problems. Here, the impact of politics, $LCV(t_1-t_0)$, on changes in policy outputs, Toxic releases(t_2-t_1), which is assumed to be demonstrable of the underlying implementation behaviors, is conditional on the values of policies, Expenditures(t_1-t_0), and problems, Toxic releases(t_1-t_0), so that political changes again do not have a consistent impact on how state environmental protection policies are implemented. As a corollary to this, and more importantly, these findings indicate that policy changes alone do not have a consistent impact on policy implementation; rather, policies combined with politics and problems drive whether there is an institutional-level shift in how policies are implemented. This relationship is further complicated by the process capacities of state agencies (model 2). While the interaction between streams is significant for states with both high and low process capacities, the directional differences are important, as they indicate that the substance of that interaction is not consistent. Specifically, for states with low process capacities (lower right corner), there appear to be only marginal differences that manifest as a result of changes in politics, policies, or problems; in other words, changes in the streams have little effect on outputs where state agencies have difficulty formalizing organizational rules that galvanize implementation behaviors.

In contrast, for states with high process capacities (upper right corner), there are again only marginal differences as a result of politics, policies, or problems where one or more of the streams is at mean levels. However, if all three streams increase by maximum levels, there is a sharp decline in toxic releases, indicating a substantive difference in how policies are implemented. On the one hand, this would suggest that policy changes only have an impact on implementation outputs if they are combined with extreme political and problem conditions and agencies have the capacity to reformulate rules and behaviors to adapt to those changing conditions. On the other hand, it may also indicate that even agencies with the capacity to adapt to changing conditions have little incentive to do so unless the perfect storm hits. It also shows that agencies are capable of withstanding the challenges that come along when there are changes in only one or two streams (e.g., budget disruption, shift in political winds, environmental disaster). Of course, these findings support the coupling hypotheses, but the correlation of residuals and the Breusch-Pagan test also indicate that both equations are correlated, supporting the interdependence hypothesis as well. That is, the process by which expenditure decisions are made is not independent of the process by which implementation occurs.

From a broad perspective, this further emphasizes that at the institutional level, status quos are difficult to alter unless there is a set of external conditions that reframe the context of implementation and an internal capacity to respond to those conditions effectively. As complicated as the SUR results may seem, what this data is saying is relatively easy to understand in practical terms. Specifically, if there is a political shift toward environmentalism, legislatures may not immediately respond by throwing more money at environmental protection, particularly if environmental indicators do not suggest a problem or if budgets have been tight in recent years. However, if this shift is coupled with increasing pollution and spending increases from previous years, then state legislatures may feel they have to respond to a problem that is getting worse, that has political support, and that they have already invested substantial resources into. Otherwise, they will face scrutiny from interest groups or citizens who question their competence. Thus, legislators will likely vote to increase environmental spending in that budget cycle in hopes that it will either solve the problem or dissipate the political interest. Of course, without new resources or new requirements from policymakers, program managers are unlikely to send signals to implementers about behavioral shifts, so the status quo remains intact. Therefore, implementation is unlikely to change without policy change.

But even if there is policy change, if pollution levels off, managers will rationalize maintaining the status quo by arguing that making changes may aggravate the problem or that what they are doing works. Alternatively, if political interest in the environment disappears as soon as the legislature passes a budget increase, then there is no pressure on implementers to change either. In contrast, when new resources are coupled with a sustained political interest in the environmental and rising pollution indicators, agency executives and program managers likely feel pressure to do something differently. Of course, if they ignore these conditions, they will face scrutiny, as the spotlight is now on administrators rather than policymakers. Thus, managers respond by sending signals to implementers on how to change their behaviors (e.g., more inspections, stronger enforcement tactics). But in order for those signals to be effective in shifting behavior, organizations need to have the capacity to promulgate rules and procedures that guide implementers in a new direction. Where this is lacking, implementers fall back on old behaviors, resulting in the same outputs as before.

How Ideas Become Change

Now let us consider how the complicated mechanisms that connect policies, implementation, and the world come together to tell a story about how ideas become change. Ideas start in policy networks, where experts research and analyze potential solutions to social or environmental problems. Those ideas are vetted and revised as they percolate through the network, until they are viewed as legitimate options. Then comes the waiting game: waiting until the time is right for a particular policy solution to be matched with a problem and politics. Even though a proposed policy may have gained momentum in a policy network, to continue to propel it forward, it needs the impetus that comes with a problem that it can solve. Until that happens, policy ideas float around networks waiting on their moment. In many cases, those problems become apparent through a focusing event that unexpectedly pulls everyone's attention toward it, but it may happen in more subtle ways as policymakers or citizens shift awareness and focus between competing interests. The politics of the day also need to be amenable to the solution. Certainly, any observer of American politics has noticed that good ideas are often cast aside if they challenge the prevailing rhetoric or doctrine of the majority party.

With that perfect storm of an idea, a problem, and the right politics, entrepreneurs can seize the moment and convince policymakers that this is something they should consider further. Now the idea is on the agenda, and policymakers are examining its pros and cons. Administrative leaders and interest groups are weighing in. During this time, policies are written out, and then rewritten and rewritten, as consensus and compromise are built. For better or worse, this often amplifies ambiguities as policies become less complete than their original proposals in some ways, and the final product on paper is often neither clear nor objective. Just like before, entrepreneurs are waiting on that perfect storm, so they construct a cogent narrative for policymakers in order to convince them that the idea they are selling is the perfect solution to the problem at hand, not only practically but also politically. Many ideas are proposed; fewer get on the agenda; and even fewer make it to the next step. When fortunate, entrepreneurs can coast on the problem and political conditions that pushed an idea onto the agenda in the first place. When unfortunate, they have to fight to keep the policy's place in line as they wait for attention to shift in their favor; otherwise, the idea disappears from the agenda. The key to their craft is framing the narrative, so decision-makers only pay attention to information that sells their ideas.

After all, in an ambiguous world, policymakers could be convinced that any idea is good or bad, because "who is paying attention to what, when" is often more important than the technical merits or political realities. Of course, when bad policies are adopted, it tends to be because policymakers are paying attention to the wrong things. If entrepreneurs are successful here, policies are adopted, and the ball is thrown into the implementation court. Specifically, policies trigger administrators to respond, but that response is not always how policymakers, entrepreneurs, or policy experts predict it to be. That concrete idea that a policy expert once had is now a policy-as-written with inherent ambiguities of theory and language that require others to interpret its meaning. As the original idea proposed has filtered through legislators and bureaucrats, its meaning and purposes have shifted back and forth, making it altogether unclear what needs to be done or how to do it. Thus, the first step in acting is that administrative leaders and program managers have to figure out what the policy means and how to communicate that meaning to implementers on the operational front lines.

While program managers can send signals to implementers on how to think about policies, implementers tend to fall back on their intuition and extend existing patterns of doing things to new areas. Often, this intuition is grounded on learned experiences with rules, procedures, and informal behavioral norms, so that implementers' judgments are hemmed in by the boundaries set by organizations on what information they have available and how they are trained to understand that information. This creates institutional barriers buttressing existing ways of doing things, and making it risky for implementers to try something different. Thus, the default for a new policy is often that it is simply layered on top of other policies, as implementers interpret this new idea in a way that allows them to continue business-as-usual. In essence, this means that practical changes do not always follow a new policy. However, skilled managers can craft narratives around these policies, targeted at implementers. By doing so, they can trigger a more deliberative thinking process, so that implementers reformulate their mental models of how they do their jobs, replacing existing coping mechanisms with new decision rules.

Nevertheless, once implementers start putting a policy into practice, they are often subject to the demands of the target population and attuned to the circumstances at the street level. Even as the weight of organizations bear down on them, implementers are not ignorant of the demands of the people they serve, so policies are adjusted to make them functional. This entails tweaks to how they understand the policy and to how they imple-ment it in response to feedback from citizens. That sense of functionality is often grounded in reducing the amount of conflict that implementers face in the process of doing their jobs, and requires experimenting with different ways of doing things. When an implementer finds a way that works, others often borrow that strategy or tactic, so it spreads across organizations. Unfortunately, at times, this means that implementers may engage in behaviors that are counterproductive to policy or organizational goals. To combat this, managers can build processes around practices that are functional and also advance their goals, in order to encourage preferred behaviors and discourage alternatives. Practices then become galvanized across organizations as implementers settle into a specific way of doing things; in turn, this becomes engrained in implementers' intuition and serves as a new status quo.

The behavioral norms of implementers become how policies work in practice, which may not be the same as envisioned by policymakers when they adopted the policy or by policy experts who originally developed the idea. These practical norms also begin to affect how other agencies or NGOs do business, as they try to align their organizations and practices with those of key policy actors to remove institutional barriers for cooperation. Failing to adapt to the business practices of others often means that organizations are effectively walling themselves off from the broader network and, over time, limiting their ability to effectively participate in governance. Collectively, these norms across organizations impress upon target populations what acceptable behaviors are, what rules and regulations mean, and/or how the government values competing interests, among other things. As a result, the policies-in-practice nudge target populations to behave in one way or another, which ultimately begins affecting problem conditions systematically. Crucially, it requires systematic practices to affect broad social or environmental conditions, as isolated practices will only contribute to isolated success or failure.

If policies and practices work as hoped, then problem conditions begin to dissipate as the underlying human behaviors that contribute to them in the first place shift in a positive direction. In turn, this signals to policymakers that policies are working, and because the problem is no longer attention grabbing, further policy adoptions become unnecessary. Subsequently, policymakers and other actors move on to the next problem. In contrast, if practices fail to nudge target populations in the right direction, then problems remain and continue to get attention, so policymakers start considering other new ideas and the cycle starts over. For better or worse, some policy actors may perceive outputs and outcomes differently, so where one sees success, others may find the need for further policy change. Of course, this stirs debate both within policy venues (e.g., legislatures) and across broader governance networks. In either case, policy actors adapt and their interdependent efforts form a comprehensive governance scheme that attaches specific actions by individuals to the broader shared goals of a network. In sum, while policies do not magically fix social or environmental problems, there is a pathway from new ideas to better outcomes that follows through policy implementation, and that is imperative to democracy.

7

So, What?

Over the preceding chapters, I have examined how policies-in-theory becomes policies-in-practice through the construction and deconstruction of behavioral norms. As I have argued, there is an inherent gap between the theoretical or written forms and the practical manifestation of policies—a gap that results from policymakers shifting decision-making authority to implementers. It is within this gap that policy success and failure is often determined. The key challenge for policy implementation, then, centers on how they come to understand what a policy means, where the aggregate norms of behaviors manifest to affect socio-environmental conditions at the institutional level. Specifically, how implementers ascribe meaning to a policy dictates which course of action they chart and how policies work in practice, as opposed to how they were designed to work. Managers and organizations are thus often trying to shape how implementers interpret policy, which leads to interactions between policy functionality pioneered in response to real-world circumstances and organizational processes developed to guide implementers to preferred behaviors. This system is inherently oriented toward upholding status quos, but there are also built-in mechanisms that allow for changes to occur under the right conditions. On the one hand, this theory explains why policies work as they do, and on the other hand, it also explains what it takes for policies-in-practice to actually change. The implications for democratic governance are numerous and pervasive, as this addresses the core issues of how societies solve problems through collective choice and action.

The goal of this chapter is to answer the questions every reader is likely asking at this point: so what? Why does any of this matter? Consequently, I use this chapter to distill the contentions and findings from the preceding pages into a useful set of conclusions about what this theory means for understanding policy implementation and, more broadly, democratic governance. First, I provide 10 summative points aimed at informing how policy implementers and program managers chip away the edges of the square peg that is policy so it fits in the round hole that is reality. These broad takeaways summarize the theoretical contentions of the preceding chapters. Second, I consider this theory's contributions to the broader scholarship on policy implementation and democratic governance, as well as how it expands the applicability of the multiple streams framework (MSF). Additionally, I consider some of the empirical challenges encountered here, and offer suggestions for future research. Finally, I conclude by considering some of the implications for democratic governance and how it informs one's understanding of why policies succeed or fail.

Summative Points on Policy Implementation

1. *Implementation is a balancing act between serving the public interest and maintaining public institutions.* On the one hand, serving the public interest casts implementers as political actors who are change oriented and responsive to policymakers; on the other hand, maintaining public institutions casts implementers as administrators who are value neutral and oriented toward creating stability. While the public interest may not always be detrimental to the long-term viability of public institutions, at times these competing forces push and pull implementers in different directions and present challenges for how they think about the purposes and goals of their actions. This creates an ebb and flow to implementation where status quos are constructed and deconstructed as public interest and institutions conflict, compete, and cooperate to shape how policies work. When the administration of institutions dominates implementation, the focus tends to be on upholding status quos, so policies are an extension of organizational norms, rather than taking on a life of their own. At opportune times, though, the prevailing public interest snuffs out institutional imperatives, so that the focus shifts to changing institutions to fit policy and new status quos take shape. Of course, this ebb and flow

is also imperative to how democratic governance plays out as it shapes public services and the interactions between citizens and their government.

2. *Ambiguity permeates policy, and the key challenge for implementation is coping with it.* Dealing with different ways of thinking about the same phenomenon is a unique conundrum, as it requires people to ascribe meanings to events without clear and objective evidence of accuracy or validity. Of course, this means that more information does not eliminate ambiguity, in the same way it does uncertainty, so it is a challenge that persists even as people come to a shared understanding. Policymakers often cope with ambiguity by leaving policies incomplete and passing the buck to implementers as a means of creating consensus. In turn, implementers become the de facto "deciders" of what policy means as they apply it to real-world circumstances, and how they decide what policy means often becomes the basis of policies-in-practice. On the one hand, this raises normative concerns about the quality of democracy, and leads to inconsistencies and unpredictability. On the other hand, it also allows implementers to better interpret policy in a way that matches the real challenges faced on the street level, and to provide services that are responsive to the changing wants and needs of citizens. Rather than run from ambiguity, implementers and managers must be thoughtful about how they are coping with it and the implications of choosing one interpretation over another.

3. *How meaning is ascribed to policy drives action.* Implementation is where ideas are translated into actions, so interpreting (or misinterpreting) the ideas that underlie policies is among the first steps. When policy can be interpreted in numerous different ways, how implementers come to understand its purpose and goals is crucial to the logic they use to determine what course of action is warranted. This means one of the key issues for coping with ambiguity is making enough sense of what is going on to decide what to do and how to do it. Unfortunately, policymakers do not always convey meaning and intent well enough in policy statements for it to be indisputable, so how policy is designed in theory may not align with how policy is understood during implementation. Where implementers respond to policies intuitively and come to understand policy as fitting into their existing ways of doing things, status quos are upheld and prevailing behavioral patterns are extended to new places. But where policy is interpreted in a way that challenges existing mental models, behavioral norms are recalibrated as implementers engage in a more deliberative thought process about how to connect the dots between ideas and actions.

4. *Policy implementers are not a discrete group.* While one most often thinks of street-level bureaucrats, like cops or teachers, implementers are a large, diverse group of actors who possess some power over how policies work. Implementers as a group are often ill defined by law or practice, particularly where they operate both inside and outside of government agencies. As such, this group tends to be fluid and dynamic as policies are implemented continually across numerous times and places. To complicate matters, implementation is only part of what most public servants do, so that many implement policies as part of their job responsibilities but few focus solely on implementation. Consequently, it is often difficult to understand who is responsible for or contributes to shared behavioral norms around policies-in-practice. This means that while not every policy implementer is experienced or thoughtful in translating policy-in-theory into policy-in-practice, they do affect the efficacy of collective action. Of course, this creates complex questions about democratic accountability, particularly surrounding out-sourcing and hollowed-out government, when it comes to drawing a causal pathway between citizens and those responsible for making policy choices.

5. *Intuition and organization reinforce status quos.* There are biases hardwired into people's brains that affect how they process information, so that who is paying attention to what is often the most crucial component in the decisions they make. Naturally, people rely chiefly on their intuition to make quick judgments, so they often do not fully analyze the situation or consider all relevant information. Of course, the reliance on intuition is even more imperative for those who are faced with time constraints in complex, volatile, and/or uncertain circumstances, where deliberative thinking becomes a luxury. Consequently, when implementers use intuitive judgments, they extend existing ways of thinking about what a policy means to new circumstances. By extension, this upholds the status quos by repeating the same behaviors over and over, unless they are forced to recalibrate their mental model of the world. Organizational structures often play on these mechanisms by biasing how implementers search for and analyze information. Over time, intuitive judgments often become grounded in the logic created by organizations, as formal managerial tools or organizational cultures send signals about which ways of thinking are acceptable. This can be a positive where one wants to create consensus around policy meanings and consistency in practices, but it can also be a significant barrier to change.

6. *Changing behaviors requires triggering deliberative thinking.* While intuition is the most common way in which people make decisions, there is also higher-order thinking where people are more likely to consider additional information and undertake intensive analyses that lead to behaviors that depart from the status quo. In order to get to it, though, people need to be triggered, which often requires them to face negative feedback that challenges the mental model that they have used to make intuitive choices. If this feedback only suggests that small changes are needed, people will use their intuition as an anchor and only adjust to fit the circumstances; but if feedback suggests that big changes are necessary, people are likely to abandon their intuition and reformulate how they see the world almost entirely. Of course, the downside of challenging existing status quos is that one can never be sure whether replacement behaviors will be an improvement or not. Thus, coupling policy interpretations with problems and politics is a crucial mechanism for challenging someone's mental model as it frames a cogent narrative about how one should shift one's perception of the world, and presents a clear causal pathway to new behavioral norms.

7. *Managers are responsible for organizing anarchy.* Where ambiguity reigns, logic has to be superimposed so actors can make rational choices based on a shared understanding of the world; this is the purpose and goal of organizations. Imposing logic is an exercise in combating ambiguity by manipulating policy actors into thinking in certain ways. This is accomplished by sending signals about organizational preferences, clarifying how to use organizational technology, and/or setting rules for who makes decisions. Since they are often situated between organizational leaders/policymakers and implementers, managers are uniquely positioned to filter messages passed between these groups, providing opportunity to shape both the logics of organizations and how their subordinates interpret what is going on around them. Managers do this to influence how implementers understand the organization in general and policy in specific, so that implementers follow the decision logic that is most likely to result in behaviors that align with managerial preferences. Of course, managers have many tools at their disposal to guide what information is used in decision-making (e.g., information management) and/or altering the decision calculus of behaviors (e.g., administrative procedures), but the most effective is socializing organizational members into behavioral patterns.

8. *Managerial skill is the ability to lead through ambiguity.* Managers are often required to fight against ambiguity and use it to their advantage at the same time, as they balance competing pressure to be both a conservator and an entrepreneur. While organizations are designed to facilitate the exertion of power over organizational actors, the authorities granted to managers are frequently not enough to force ways of thinking onto implementers. This means that managers must rely more on influencing how people think and decoding organized anarchies than on their technical skills. To this end, managerial skill is grounded in how one leverages different sources of power to manipulate the thinking of others about the organization in general and policies in specific. If it is done successfully, managers elicit behaviors that align with their preferences. Here, manipulation involves calibrating narratives by framing and reframing how they present information in order to both appeal to the self-rational nature of individuals and alter their perceptions of a shared understanding of the world. Playing on cognitive biases by coupling policy, politics, and problems streams is key to this, as it affects how organizational actors decide what information is relevant and what it means in a broader context.

9. *Building processes and making policies functional should go hand-in-hand.* Whether they are intuitive or deliberative, implementer choices tend to be used to make policy functional in order to gain buy-in from stakeholders and reduce negative feedback. This is an exercise in coping with ambiguity by field-testing different ways of ascribing meanings to how a policy should work. On the other hand, organizations build formalized processes that galvanize behavioral norms and create consistency in how a policy will work. This is an exercise in coping with uncertainty, designed to increase predictability in implementation behaviors and reduce the static that may affect how implementers perceive the issues at hand when applying policy. Ideally, processes are built around successful experiments in functionality, so how policies should work and how they will work align. If done well, this means that processes advance policy goals and are met with positive feedback. Where processes and functions become misaligned, though, red tape tends to emerge, as implementation behaviors fail to satisfy stakeholders, and implementers face pressure to deviate from rules perceived as arbitrary. This puts pressure on managers to effectively understand what makes policies functional when building processes. Additionally, this means that processes need to adjust iteratively as functionality adapts to changing political and problem parameters.

10. *Macro-level change starts at the micro level.* Policy is meant to solve problems by creating a systematic change in the status quos around certain conditions that fail to meet expectations for what ought to be. While policy is often designed with the macro level in mind, there has to be a causal pathway that connects micro-level behaviors to the whole-sale changes needed to fix systematic problems, and mechanisms to hold implementers accountable for those behaviors. Of course, the natural tendency will always be to defer to the status quo, so widespread change is no easy task for individuals or institutions. Achieving change requires a shift in the behavioral norms of individual implementers, which are grounded in their policy interpretations. Specifically, as an implementer begins to think differently about what a policy means, she begins to act differently too. Over time, if these changes are met with positive feedback and encouraged, they are likely to spread to other implementers, and eventually a new behavioral norm will replace the old one. This new behavioral norm should lead to changes in conditions at an institutional level, which will then allow one to understand whether a policy has been successful in solving the problem it was intended to solve. Essentially, one needs to think about the micro level to achieve change at the macro level, and how this occurs is crucial to defining the character and quality of democratic governance.

Implications for Theory

Possibly the most novel contribution of this work is the deployment of MSF to explain implementation. Although MSF is one of the most widely used theories of agenda setting and policy adoption, there have been few applications to implementation and to understanding the whole policy process from ideas to outcomes (Herweg, Zahariadis, & Zohlnhöfer, 2018). While several scholars have demonstrated the potential of MSF to explain more than just why policies are adopted (e.g., Zahariadis & Exadaktylos, 2016; Fowler, 2019b; Howlett, 2019), the preceding chapters represent the most developed articulation of how MSF accounts for the dynamics of implementation, as well as how implementation fits within the broader policy process. The key theoretical contribution in this regard is that it allows for a comprehensive view of how policy is adopted, becomes actions, and affects social outcomes, rather than a more narrowly defined set of research questions that only consider why issues rise to the agenda and/ or become law. From this perspective, one can argue that ambiguity is a foundational concept for how choices are made in policy processes; the only thing that changes is who is making decisions, for what purpose, and to what outcome. Notably, limitations in addressing implementation and offering a comprehensive framework to understand policy cycles have been at the center of MSF criticisms, particularly as it applies to its ability to inform and guide democratic governance (Herweg, Zahariadis, & Zohlnhöfer, 2018; Fowler, 2022).

One advantage of deploying MSF to examine policy implementation is that in addition to the core theoretical structure, it may also be possible to adapt and apply proposed hypotheses from agenda setting and/or policy adoption as well. In general, implementation theory suffers from a dearth of testable hypotheses derived from a central theoretical framework, which is certainly one reason why the list of variables that affect implementation continues to grow (Meier, 1999; O'Toole, 2000). While falsifiable hypotheses are an important step in theoretical development, they are also crucial to a more consistent identity in implementation studies by focusing scholars on a core set of propositions to work from. Additionally, hypotheses can also be used as a basis to provide more sophisticated guidance to implementers, managers, and policymakers seeking to understand how to better organize efforts to close the gap between policy-as-written and policy-in-practice. To this end, table 7.1 proposes several hypotheses based on Herweg, Zahariadis, & Zohlnhöfer's (2018) listing of MSF hypotheses from extant MSF scholarship (see chapter 1). Most obviously, the coupling hypothesis suggests that a change in implementation behavior results from the same mechanism as an agenda change.

While I have not gone so far as to explicitly test MSF hypotheses other than the coupling hypotheses in the preceding chapters, they do have the potential to offer additional insights into how behavioral norms of implementers are constructed and deconstructed. For instance, from the agenda-setting hypotheses, one can infer that implementation behaviors are more likely to become norms among implementers if they fit the general ideology of the government and/or the selection criteria used by implementers. Alternatively, from the policy adoption hypotheses, one can infer that changes in how policies are implemented are more likely if proposed policy interpretations are put forward by elected leaders, if they are supported by the government or majority party of government, or if the problem to be solved is salient to the public. Logically, this

Table 7.1. Potential MSF Hypotheses for Implementation

- Changes in norms of implementation behavior become more likely if a policy window opens, the streams are ready for coupling, and a policy entrepreneur promotes a policy interpretation.
- Implementation behaviors that fit the general ideology of government have a better chance of becoming norms among implementers.
- Implementation behaviors are more likely to become norms if they fit the selection criteria used by implementers.
- As implementers become less integrated, new policy interpretations are more likely to emerge.
- Implementation windows open following policy adoption.
- Implementation windows open in the problem stream as a result of a change of indicators, focusing events, or feedback.
- Implementation windows open in the political stream as a result of changes in legislatures, election of a new government, interest group campaigns, or a change in national mood.
- Changes in how policies are implemented are more likely if the proposed reinterpretation is put forward by an elected leader in government.
- Changes in how policies are implemented are more likely if the proposed reinterpretation is put forward by a government or majority party that is not constrained by other veto actors.
- Changes in how policies are implemented are more likely if the problem that the policy is supposed to solve is salient among the voters.

Source: Author.

tracks with arguments concerning how the selection between alternatives becomes biased by political pressures and motivations to stave off challenges to legitimacy and validity of administrative decision-making. The importance here is that the extant MSF literature lays the groundwork for policy implementation hypotheses from which a research agenda can be built. In sum, the theoretical contributions here for both implementation studies and MSF are substantial.

Furthermore, implementation scholars have long struggled with finding consensus on defining key research questions, concepts, and units of analysis, which has largely splintered implementation studies. Although many have attempted to reconcile these debates, unfortunately, there has been insufficient progress in developing a framework that articulates a cohesive vision for how implementation plays out across sites (O'Toole,

2000; deLeon & deLeon, 2002; Saetren, 2005, 2014). In general, I argue that the core research questions of policy implementation hover around the construction and deconstruction of status quos in behavioral norms among implementers, such as "What behavioral norms exist around specific policy problems?" "What role does policy play in shaping those norms?" "How do norms align with the intents of policymakers?" and/or "How do norms impact policy outcomes?" I also show that these research questions can be applied at micro, meso, and/or macro levels, as individual behaviors aggregate across organizations and institutions to impact social and environmental conditions. Certainly, this would imply there is more than one unit of analysis to work with in implementation research, ranging from decisions to organizational processes and policy systems. In large part, this thinking is influenced by the approach used by the Institutional Analysis and Development framework to connect and organize concepts operating at different analytical levels in complex governance systems (Schlager & Cox, 2018).

I believe three theoretical concepts are particularly crucial in explaining how policy implementation plays out: policies-in-practice, ambiguity, and status quos. Notably, these concepts can be deployed across units of analysis and provide insights into both micro-level and institutional-level patterns. First, policy-in-practice represents the core idea that policy as practiced is a fundamentally different concept than policy-in-theory. This occurs at both the micro level, where implementers come to ascribe meaning to policy, and the macro level, where practices aggregate together to from a set of behavioral norms. Second, ambiguity accounts for how and why the same policy may manifest in different ways during implementation, as interpretations differ based on how one thinks about the same policy under different circumstances. Implicit here is the tension between social constructivism and rational choice approaches to policy, which are often thought of as competing or contradictory (Stone, 2011). However, ambiguity as a core concept allows for inferences from both to add depth to understanding decision-making parameters, as one can make rational choices within a socially constructed world. At both micro and macro levels, this helps to unpack how and why implementers come to seemingly objective conclusions about subjective enterprises, as well as how one uses tactics to manipulate thinking about policy, problems, or politics.

Third, status quos identify the resistance to change and the mechanisms in place that buttress existing ways of doing things as well as those needed to trigger change. At micro levels, this ties directly to cognitive processing and how the human mind is hardwired to search for and analyze information, as intuitive and deliberative thinking work in tandem. At the macro level, this is grounded in the tension between public policy and public administration, as one force pushes for change and the other, for stability. Particularly novel here is thinking about policy implementation as sitting at an intersection between executing the public interest and maintaining public institutions, which carries many implications for understanding the broader organization and operations of government. By application of these concepts, the answers to many implementation research questions lie in examining how policies-in-practice compare to policies-in-theory or policies-as-written, how ambiguity has affected the gap between the former and latter, and how the construction or deconstruction of status quos affects whether that gap can be closed. Each of these concepts is as important in understanding individual behavior as it is in understanding collective action occurring within and across institutions. By extension, these concepts also lay the groundwork for how other theoretical concepts, drawn from political science, public policy, public administration, cognitive sciences, and other academic fields, can be incorporated into implementation studies, adding further depth and sophistication to how ideas are translated into both individual and collective action.

Importantly, this theory does not discard findings from early work. Rather, it provides a framework to understand why there are "47 variables completely explaining 5 cases" (Meier, 1999, p. 6) and how the diversity of ideas encountered in implementation research can be connected. Certainly, arguments concerning how implementers make sense of ambiguous situations are influenced by earlier works on bottom-up implementation. At the same time, arguments about the crucial roles program managers and organizations play in shaping how implementers behave rely on top-down theories. From this perspective, bottom-up and top-down are less diametrically opposed and more a consequence of different units of analysis, and observations from both are compatible with this theoretical framework. This is notable given that the top-down versus bottom-up debate weighed down efforts to push implementation studies forward for years, although this debate is largely seen as antiquated today (O'Toole, 2000). Furthermore, these arguments do not fundamentally oppose other attempts at developing third-generation theories, such as Goggin et al.'s (1990) theory of implementation in a federal system, Matland's (1995) ambiguity-conflict contingency theory, or Winter's (2012) systems model of implementation; instead, this work tries to place those theories into a broader framework that thinks about implementation at multiple levels that are not principally grounded by any technical dimensions that fluctuate between jurisdictions.

Empirical Challenges and Future Research

As one can imagine, the challenges of obtaining and analyzing empirical evidence to support the theoretical contentions in the preceding chapters were numerous. While "Methods Memos" (see Appendix) discuss some of the specific issues that arose, there are also several broader issues that deserve discussion. First and foremost, in an ideal world, one could track implementation of a single policy as it moved from individual-level behaviors through managers and organizational systems to become processes and then observed as institutional-level changes in social or environmental outcomes. But research never happens in an ideal world, so I was forced to make trade-offs: I rely on a mixed-methods approach while focusing on environmental policy as a consistent case study across chapters. On the one hand, this provides a sophisticated and broad look at the different moving parts that occur in policy implementation, and balances limitations that occur when one relies on a single case, methodological approach, and/ or analytical tool. On the other hand, this does not provide a complete empirical picture of the complexities of policy implementation, as data from individual chapters are not fully connected to each other, so there is a lack of comprehensiveness, so to speak. While this does not affect the validity or reliability of results from individual chapters, it does suggest that one should be cautious in thinking through the specific ways in which the entire empirical picture painted in this volume comes together.

Second, this project requires the observation and modeling of practical circumstances that implementers face in the real world. On the one hand, this creates issues of the observer effect, whereby observing a natural phenomenon inevitably affects it (e.g., Spano, 2006; Monahan & Fisher, 2010). For instance, it is likely that simply by discussing implementation with interviewees (see chapter 4), I cued them to think differently about how they do their job and inadvertently led them to answers that they may not have otherwise explicitly stated. But these effects likely also occur in the secondary data obtained from government agencies, such as EPA's program evaluation reports (see chapter 5). In this case, observations may be biased by either evaluators with a specific agenda (i.e., rule compliance) or state agencies attempting to "game the system" (e.g., Fowler, 2020a). On the other hand, trying to get around these effects with controlled experiments removes the complex and ambiguous circumstances that implementers face on the job. Certainly, this is an issue with the survey experiments, where respondents do not have to deal with the consequences of their choices (see chapter 3). Essentially, it is nearly impossible to effectively and accurately observe how implementers do their jobs. Thus, one has to recognize that observations here are not completely independent of this analysis.

Of course, an irony here is also that one of the biggest challenges in examining ambiguity is that ambiguity is difficult to model. There are inherent flaws in any attempt to boil the countless variables that impact how and why people behave as they do into a model that uses the fewest possible; unfortunately, this is the key challenge for all social sciences (Simon, 2004; Gunitsky, 2019). Given the too many variables problem that stretches across previous implementation research, I believe parsimony is crucial. Nevertheless, issues like job complexity (i.e., everyone is a policy implementer but no one focuses solely on implementing a single policy), serial versus concurrent processing (i.e., is there an order here or does everything occur simultaneously?), and power (i.e., who do people decide to listen to?) make this easier said than done, particularly as one thinks about how these issues manifest in empirical models. While there are valid theoretical explanations that underlie these empirics, modeling these dynamics is difficult. Thus, I was forced to make assumptions about innate human behaviors that do not always occur through a conscious, organized process. This inevitably leads to unexplained variance, where the predictor variables examined fail to completely explain the phenomena occurring.

Third, and by extension, there are also issues at play that cannot be meaningfully observed, requiring inferences to be made based on what is observable. For instance, with the survey experiments (chapter 3), there is no real mechanism to observe the internal dynamics of decision processes; instead, I can only observe the outcomes of those processes and make inferences about why differences emerge. Of course, this is again a common problem in social and behavioral sciences where scholars are attempting to explain facets of the human experience that are impossible to effectively capture as they manifest in the real world. This is especially difficult when dynamics play out across decentralized, multi-level systems so that there is no one "smoking gun" to observe. While the underlying theory here provides a valid explanation for the evidence presented, there are potentially other legitimate explanations that can only be proved or disproved with additional data. I have considered some of those within the discussion of individual results, but others may exist and should be examined by scholars in order to further develop the collective understanding of implementation dynamics.

These issues suggest there is a need for further development and application of this theoretical framework to policy implementation across jurisdictions, organizations, policies, and time. Most readily, this requires testing of hypotheses (see above) within different contexts. Further research should examine how these dynamics may be affected by the cultural, political, or institutional norms of jurisdictions, such as implementation by federal versus state or local agencies or implementing a policy in Texas versus California or in urban versus rural areas. Given the diversity of jurisdictions in the United States, as well as those across the globe, and the increasing levels of political conflict within society, it is crucial to understand how lessons for effective implementation transfer between places. This also applies to understanding organizations that have overlapping jurisdictions or that are designed to achieve different missions but operating within the same policy spaces. For instance, energy policy is often an intergovernmental affair, and in some states, it is treated as an issue of utility regulation, while in other states, it is a matter of environmental protection or economic development. Of course, there is evidence to suggest that these mission-based differences have led to operational differences in programs (Fowler, 2015). But does this mean that policies are implemented differently or that the process of implementation is different?

Furthermore, scholars should also explore these dynamics within the context of different types of policies, both in terms of both technical dimensions and as they relate to policy problems. Certainly, the degree and types of ambiguity that emerge in the application of social policies are likely to contribute to a different context for implementation as compared to a technical policy for environmental management. What does this mean for the transferability of lessons learned across policy areas or from specific policies? Finally, there is also the question of how well this framework explains whether implementation has changed or will change over time. A casual re-reading of Pressman and Wildavsky's (1984) *Implementation* is a good reminder of how difficult implementation has always been, but reading it also raises the question of what has changed in the decades since the authors observed how good intentions in Washington are dashed in Oakland. In other words, how long can one expect the lessons of implementation to stay good for? In sum, this volume should be seen as an opening salvo into understanding implementation through organized anarchies, rather than a closing statement, as there are countless open questions, both theoretically and empirically.

Implications for Democratic Governance

So, what does this tell us about why policies succeed or fail? Well, it tells us that policy success depends on whether public servants change the way they think and act every day as they ask themselves "How does this policy apply to this situation?" Of course, that question is at the core of how policy-in-practice works, and it is not always a direct manifestation of policy-in-theory as it filters through organizations. Specifically, where public servants continue to find the same answer over and over again, the status quo remains unchanged, and the impact of new policies may be inconsequential. On the other hand, where policy causes public servants to rethink how they behave, existing status quos are replaced by new ones, and the social or environmental conditions that result from the behavioral patterns of public servants begin to change. To quote a friend, "If you do what you've always done, you'll get what you've always gotten." Thus, policy success and failure are often caught up in the question of whether one wants to see public servants change their behaviors. While the emphasis of policy is often on change, there may be times where stopping change is the ultimate goal (i.e., "don't fix what ain't broke"), which is particularly on display with the culture wars of recent years.

Surely, this helps us understand better why Supreme Court rulings from the mid-20th century, like *Brown v. Board of Education* (1954), did not end the scourge of racism in public education across the country. Some state and local leaders hid behind phrases like "with all deliberate speed" to stop public servants from rethinking how they provide public services to people of color. Certainly, there is enough ambiguity in that phrase to allow one to believe that they are complying with the intent of the court's ruling, but still fail to provide racially integrated services. But each new ruling chipped away at that way of thinking, little by little, by making the court's stance on school integration less and less ambiguous, until the mental gymnastics necessary to square the practice of school segregation and the prevailing legal interpretations became too much for the masses to perform on a routine basis (Daugherty & Bolton, 2008;

Ogletree, 2004). Of course, Supreme Court rulings and federal laws did not solve the problems of institutionalized racism in America, but they did provide a basis for shifting how public servants interpreted the meanings of policy and their responsibilities as agents of democracies who have an obligation to comply with the law and respond to citizen demands.

More recently, successes and failures in responding to the COVID-19 pandemic are largely driven by a competition between policy narratives. On one side, scientists and public health experts consistently contended that COVID-19 is a clear and present danger to public health, and there is/was a needed change in the status quo in order to contain it (e.g., wearing masks, social distancing). On the other side, some believe/believed that the threat is overblown and altering status quos is too big of a risk to individual freedom or the economy (Grossman et al., 2020; Rutledge, 2020). Implementation of COVID policies, though, is complicated by the fact that society must rely on citizens as policy implementers to do things like wear masks, socially distance, or get vaccinated. Unfortunately, this removes many of the organizational tools that program managers rely on to guide behaviors, and instead requires elected officials and other public leaders to use their bully pulpit to send signals to citizens on how to behave (Mintrom & O'Connor, 2020). Further, it has also shifted a significant amount of responsibility to NGOs as employers and service providers to set rules for their stakeholders, in the absence of a consistent government policy. Thus, whether COVID policies are effectively implemented largely relies on the skills of local leaders, which helps explain why some states have done well with containment initially and vaccination roll-outs later, and others have languished on both accounts (Gupta et al. 2020).

However, there are also some examples of policy successes to consider here, even if they are few and far between. While not one specific policy, community-based policing has largely been regarded as successful in many cities, such as Dallas or Seattle, where it has been implemented. Its key tenet is to establish a deeper connection between communities and the police officers who serve those communities in order to create a greater sense of accountability for both groups; this is in contrast to more traditional policing tactics that focus on responding to crime after it occurs. Although there are some criticisms, and community-based policing does not solve issues such as racial profiling or corruption, advocates argue that this approach works by shifting the discourse between police and communities, so that the goal becomes solving community problems, rather than simply arresting criminals. Overall, this tends to lead to more positive interactions as community members build trust with local officers (Reed, 1999; Davis, 2010; Miller, Hess, & Orthmann, 2013). At the core of this is a revision in how police see their roles in society and the communities that they serve; that is, they become a partner in the community as opposed to a mechanism of social control.

Certainly, the implications for democratic governance are clear: the power of the people hinges on the ability to turn ideas into actions, and that pathway runs through policy implementation. For better or worse, the good ideas hatched in capitol buildings or city halls are dashed when they run into realities of the office buildings or public spaces where policies are actually practiced. The ideas behind policies are not necessarily always flawed, but reality is hard to explain or predict. It is nearly impossible for policymakers to envision all the scenarios that implementers are likely to run into, while any experienced public employee can tell you numerous tales of the unbelievable and inconceivable that are stranger than fiction. This means far too often policy implementation is an exercise in fitting a square peg into a round hole, where policymakers have misestimated the space they are trying to plug. While the natural inclination of most is to hammer away as they try to force the peg in the hole, the well-seasoned in this game know that the most effective approach is to chip away at the peg's edges so it fits without breaking something beyond repair. This is where implementers find themselves time and time again, figuring out how to reshape the peg by rethinking what a policy means. At the end of the day, it is messy and difficult, but those who are persistent find ways to make it work.

Executing the ideas that are at the foundation of government is often harder than coming up with the ideas to start with (Wilson, 1887). It has only gotten harder as society has developed, economically and politically, and public agencies are now only players in a larger governance scheme that includes a myriad of decentralized participants. Further, many "new" policy proposals are just rehashing or repackaging of old ideas that failed to meet their potential, and thoughtfulness has given way to polarization and incivility in political debate. As Derthick (2011) points out, "much of the activity of American policymaking consists of attempts not to pass new laws but to invest old ones with new meanings" (p. 56). Some may even say that America has entered a "post-idea" era, where critical thinking has taken a back seat to punditry in public discourse (Sterling, 2011); anyone who observed American politics during the Trump presidency is likely to agree. To this end, the core challenges of governance moving forward are likely to be less about coming up with new ideas and more about figuring out how to make existing ideas work in practice. For better or worse, the power to make the positive changes that societies so desperately need is shifting more and more to the army of public servants, as elected officials have gotten lost in politics.

Appendix
Methods Memos

Methods Memo for Chapter 3

Survey experiments were conducted in partnership with Dr. Stephen Utych.[1] In general, experiments ask respondents to imagine they are responsible for implementing a new law, and then rate their support for different tools for doing so. The experimental treatments rely on providing differing information on the political and problem conditions to determine how fluctuations may bias preferences. We used a 3×2 factorial design, where there are two independent variables with three categorical variations (Auspurg & Hinz, 2015). The two independent variables were political and proble m conditions. While policy is included in the experiment, it is held constant across respondents. This created 10 groups in total: nine treatment groups (varying information on politics/problems) and one control group (no information). The survey experiment was conducted using Lucid, an opt-in online survey panel that recruits participants to match national demographic percentages, making it an increasingly popular tool in the social sciences (Coppock & McClellan, 2019). We recruited 3,300 participants for the experiment, giving sufficient respondents per group to make comparisons. In general, the sample is younger, whiter, and more educated than the general population; I correct for this in statistical models by controlling for demographic factors. Table A3.1 provides a breakdown of participants.

---

1. Dr. Utych is an independent researcher. He has authored more than a dozen studies on political psychology using survey experimental methodologies (e.g., Utych [2022]; Utych & Fowler [2021]). This portion of this project would not be possible without his expertise and advice.

Table A3.1. Demographic Breakdown of Survey Participants

Gender	%
Male	49.5
Female	50.5
Race	%
White	73.2
African American/Black	13.1
Hispanic/Latinx	5.9
Asian	4.5
Native American	1.2
Other	2.1
Education	%
Less than high school	3.62
High school or equivalent	22.01
Some college	31.47
Bachelor's degree	25.57
Advanced degree	17.34
Age	%
18–44	55.3
45–64	28.8
65+	15.9
Mean age: 44.4	

Source: Author.

Respondents participated in two experiments for confirmation and comparison purposes. The second experiment (not discussed in chapter 3) relied on the same general structure, but used an anti-panhandling ordinance instead. Participants received the idling experiment first and the panhandling experiment second. Experimental treatment text for the panhandling experiment is:

Imagine you are a city's police chief. In response to recent concerns about panhandling, the city council has passed an anti-panhandling law which bans in-person solicitations of monetary donations on public property. The law allows violators to be fined up to $500. This is a civil, rather than a criminal, penalty—citizens can be fined for violations, but cannot be arrested. This law is scheduled to go into effect January 1, 2021. How to enforce the new law and the specific fine schedule is left to your discretion.

A recent poll shows that public concern about panhandling has [**increased/decreased/remained the same**] since the previous poll, conducted last year, and new data shows incidences of panhandling have [**increased/decreased/remained the same**] over the past year.

Additionally, there was an unrelated task in between the two experiments so that respondents would cognitively focus on a different task between experiments. Respondents were randomly assigned political and problem conditions. While the same general implementation tools were used as dependent variables in both experiments, there are slight wording variations to fit the different policies. Both street-level (e.g., enforce all violations, increase patrols) and office-based (e.g., planning committee, grant program) implementation tools were included as options to provide respondents an array of potential tactics. The experiments were specifically designed so that one scenario (i.e., idling) followed a more ambiguous causal pathway from implementation tool to problem-solving than the other (i.e., panhandling). That is, one could assume that the average person would find the relationship between limiting vehicle idling and air pollution to be more ambiguous than that between banning panhandling and panhandling incidences. Since these are hypothetical choices that are not subject to real-world pressures, this experiment does not directly provide evidence of the type of intuitive versus deliberative thinking that occurs in actual implementation, but is still informative of how people react to information when formulating behavioral preferences (Kuhberger, Schulte-Mecklenbeck, & Perner, 2002).

Specifically, it provides evidence as to whether information about political and problem conditions trigger a shift in respondent preferences. From this, one can infer under what conditions respondents rely on intuitive, quick decisions when responding and under what conditions respondents provide more in-depth thought to their responses, as system 1 and system 2 thinking should lead to discernible differences. For instance, if there is no statistically significant difference between control and treatment groups, then one can infer that both sets of respondents relied on intuitive judgments that either produced the same response or no discernible variation in responses. However, if there are statistically significant differences, one can infer that the political/problem conditions trigger respondents to engage in deliberative thinking that resulted in a different pattern of preferences. The null hypothesis is that respondents will use intuitive judgments when rating their preferences so that there is no substantive difference between control and treatment groups. The research hypothesis is that when additional information is provided that indicates a changing situation, respondents will engage in more deliberative thinking about their preferences so that there is a substantive difference between control and treatment groups.

In order to consider the implications of problematic preferences among respondents, I use a set of interrelated questions designed to capture respondent beliefs/attitudes toward the environment and the homeless. Questions on the environment are discussed in chapter 3's main text. Questions used to measure preferences related to homelessness are below (rated from strongly disagree to strongly agree):

1. People who beg for money do so only because they are too lazy to work [recoded];

2. Homeless people and vagrants are a public nuisance [recoded];

3. I give money to people that are having "hard times";

4. We have a public responsibility to support people that are homeless.

Respondents were provided these questions before the experimental text to cue them to consider their broader attitudes about the policy issues at hand. One environmental question and two homeless questions were recoded so that the response categories were aligned to represent the same ideological positions. I calculated the variance across each set of questions and organized the variance into three categories (low, moderate, and high) separated at the 33rd and 66th percentile values, respectively. I assume that lower variance indicates a more rigid set of beliefs/attitudes about the environment or homelessness, respectively, while a higher variance indicates respondents have less formulated beliefs/attitudes; moderate variance is around the mean level of variance, representing a benchmark for where an average person would likely fall. While respondents in the low (43.0% in idling and 35.0% in panhandling) and high sub-samples (43.8% and 34.6%) were relatively evenly distributed, the moderate sub-sample was relatively smaller in both experiments (13.3% and 30.5%).

I use ordinal logistic regression with respondents' preferences for each implementation tool as dependent variables, with coefficients reported in the full results (see tables A3.2 through A3.5). The key predictor variables are indicators for the nine treatment conditions, with the control group as the suppressed base category for comparison in the initial analyses. In models comparing sub-samples based on problematic preferences, the base comparison category is the control group with moderate variance, so that other groups are compared to those that received no information on political or problem conditions and express a moderate degree of variance in their beliefs/attitudes about the respective policy issues. Results indicate whether preferences of respondents vary based on additional information about conditions, as compared to respondents with no information. Standard diagnostic tests indicate that no assumption of ordinal logistic were violated (e.g., multicollinearity) (Menard, 2001). I also include race, age, gender, and education[2] to increase statistical efficiency of the models and control for any effects demographic characteristics have in biasing preferences.

Findings were generally consistent between experiments, although respondents appear to be more responsive to problem and/or political conditions in the panhandling experiment as compared to the idling experiment. Additionally, preferences for implementation tools were inconsistent, so it is likely that shifts in preferences were tied to an interaction between conditional changes and the specific policy at hand. This may be because the panhandling experiment presents a less ambiguous causal pathway between policy implementation and the problem, as compared to the idling experiment. It is likely that respondents could more easily imagine how their actions impact the efficacy of the policy when it comes to something as straightforward as banning panhandling, as compared to a more complicated pathway between implementation actions and outcomes when limiting automobile idling in public spaces. Despite this, the results from the second experiment largely confirm the findings from the first, and further support the conclusions that respondents only respond to conditional changes when formulating their preferences under certain circumstances.

While findings are relatively robust and provide evidence to the underlying theory, there are two notable limitations to the experimental

---

2. Gender is coded 1 for male and 0 for female. White is coded 1 for white, and 0 for all other races. Education is an ordinal variable on a 7-point scale ranging from (1) 8th grade to (7) advanced degree. Age is a count variable.

Table A3.2. Full Results for Idling Experiment

	Media campaign	Install signs	Enforce only flagrant	Enforce all violations	Increase patrols	Create tip line	Private contractor	Tax incentive	Planning committee	Do nothing
Increase/improve	-0.156	-0.206	-0.126	-0.175	-0.0342	-0.0525	-0.0380	-0.198	-0.243	-0.0269
	(0.139)	(0.141)	(0.139)	(0.139)	(0.139)	(0.140)	(0.140)	(0.140)	(0.140)	(0.139)
Increase/same	-0.178	-0.238	-0.121	-0.0709	-0.118	-0.0392	-0.0845	-0.258	-0.119	-0.220
	(0.142)	(0.142)	(0.141)	(0.141)	(0.141)	(0.142)	(0.141)	(0.142)	(0.143)	(0.142)
Increase/worse	-0.0520	-0.199	-0.272	0.0103	0.0304	0.127	-0.0764	-0.229	-0.102	-0.167
	(0.141)	(0.143)	(0.141)	(0.140)	(0.141)	(0.141)	(0.142)	(0.140)	(0.142)	(0.142)
Same/improve	-0.0193	-0.295*	-0.160	0.00150	-0.0707	-0.0605	-0.0212	-0.175	-0.126	-0.189
	(0.143)	(0.145)	(0.141)	(0.141)	(0.140)	(0.141)	(0.142)	(0.141)	(0.142)	(0.141)
Same/same	-0.167	-0.203	-0.0852	-0.0975	-0.139	-0.0530	0.0697	-0.236	-0.0652	-0.128
	(0.139)	(0.143)	(0.139)	(0.140)	(0.140)	(0.140)	(0.140)	(0.139)	(0.140)	(0.139)
Same/worse	-0.196	-0.302*	-0.292*	-0.0749	-0.267	-0.0731	0.0836	-0.359*	-0.167	-0.207
	(0.142)	(0.143)	(0.141)	(0.142)	(0.141)	(0.142)	(0.143)	(0.143)	(0.143)	(0.141)
Decrease/improve	-0.0976	-0.110	-0.263	0.0157	-0.217	0.0844	0.0324	-0.161	-0.0616	-0.178
	(0.143)	(0.144)	(0.141)	(0.143)	(0.142)	(0.143)	(0.143)	(0.143)	(0.143)	(0.142)
Decrease/same	0.0164	-0.106	0.00689	-0.000640	-0.206	0.00764	0.157	-0.0856	-0.0951	-0.0651
	(0.141)	(0.143)	(0.141)	(0.140)	(0.140)	(0.142)	(0.140)	(0.141)	(0.140)	(0.141)
Decrease/worse	0.0428	-0.263	-0.308*	-0.0457	-0.0267	-0.0719	-0.110	-0.142	0.104	-0.253
	(0.143)	(0.143)	(0.142)	(0.142)	(0.141)	(0.142)	(0.142)	(0.141)	(0.144)	(0.141)
Age	0.0130‡	0.0155‡	0.000238	-0.00846‡	-0.00462*	-0.0149‡	-0.0188‡	0.00780‡	-0.00199	0.00135
	(0.00197)	(0.00196)	(0.00193)	(0.00194)	(0.00194)	(0.00195)	(0.00196)	(0.00196)	(0.00194)	(0.00194)
Gender	0.123	0.199†	-0.392‡	-0.326‡	-0.284‡	-0.189†	-0.183†	0.0782	-0.0548	-0.299‡
	(0.0640)	(0.0640)	(0.0640)	(0.0639)	(0.0641)	(0.0636)	(0.0638)	(0.0639)	(0.0638)	(0.0640)
White	0.296‡	0.429‡	0.162*	0.0310	0.167*	0.0484	0.0630	0.395‡	0.181*	0.458‡
	(0.0770)	(0.0779)	(0.0757)	(0.0758)	(0.0760)	(0.0755)	(0.0765)	(0.0772)	(0.0765)	(0.0769)
Education	0.119‡	0.138‡	0.0854‡	0.0905‡	0.114‡	0.0764‡	0.0778‡	0.110‡	0.128‡	0.104‡
	(0.0166)	(0.0167)	(0.0165)	(0.0164)	(0.0166)	(0.0164)	(0.0165)	(0.0166)	(0.0166)	(0.0167)

	(1)	(2)	(3)	(4)	(5)	(6)	(7)	(8)	(9)	(10)
Cut1	-1.451‡	-1.296‡	-2.520‡	-2.351‡	-2.120‡	-2.434‡	-2.307‡	-1.602‡	-2.231‡	-1.867‡
	(0.190)	(0.192)	(0.188)	(0.186)	(0.185)	(0.186)	(0.185)	(0.188)	(0.190)	(0.187)
Cut2	-0.775‡	-0.668‡	-1.804‡	-1.640‡	-1.461‡	-1.828‡	-1.578‡	-0.955‡	-1.525‡	-1.108‡
	(0.183)	(0.186)	(0.184)	(0.183)	(0.182)	(0.184)	(0.183)	(0.183)	(0.184)	(0.184)
Cut3	-0.334	-0.127	-1.194‡	-1.019‡	-0.874‡	-1.315‡	-1.004‡	-0.500†	-0.987‡	-0.496†
	(0.181)	(0.184)	(0.182)	(0.182)	(0.181)	(0.182)	(0.182)	(0.181)	(0.182)	(0.183)
Cut4	0.803‡	1.057‡	-0.109	-0.0761	0.188	-0.361*	0.00484	0.568†	0.182	0.710‡
	(0.181)	(0.185)	(0.180)	(0.181)	(0.181)	(0.181)	(0.181)	(0.182)	(0.182)	(0.183)
Cut5	1.692‡	1.972‡	0.754‡	0.747‡	1.154‡	0.444*	0.834‡	1.425‡	1.125‡	1.590‡
	(0.184)	(0.187)	(0.181)	(0.182)	(0.182)	(0.181)	(0.182)	(0.184)	(0.183)	(0.185)
Cut6	2.801‡	3.116‡	1.747‡	1.745‡	2.151‡	1.419‡	1.769‡	2.434‡	2.313‡	2.517‡
	(0.187)	(0.191)	(0.184)	(0.186)	(0.187)	(0.184)	(0.187)	(0.186)	(0.187)	(0.189)
R^2	.0147	.0221	.0080	.0072	.0082	.0082	.0113	.0117	.0072	.0114
N	3153	3161	3157	3156	3156	3162	3160	3153	3162	3155

Note: Standard errors in parentheses. P-value = * < .05, † < .01, ‡ < .001.
Source: Author.

Table A3.3. Full Results for Idling Experiment by Problematic Preferences Sub-groups

	Media campaign	Install signs	Enforce only flagrant	Enforce all violations	Increase patrols	Create tip line	Private contractor	Tax incentive	Planning committee	Do nothing
Moderate variance										
Increase/improve	-0.137	0.0361	-0.476	-0.164	0.463	-0.147	-0.0994	-0.0162	-0.0992	-0.00232
	(0.373)	(0.387)	(0.380)	(0.389)	(0.372)	(0.375)	(0.378)	(0.391)	(0.390)	(0.384)
Increase/same	0.159	0.0241	-0.332	-0.146	0.0503	-0.252	-0.0686	-0.369	0.646	0.627
	(0.379)	(0.377)	(0.378)	(0.382)	(0.368)	(0.369)	(0.371)	(0.366)	(0.385)	(0.388)
Increase/worse	0.585	0.585	-0.445	0.180	0.418	0.0518	-0.132	0.0700	0.419	0.445
	(0.393)	(0.391)	(0.386)	(0.395)	(0.382)	(0.376)	(0.390)	(0.370)	(0.397)	(0.401)
Same/improve	0.426	-0.120	-0.372	0.107	0.149	0.00336	0.102	-0.189	0.245	0.378
	(0.395)	(0.381)	(0.373)	(0.395)	(0.369)	(0.371)	(0.383)	(0.379)	(0.381)	(0.386)
Same/same	0.357	0.233	-0.321	0.398	0.674	0.469	**0.844***	0.258	0.733	0.651
	(0.391)	(0.398)	(0.387)	(0.397)	(0.385)	(0.382)	(0.386)	(0.386)	(0.395)	(0.391)
Same/worse	-0.154	-0.148	-0.385	0.00891	-0.0178	-0.273	0.253	-0.414	-0.0496	0.665
	(0.368)	(0.377)	(0.371)	(0.376)	(0.367)	(0.368)	(0.370)	(0.366)	(0.381)	(0.376)
Decrease/improve	-0.172	-0.0516	-0.390	-0.145	-0.0151	-0.261	0.221	-0.216	-0.117	0.532
	(0.392)	(0.388)	(0.391)	(0.396)	(0.388)	(0.399)	(0.389)	(0.393)	(0.405)	(0.396)
Decrease/same	-0.171	0.307	-0.210	0.259	0.430	0.0539	0.197	-0.164	-0.0252	0.446
	(0.386)	(0.394)	(0.384)	(0.383)	(0.375)	(0.371)	(0.390)	(0.375)	(0.386)	(0.395)
Decrease/worse	0.348	0.439	**-0.807***	0.203	0.585	-0.0629	0.202	-0.0250	0.839*	0.145
	(0.393)	(0.392)	(0.391)	(0.397)	(0.380)	(0.387)	(0.390)	(0.384)	(0.390)	(0.398)

High variance

Control group	0.264	0.439	0.0284	0.375	0.518	0.132	0.461	0.310	0.588	0.690*
	(0.317)	(0.320)	(0.312)	(0.326)	(0.305)	(0.312)	(0.313)	(0.309)	(0.326)	(0.321)
Increase/improve	0.400	0.381	−0.218	0.564	0.710*	0.316	0.649*	0.221	0.660*	0.496
	(0.314)	(0.317)	(0.311)	(0.324)	(0.305)	(0.309)	(0.312)	(0.307)	(0.322)	(0.318)
Increase/same	0.285	0.443	−0.155	0.740*	0.723*	0.457	0.632*	0.169	0.470	0.251
	(0.318)	(0.321)	(0.314)	(0.328)	(0.308)	(0.314)	(0.314)	(0.313)	(0.328)	(0.322)
Increase/worse	0.268	−0.0360	−0.504	0.447	0.575	0.528	0.517	−0.100	0.458	0.334
	(0.321)	(0.323)	(0.319)	(0.328)	(0.310)	(0.314)	(0.317)	(0.311)	(0.330)	(0.323)
Same/improve	0.548	0.293	−0.0138	0.585	0.788*	0.355	0.744*	0.230	0.751*	0.353
	(0.319)	(0.322)	(0.316)	(0.328)	(0.307)	(0.311)	(0.316)	(0.312)	(0.327)	(0.322)
Same/same	0.0772	0.330	−0.244	0.281	0.395	0.0272	0.465	0.0603	0.423	0.364
	(0.315)	(0.320)	(0.313)	(0.326)	(0.305)	(0.310)	(0.312)	(0.308)	(0.322)	(0.321)
Same/worse	0.116	0.0100	−0.477	0.442	0.264	0.378	0.711*	−0.0132	0.557	0.206
	(0.320)	(0.323)	(0.319)	(0.329)	(0.311)	(0.315)	(0.320)	(0.315)	(0.329)	(0.323)
Decrease/improve	0.478	0.678*	−0.342	0.658*	0.598*	0.471	0.763*	0.363	0.935†	0.510
	(0.314)	(0.317)	(0.311)	(0.324)	(0.303)	(0.309)	(0.312)	(0.307)	(0.322)	(0.319)
Decrease/same	0.591	0.576	0.0459	0.479	0.244	0.229	0.696*	0.181	0.755*	0.526
	(0.315)	(0.318)	(0.313)	(0.323)	(0.304)	(0.312)	(0.312)	(0.310)	(0.322)	(0.320)
Decrease/worse	0.341	−0.0720	−0.325	0.256	0.485	0.0939	0.360	0.0203	0.605	0.328
	(0.318)	(0.319)	(0.318)	(0.326)	(0.309)	(0.311)	(0.316)	(0.311)	(0.330)	(0.321)

continued on next page

Table A3.3. Continued.

	Media campaign	Install signs	Enforce only flagrant	Enforce all violations	Increase patrols	Create tip line	Private contractor	Tax incentive	Planning committee	Do nothing
Low variance										
Control group	0.405	0.377	−0.145	0.541	0.615*	0.284	0.612	0.204	0.690*	0.640*
	(0.316)	(0.322)	(0.316)	(0.327)	(0.307)	(0.313)	(0.317)	(0.309)	(0.324)	(0.320)
Increase/improve	0.252	0.193	−0.132	0.208	0.391	0.245	0.445	−0.00871	0.338	0.653*
	(0.314)	(0.317)	(0.312)	(0.324)	(0.304)	(0.310)	(0.313)	(0.309)	(0.323)	(0.319)
Increase/same	0.0291	−0.0667	−0.223	0.212	0.229	0.118	0.283	−0.00354	0.433	0.282
	(0.317)	(0.317)	(0.316)	(0.324)	(0.306)	(0.308)	(0.313)	(0.309)	(0.325)	(0.321)
Increase/worse	0.149	0.178	−0.199	0.510	0.496	0.283	0.386	−0.00943	0.468	0.386
	(0.312)	(0.316)	(0.311)	(0.321)	(0.303)	(0.306)	(0.311)	(0.305)	(0.321)	(0.319)
Same/improve	0.140	0.0270	−0.382	0.473	0.289	0.0749	0.297	0.0265	0.352	0.316
	(0.315)	(0.320)	(0.311)	(0.325)	(0.305)	(0.308)	(0.314)	(0.308)	(0.323)	(0.320)
Same/same	0.334	0.149	−0.0909	0.461	0.356	0.285	0.553	−0.0345	0.688*	0.329
	(0.312)	(0.315)	(0.310)	(0.322)	(0.305)	(0.307)	(0.311)	(0.304)	(0.321)	(0.317)
Same/worse	0.291	0.251	−0.242	0.437	0.320	0.0704	0.564	−0.117	0.477	0.324
	(0.313)	(0.316)	(0.313)	(0.324)	(0.304)	(0.307)	(0.313)	(0.308)	(0.324)	(0.319)
Decrease/improve	0.177	0.0500	−0.342	0.474	0.0694	0.344	0.325	−0.0871	0.325	0.124
	(0.320)	(0.322)	(0.319)	(0.330)	(0.312)	(0.315)	(0.318)	(0.314)	(0.326)	(0.323)
Decrease/same	0.330	−0.00562	−0.165	0.473	0.386	0.320	0.691*	0.260	0.414	0.384
	(0.317)	(0.319)	(0.315)	(0.326)	(0.306)	(0.311)	(0.311)	(0.308)	(0.323)	(0.321)
Decrease/worse	0.385	0.220	−0.308	0.567	0.471	0.282	0.397	0.208	0.716*	0.295
	(0.314)	(0.317)	(0.312)	(0.324)	(0.304)	(0.308)	(0.311)	(0.306)	(0.323)	(0.318)

	(1)	(2)	(3)	(4)	(5)	(6)	(7)	(8)	(9)	(10)
Belief 1	-0.220‡	-0.203‡	0.0495*	-0.142‡	-0.151‡	-0.151‡	-0.101‡	-0.133‡	-0.193‡	0.0250
	(0.0237)	(0.0236)	(0.0234)	(0.0234)	(0.0235)	(0.0235)	(0.0232)	(0.0234)	(0.0238)	(0.0232)
Belief 2	-0.248‡	-0.215‡	0.0415*	-0.137‡	-0.0925‡	-0.150‡	-0.0786‡	-0.194‡	-0.213‡	0.0833‡
	(0.0200)	(0.0198)	(0.0191)	(0.0194)	(0.0195)	(0.0195)	(0.0192)	(0.0196)	(0.0198)	(0.0194)
Belief 3	-0.0182	0.0215	0.0543*	-0.0470	-0.00952	-0.0537*	0.0220	0.00976	-0.0109	0.127‡
	(0.0249)	(0.0249)	(0.0248)	(0.0247)	(0.0251)	(0.0250)	(0.0248)	(0.0247)	(0.0251)	(0.0248)
Age	0.00991‡	0.0127‡	0.00138	-0.0114‡	-0.006887†	-0.0183‡	-0.0201‡	0.00535‡	-0.00528†	0.00266
	(0.00201)	(0.00200)	(0.00196)	(0.00198)	(0.00198)	(0.00199)	(0.00200)	(0.00199)	(0.00198)	(0.00197)
Gender	-0.0154	0.0964	-0.362‡	-0.420‡	-0.343‡	-0.296‡	-0.225‡	-0.0274	-0.177†	-0.238‡
	(0.0655)	(0.0655)	(0.0652)	(0.0652)	(0.0652)	(0.0649)	(0.0651)	(0.0652)	(0.0651)	(0.0651)
White	0.336‡	0.467‡	0.139	0.0529	0.185*	0.0609	0.0632	0.388‡	0.207†	0.444‡
	(0.0781)	(0.0786)	(0.0763)	(0.0768)	(0.0768)	(0.0765)	(0.0769)	(0.0777)	(0.0774)	(0.0775)
Education	0.109‡	0.128‡	0.0844‡	0.0805‡	0.105‡	0.0630‡	0.0720‡	0.102‡	0.113‡	0.103‡
	(0.0168)	(0.0169)	(0.0167)	(0.0166)	(0.0167)	(0.0166)	(0.0166)	(0.0168)	(0.0168)	(0.0168)
Cut1	-3.292‡	-2.672‡	-2.054‡	-3.370‡	-2.711‡	-3.833‡	-2.535‡	-2.805‡	-3.545‡	-0.441
	(0.336)	(0.339)	(0.329)	(0.339)	(0.321)	(0.327)	(0.329)	(0.326)	(0.343)	(0.334)
Cut2	-2.579‡	-2.023‡	-1.331‡	-2.627‡	-2.035‡	-3.200‡	-1.797‡	-2.143‡	-2.813‡	0.331
	(0.332)	(0.335)	(0.327)	(0.337)	(0.319)	(0.325)	(0.327)	(0.323)	(0.339)	(0.333)
Cut3	-2.110‡	-1.453‡	-0.720*	-1.983‡	-1.429‡	-2.659‡	-1.214‡	-1.675‡	-2.240‡	0.956‡
	(0.330)	(0.334)	(0.326)	(0.335)	(0.318)	(0.323)	(0.326)	(0.322)	(0.337)	(0.333)
Cut4	-0.866†	-0.194	0.380	-0.997‡	-0.332	-1.655‡	-0.184	-0.558	-0.975†	2.195‡
	(0.328)	(0.333)	(0.325)	(0.334)	(0.317)	(0.321)	(0.326)	(0.321)	(0.336)	(0.335)
Cut5	0.117	0.789*	1.253‡	-0.131	0.660*	-0.809*	0.662*	0.346	0.0484	3.090‡
	(0.328)	(0.333)	(0.326)	(0.334)	(0.318)	(0.321)	(0.326)	(0.321)	(0.335)	(0.337)
Cut6	1.344‡	2.026‡	2.255‡	0.900‡	1.685‡	0.203	1.618‡	1.409‡	1.312‡	4.035‡
	(0.329)	(0.334)	(0.328)	(0.336)	(0.320)	(0.322)	(0.329)	(0.322)	(0.336)	(0.340)
R^2	.0567	.0546	.0120	.0258	.0210	.0290	.0192	.0322	.0397	.0207
N	3139	3147	3143	3143	3142	3148	3146	3139	3148	3141

Note: Standard errors in parentheses. P-value = * < .05, † < .01, ‡ < .001.

Source: Author.

Table A3.4. Results for Panhandling Experiment

	Media campaign	Install signs	Enforce only flagrant	Enforce all violations	Increase patrols	Create tip line	Private contractor	Tax incentive	Planning committee	Do nothing
Increase/increase	0.136	0.110	**-0.350***	**0.277***	0.198	0.108	-0.0702	-0.219	-0.118	-0.229
	(0.141)	(0.143)	(0.141)	(0.139)	(0.141)	(0.140)	(0.142)	(0.141)	(0.142)	(0.143)
Increase/same	0.0490	0.0337	0.0629	-0.0270	0.196	0.156	0.0286	-0.0482	-0.0968	-0.171
	(0.143)	(0.142)	(0.141)	(0.141)	(0.143)	(0.143)	(0.141)	(0.142)	(0.142)	(0.143)
Increase/decrease	0.135	0.0745	-0.0694	0.168	0.215	0.105	-0.0745	-0.223	0.00434	0.0507
	(0.141)	(0.143)	(0.141)	(0.142)	(0.141)	(0.142)	(0.140)	(0.141)	(0.141)	(0.142)
Same/increase	0.0801	-0.127	-0.154	0.116	0.181	-0.0137	-0.111	-0.0888	-0.0976	-0.143
	(0.141)	(0.143)	(0.141)	(0.140)	(0.141)	(0.141)	(0.140)	(0.140)	(0.142)	(0.142)
Same/same	0.122	0.0492	-0.0831	0.00722	0.0974	-0.0933	-0.0949	-0.244	-0.127	0.0293
	(0.144)	(0.143)	(0.141)	(0.140)	(0.142)	(0.143)	(0.141)	(0.142)	(0.142)	(0.142)
Same/decrease	-0.0261	-0.0512	-0.00835	0.0726	0.0876	0.191	-0.0965	**-0.288***	-0.164	0.0706
	(0.141)	(0.143)	(0.140)	(0.142)	(0.142)	(0.143)	(0.142)	(0.141)	(0.142)	(0.142)
Decrease/increase	0.170	-0.0240	-0.127	0.0791	**0.355***	-0.0196	0.0694	-0.111	-0.0276	0.0224
	(0.143)	(0.144)	(0.141)	(0.139)	(0.140)	(0.141)	(0.141)	(0.139)	(0.140)	(0.142)
Decrease/same	0.0322	-0.129	0.170	-0.0527	0.0596	-0.116	-0.0959	0.000554	-0.0835	0.0812
	(0.140)	(0.141)	(0.141)	(0.140)	(0.141)	(0.142)	(0.141)	(0.140)	(0.141)	(0.141)
Decrease/decrease	0.0319	-0.0923	-0.197	0.0255	0.0651	-0.0728	-0.171	-0.0962	-0.0819	0.0543
	(0.143)	(0.144)	(0.142)	(0.141)	(0.142)	(0.143)	(0.143)	(0.142)	(0.143)	(0.142)

Age	0.0164‡	0.0270‡	0.00196	0.0000814	-0.00166	-0.0108‡	-0.0234‡	-0.00837‡	0.00559†	-0.00867‡
	(0.00196)	(0.00203)	(0.00195)	(0.00194)	(0.00194)	(0.00196)	(0.00198)	(0.00196)	(0.00196)	(0.00195)
Gender	0.0368	0.181†	-0.141*	-0.222‡	-0.327‡	-0.210‡	-0.233‡	0.0415	-0.0740	-0.434‡
	(0.0635)	(0.0644)	(0.0635)	(0.0635)	(0.0638)	(0.0636)	(0.0638)	(0.0637)	(0.0641)	(0.0641)
White	0.353‡	0.492‡	0.240†	0.229‡	0.294‡	0.281‡	0.103	0.125	0.148	0.0839
	(0.0767)	(0.0782)	(0.0754)	(0.0762)	(0.0764)	(0.0762)	(0.0760)	(0.0765)	(0.0775)	(0.0762)
Education	0.0996‡	0.114‡	0.0925‡	0.0653‡	0.0837‡	0.0724‡	0.0519†	0.107‡	0.130‡	0.0507†
	(0.0165)	(0.0167)	(0.0165)	(0.0165)	(0.0165)	(0.0165)	(0.0165)	(0.0165)	(0.0167)	(0.0165)
Cut1	-1.393‡	-0.993‡	-2.202‡	-2.162‡	-2.330‡	-2.450‡	-2.649‡	-2.397‡	-2.179‡	-2.867‡
	(0.191)	(0.196)	(0.190)	(0.187)	(0.189)	(0.189)	(0.188)	(0.191)	(0.195)	(0.189)
Cut2	-0.667‡	-0.193	-1.339‡	-1.458‡	-1.525‡	-1.761‡	-1.946‡	-1.716‡	-1.548‡	-2.126‡
	(0.184)	(0.187)	(0.184)	(0.183)	(0.184)	(0.185)	(0.185)	(0.186)	(0.188)	(0.185)
Cut3	-0.0117	0.427*	-0.665‡	-0.858‡	-0.887‡	-1.270‡	-1.398‡	-1.141‡	-1.053‡	-1.514‡
	(0.182)	(0.184)	(0.182)	(0.181)	(0.182)	(0.183)	(0.184)	(0.184)	(0.185)	(0.183)
Cut4	1.069‡	1.350‡	0.239	0.126	0.0977	-0.296	-0.459*	-0.204	0.179	-0.327
	(0.182)	(0.185)	(0.182)	(0.180)	(0.181)	(0.182)	(0.182)	(0.183)	(0.184)	(0.181)
Cut5	1.907‡	2.297‡	1.058‡	0.944‡	0.967‡	0.524†	0.258	0.595†	1.166‡	0.449*
	(0.185)	(0.189)	(0.183)	(0.181)	(0.182)	(0.183)	(0.183)	(0.184)	(0.186)	(0.182)
Cut6	3.076‡	3.606‡	2.111‡	2.065‡	2.055‡	1.660‡	1.180‡	1.574‡	2.339‡	1.495‡
	(0.189)	(0.194)	(0.186)	(0.185)	(0.186)	(0.186)	(0.187)	(0.186)	(0.189)	(0.186)
R^2	.0168	.0357	.0068	.0049	.0078	.0070	.0148	.0060	.0089	.0079
N	3169	3162	3159	3153	3155	3150	3149	3148	3142	3146

Note: Standard errors in parentheses. P-value = * < .05, † < .01, ‡ < .001.

Source: Author.

Table A3.5. Results for Panhandling Experiment by Problematic Preference Sub-groups

	Media campaign	Install signs	Enforce only flagrant	Enforce all violations	Increase patrols	Create tip line	Private contractor	Tax incentive	Planning committee	Do nothing
Moderate variance										
Increase/increase	0.392	0.520*	-0.657†	0.688†	0.460	0.469*	-0.129	-0.214	0.185	-0.425
	(0.239)	(0.241)	(0.235)	(0.237)	(0.236)	(0.239)	(0.240)	(0.245)	(0.239)	(0.243)
Increase/same	0.0417	0.133	0.132	0.144	0.292	0.172	-0.123	0.000138	-0.249	-0.553*
	(0.249)	(0.250)	(0.244)	(0.247)	(0.248)	(0.253)	(0.249)	(0.256)	(0.249)	(0.249)
Increase/decrease	0.364	0.451	0.105	0.246	0.400	0.324	-0.234	-0.278	0.283	-0.251
	(0.247)	(0.251)	(0.253)	(0.251)	(0.246)	(0.254)	(0.247)	(0.254)	(0.250)	(0.252)
Same/increase	0.233	0.00892	-0.0267	-0.0696	0.135	0.00351	-0.295	-0.0678	0.0197	-0.216
	(0.245)	(0.252)	(0.248)	(0.244)	(0.244)	(0.246)	(0.240)	(0.251)	(0.245)	(0.245)
Same/same	0.470	0.642*	-0.0119	0.347	0.284	0.108	-0.0816	-0.00374	0.236	-0.252
	(0.265)	(0.268)	(0.258)	(0.264)	(0.264)	(0.271)	(0.266)	(0.268)	(0.262)	(0.262)
Same/decrease	0.234	0.0581	0.196	0.224	0.192	0.367	-0.228	-0.0881	0.0801	0.106
	(0.256)	(0.260)	(0.255)	(0.257)	(0.258)	(0.258)	(0.259)	(0.255)	(0.260)	(0.260)
Decrease/increase	0.220	0.0794	-0.0933	0.155	0.373	-0.0383	0.0359	-0.00517	0.247	-0.168
	(0.255)	(0.257)	(0.252)	(0.249)	(0.249)	(0.252)	(0.253)	(0.262)	(0.254)	(0.259)
Decrease/same	0.144	-0.0559	0.153	-0.0962	0.0141	0.00456	-0.136	0.207	-0.0253	-0.00666
	(0.245)	(0.245)	(0.246)	(0.242)	(0.243)	(0.249)	(0.250)	(0.249)	(0.245)	(0.245)
Decrease/decrease	0.265	0.412	-0.196	0.358	0.0135	0.275	-0.194	0.124	0.317	-0.264
	(0.261)	(0.263)	(0.259)	(0.258)	(0.255)	(0.264)	(0.262)	(0.267)	(0.266)	(0.262)

High variance										
Control group	0.644*	0.566*	0.347	0.585*	0.615*	0.699†	0.284	0.722†	0.881‡	0.447
	(0.257)	(0.255)	(0.250)	(0.250)	(0.253)	(0.255)	(0.257)	(0.256)	(0.252)	(0.253)
Increase/increase	0.348	0.315	0.520*	0.388	0.196	0.143	-0.0382	0.234	0.315	0.0364
	(0.255)	(0.258)	(0.255)	(0.251)	(0.253)	(0.253)	(0.260)	(0.257)	(0.259)	(0.260)
Increase/same	0.786†	0.595*	0.590'	0.409	0.778†	0.903‡	0.584*	0.406	0.724†	0.295
	(0.249)	(0.246)	(0.243)	(0.243)	(0.246)	(0.249)	(0.244)	(0.253)	(0.254)	(0.250)
Increase/decrease	0.664†	0.505*	0.325	0.644†	0.687†	0.536*	0.289	0.360	0.429	0.447
	(0.248)	(0.251)	(0.246)	(0.248)	(0.246)	(0.250)	(0.248)	(0.252)	(0.248)	(0.247)
Same/increase	0.523	0.376	0.391	0.572*	0.532*	0.492	0.205	0.773†	0.445	0.252
	(0.270)	(0.265)	(0.258)	(0.259)	(0.264)	(0.265)	(0.265)	(0.271)	(0.268)	(0.261)
Same/same	0.731†	0.402	0.409	0.523*	0.457	0.580*	0.239	0.395	0.493*	0.546*
	(0.251)	(0.246)	(0.245)	(0.244)	(0.242)	(0.246)	(0.245)	(0.254)	(0.248)	(0.245)
Same/decrease	0.371	0.499*	0.335	0.534*	0.526*	0.923‡	0.316	0.108	0.603*	0.424
	(0.247)	(0.249)	(0.241)	(0.247)	(0.243)	(0.251)	(0.247)	(0.250)	(0.250)	(0.247)
Decrease/increase	0.796†	0.443	0.364	0.408	0.711†	0.484	0.451	0.587*	0.523*	0.376
	(0.250)	(0.249)	(0.244)	(0.242)	(0.241)	(0.249)	(0.248)	(0.249)	(0.247)	(0.246)
Decrease/same	0.747†	0.473	0.628*	0.688†	0.721†	0.531*	0.614*	0.576*	0.773†	0.353
	(0.248)	(0.249)	(0.246)	(0.247)	(0.247)	(0.249)	(0.249)	(0.249)	(0.246)	(0.249)
Decrease/decrease	0.620*	0.406	0.582*	0.443	0.537*	0.330	0.267	0.497*	0.435	0.376
	(0.247)	(0.249)	(0.248)	(0.243)	(0.244)	(0.246)	(0.248)	(0.250)	(0.244)	(0.245)

cvontinued on next page

Table A3.5. Continued.

	Media campaign	Install signs	Enforce only flagrant	Enforce all violations	Increase patrols	Create tip line	Private contractor	Tax incentive	Planning committee	Do nothing
Low variance										
Control group	0.0239	0.121	0.213	0.0895	-0.113	0.0529	0.0190	0.00345	0.0646	-0.394
	(0.245)	(0.250)	(0.246)	(0.241)	(0.243)	(0.247)	(0.242)	(0.249)	(0.245)	(0.246)
Increase/increase	0.209	0.201	-0.244	0.229	0.225	0.327	-0.0178	0.0129	0.0419	-0.483*
	(0.243)	(0.250)	(0.242)	(0.241)	(0.244)	(0.247)	(0.247)	(0.251)	(0.246)	(0.245)
Increase/same	-0.0632	0.0991	0.0809	-0.138	-0.175	0.0372	-0.163	0.272	0.126	-0.334
	(0.249)	(0.250)	(0.242)	(0.248)	(0.248)	(0.253)	(0.249)	(0.254)	(0.244)	(0.246)
Increase/decrease	-0.000279	0.0507	-0.0305	0.244	0.0313	0.0928	-0.0108	-0.0574	0.261	-0.0925
	(0.243)	(0.244)	(0.236)	(0.241)	(0.238)	(0.242)	(0.241)	(0.244)	(0.240)	(0.240)
Same/increase	0.181	0.0218	-0.213	0.429	0.318	0.130	-0.0191	-0.0592	0.162	-0.424
	(0.233)	(0.237)	(0.231)	(0.233)	(0.230)	(0.235)	(0.233)	(0.237)	(0.233)	(0.234)
Same/same	0.0122	0.131	0.0618	-0.0756	0.113	-0.189	-0.124	-0.0862	-0.0278	-0.140
	(0.241)	(0.242)	(0.235)	(0.237)	(0.233)	(0.240)	(0.236)	(0.241)	(0.237)	(0.236)
Same/decrease	-0.0511	0.0693	0.0125	-0.0141	-0.122	-0.0326	-0.271	-0.196	-0.119	-0.311
	(0.240)	(0.243)	(0.238)	(0.238)	(0.238)	(0.243)	(0.242)	(0.245)	(0.239)	(0.240)
Decrease/increase	0.139	0.113	-0.0955	0.116	0.279	0.00502	-0.133	0.00161	0.0645	-0.247
	(0.242)	(0.247)	(0.236)	(0.236)	(0.236)	(0.243)	(0.244)	(0.238)	(0.237)	(0.239)
Decrease/same	-0.108	-0.0451	0.280	-0.122	-0.112	-0.176	-0.486*	0.00542	-0.186	-0.115
	(0.240)	(0.244)	(0.239)	(0.240)	(0.237)	(0.243)	(0.244)	(0.251)	(0.242)	(0.242)
Decrease/decrease	-0.245	-0.388	-0.477*	-0.0923	0.0372	-0.161	-0.333	-0.226	-0.118	-0.234
	(0.241)	(0.244)	(0.236)	(0.237)	(0.235)	(0.240)	(0.240)	(0.245)	(0.241)	(0.236)

	(1)	(2)	(3)	(4)	(5)	(6)	(7)	(8)	(9)
Belief 1	-0.0937‡	-0.0510*	-0.0524*	-0.192‡	-0.223‡	-0.191‡	0.00862	-0.0362	-0.112‡
	(0.0238)	(0.0235)	(0.0236)	(0.0238)	(0.0240)	(0.0238)	(0.0237)	(0.0239)	(0.0237)
Belief 2	-0.0736‡	-0.0714‡	-0.00244	-0.172‡	-0.164‡	-0.135‡	0.114‡	-0.0174	-0.0826‡
	(0.0236)	(0.0232)	(0.0234)	(0.0237)	(0.0238)	(0.0236)	(0.0235)	(0.0236)	(0.0236)
Belief 3	0.174‡	0.126‡	0.174‡	0.106‡	0.0959‡	0.0629†	0.208‡	0.196‡	0.156‡
	(0.0232)	(0.0232)	(0.0231)	(0.0232)	(0.0231)	(0.0231)	(0.0235)	(0.0235)	(0.0232)
Belief 4	0.219‡	0.201‡	0.220‡	0.111‡	0.133‡	0.145‡	0.400‡	0.275‡	0.163‡
	(0.0238)	(0.0238)	(0.0237)	(0.0234)	(0.0237)	(0.0237)	(0.0248)	(0.0245)	(0.0234)
Age	0.0206‡	0.0301‡	0.00438*	0.00258	0.00114	-0.00871‡	-0.00813‡	0.00846‡	-0.00583†
	(0.00202)	(0.00209)	(0.00201)	(0.00199)	(0.00199)	(0.00201)	(0.00203)	(0.00202)	(0.00201)
Gender	0.182†	0.290‡	-0.0572	0.00766	-0.0932	0.00510	0.0649	0.0332	-0.268‡
	(0.0657)	(0.0668)	(0.0657)	(0.0660)	(0.0661)	(0.0660)	(0.0665)	(0.0665)	(0.0660)
White	0.246†	0.407‡	0.156*	0.134	0.167*	0.171*	0.0640	0.100	-0.0134
	(0.0778)	(0.0792)	(0.0767)	(0.0778)	(0.0780)	(0.0777)	(0.0780)	(0.0786)	(0.0775)
Education	0.0400*	0.0649‡	0.0434‡	0.0102	0.0265	0.0201	0.0547†	0.0757‡	0.000602
	(0.0171)	(0.0172)	(0.0170)	(0.0170)	(0.0171)	(0.0170)	(0.0172)	(0.0172)	(0.0170)
Cut1	-0.191	0.108	-0.594*	-2.569‡	-2.869‡	-2.720‡	0.677*	-0.0908	-2.283‡
	(0.274)	(0.280)	(0.268)	(0.271)	(0.272)	(0.275)	(0.275)	(0.274)	(0.272)
Cut2	0.543*	0.927‡	0.281	-1.848‡	-2.041†	-2.011‡	1.428‡	0.563*	-1.531‡
	(0.270)	(0.273)	(0.265)	(0.267)	(0.267)	(0.272)	(0.273)	(0.270)	(0.269)
Cut3	1.224‡	1.572‡	0.982‡	-1.215‡	-1.373‡	-1.502‡	2.072‡	1.082‡	-0.906*
	(0.268)	(0.272)	(0.264)	(0.266)	(0.266)	(0.270)	(0.272)	(0.268)	(0.268)
Cut4	2.368‡	2.546‡	1.943‡	-0.171	-0.328	-0.473	3.141‡	2.385‡	0.349
	(0.271)	(0.274)	(0.266)	(0.265)	(0.265)	(0.269)	(0.275)	(0.270)	(0.267)
Cut5	3.277‡	3.550‡	2.832‡	0.724†	0.632*	0.423	4.090‡	3.472‡	1.205‡
	(0.274)	(0.278)	(0.269)	(0.266)	(0.265)	(0.269)	(0.279)	(0.274)	(0.269)
Cut6	4.560‡	4.933‡	3.981‡	1.966‡	1.858‡	1.675‡	5.238‡	4.772‡	2.363‡
	(0.280)	(0.284)	(0.273)	(0.269)	(0.268)	(0.273)	(0.285)	(0.280)	(0.273)
R^2	.0478	.0570	.0348	.0377	.0443	.0376	.0681	.0471	.0341
N	3132	3127	3124	3120	3119	3114	3115	3109	3112

Note: Standard errors in parentheses. P-value = * < .05, † < .01, ‡ < .001.

Source: Author.

design. First, and most important, respondents are asked to make hypothetical choices about how to implement policies that are removed from many of the real-world circumstances that make policy implementation so difficult. Although previous scholarship suggests that hypothetical choices made in experimental settings do not substantially differ from real-world choices, and survey experiments tend to be generalizable (Kuhberger, Schulte-Mecklenbeck, & Perner, 2002; Mullinix et al., 2015), implementers in the real world would be unlikely to make decisions under the same circumstances as presented in the experiments here. For instance, they would not be provided a neat package of relevant information to work from and would likely face entrepreneurs trying to influence their understanding of the situation. To this end, Barbas and Jerit (2010) indicate that participants are much more likely to respond to information in survey experiments than in natural experiments. This suggests that while findings indicate some movement in preferences, these same effects may not be as easy to elicit in the real world, where people carry the baggage of preconceptions about policy tools and pressures from organizational, social, political, and economic environments.

Second, neither experiment is sophisticated enough to understand how the coupling process works in this context. Given that the experiments do not include an explicit attempt to couple the streams or frame policy statements about how the information connects, respondents had to impose their own logic onto the information in order to ascribe meaning to it. Of course, it was necessary to leave certain aspects of the experiment ambiguous, since this is ultimately a test of how people make choices under ambiguous circumstances. The most obvious way to couple the streams would be via consequential coupling, as it requires no additional motivations and there is certainly no implication that respondents should uphold policy doctrine or satisfy political interests (Blum, 2018). To this end, one could assume that the experiments implicitly ask respondents to consider the likelihood that a specific implementation tool would reduce panhandling or air pollution. However, this is implicit, and it is possible that respondents instead ascribe other meanings or coupled streams using alternative logics, which cannot be teased apart from the existing data. In either case, some of the differences between treatment groups may be a function of how streams were coupled as opposed to using intuitive versus deliberative judgments. If so, it would not negate the core of the conclusions drawn from this data, but it would suggest that something more sophisticated is occurring.

Methods Memo for Chapter 4

I recruited 10 participants for semi-structured interviews with open-ended questions. The recruitment strategy focused, first, on identifying those from my professional network who had experience as a program manager and/or policy implementer in an environmental, natural resource, or public health agency at the federal, state, or local level in the Western United States. I focused on agencies with an environmental component to retain consistency in the policy orientation of data used in other chapters, and the Western US to provide some regional consistency in the sociopolitical, geographic, and economic context. Recruitment included former students, but none with direct knowledge or interest in the subject matter of this book. Additionally, I supplemented this by asking for further recommendations from the initial participants and from colleagues (Harvey, 2011; Aberbach & Rockman, 2017). The end result was a group of participants representing federal, state, and local agencies across four states (Arizona, Colorado, Idaho, and Oregon). Of the participants, six were currently serving as program managers supervising employees but still had some responsibilities and significant prior experience as policy implementers, while four served directly as a policy implementers without added authorities of program management. This group have between 12 and 27 years of experience working in the public sector.

Interviews were conducted over Zoom between summer 2021 and winter 2022, and ranged from approximately 30 minutes to 1 hour in length. Participation was voluntary and uncompensated. Additionally, there were no anticipated risks or benefits to participation. Following a few preliminary questions (e.g., job title, years of experience), interviews included 10 guiding questions, with follow-up questions used as appropriate:

- How much of your job is policy implementation? How often do you think of what you do in those terms?

- In your experience, how much of implementing policy is problem-solving versus rule-following?

- How much of your job do you think is left open to interpretation? How much do you think organizational rules and procedures shape that interpretation?

- Do you tend to think about policies in the same way as your co-workers? Why do you think so?

- If you're unsure, where do you look for signals about how to interpret a policy?

- How often do you refer to the letter of the law? What about media accounts or public statements from policymakers?

- When implementing policies, how responsive do you think you are to external factors? For instance, if the political environment changed, would you adapt to it?

- Think about when you first started your job, how did you learn about policies that governed what you do? (i.e., which ones mattered, what they meant, what you're supposed to do)

- Think about a time that a new policy has come up, how did you figure out what to do?

- If you think a policy intends for you to do one thing and an organizational rule something else, what do you do?

After interviews were transcribed from recordings, I performed a two-step content analysis. In the first step, I used a deductive coding method based on the theoretical framework articulated in the first half of the chapter. From this, I separated responses into three categories:

- role and rule perceptions—perceptions of the role that one plays in the organization and the purpose and impacts of organizational rules

- organizational socialization—sources and processes by which people learned the unwritten rules of organizations and policies

- decision processes—processes or metrics by which implementation decisions are made

Coding of most responses was tied to specific questions, so that interviewees generally provided perceptions that fit into all three categories during the interview. In several cases, codes reemerged across the entire interview, providing more depth to perceptions about specific issues. Then, in the second step, I focused on a thematic analysis using an inductive logic in order to distill the broader commonalities across interviews contained within each category. In this case, I began with a general set of codes that were iteratively refined as I reviewed interview transcripts, ultimately leading to several themes within each broad category (Roulston, 2013; Aberbach & Rockman, 2017).

Of course, there are ethical and methodological limitations associated with using interviews in social science data. Most importantly, "the valuable flexibility of open-ended questioning exacerbates the validity and reliability issues that are part and parcel of this approach" (Berry, 2017, p. 679). In other words, interviewing naturally creates limitations to how well responses would be recreated if another researcher were to interview the same interviewees or if one were to ask other interviewees in similar positions the same questions. Furthermore, there is also the issue of whether interviewees are cued to certain responses, which may occur directly through question wording or more implicitly through the body language of the interviewer. While interview data is kept anonymous, there may also be concerns that some questions put interviewees at risk in some form or another, potentially biasing their responses (Roulston, 2013; Berry, 2017). In at least one case, a potential interviewee declined participating due to fears that her comments would be taken out of context and used against her in what was an ongoing politicization of her administrative unit. Certainly, this also suggests there could be some self-selection bias in the interview pool, where those who voluntarily participated may not be completely representative of the entire pool of potential interviewees (Robinson, 2014).

Methods Memo for Chapter 5

State Review Framework for Compliance and Enforcement Performance (SRF) evaluations are the result of a partnership between EPA, state environmental agencies, and the Environmental Council of the States (ECOS) to develop a uniform assessment tool capable of fairly and consistently evaluating the implementation and management of the CAA, as well as the Clean Water Act (CWA) of 1977 (and related acts) and Resource Conservation and Recovery Act (RCRA) of 1976, by state and territorial governments. As stated by EPA, SRF's purpose is to "to evaluate state performance to (a) provide a consistent level of environmental and public health protection across states; and (b) develop a consistent mechanism by which EPA Regions, working collaboratively with their states, can ensure that authorized state agencies meet agreed-upon performance levels" (US EPA, 2005, p. 1). In practice, EPA evaluators are deployed from regional offices and review data entered into national databases managed by EPA as well as samples of state files. Evaluators are also supposed to collaborate with state agencies during this process to ensure a mutual understanding of program practices and areas of needed improvement. SRF has undergone three cycles: the first between 2004 and 2007, the second between 2009 and 2013, and the third between 2015 and 2019. A fourth cycle began in 2021. Between the first and second cycle, the evaluation instrument was revised into its current form that evaluates 12 program elements.

There is a three-category rating system used for evaluation: area for state improvement (i.e., significant problems that have not occurred randomly and require follow-up); area for state attention (i.e., minor issues that can likely be self-corrected); and meets expectations (i.e., no issues identified). See table A5.1 for descriptive statistics of ratings by program element. Additionally, during the second cycle, the good practice distinction was defined as "activities, processes, or policies that the SRF data metrics and/or the file reviews show are being implemented exceptionally well. . . . Additionally, the report may single out specific innovative or noteworthy activities, process, or policies that have the potential to be replicated by other States and that can be highlighted as a practice for other states to emulate" (US EPA, 2010, p. 3).

After reviewing the SRF reports for CAA programs from the 2009 to 2013 cycle, I identified 28 good practices across nine program elements. No CAA good practices were identified for timeliness of data entry, identification of alleged violations, and timely and appropriate enforcement action. Good practices were identified in 13 states. For the qualitative analysis of best practices (stage 1), I used two questions to guide coding: 1) is the practice a result of a formalized mechanism that is delineated in reports and can be replicated by others? and/or 2) is the practice left vaguely defined in reports in terms of how operation connects to positive outcomes? If yes to the first question, then the practice was coded as a process; if yes to the second question, then the practice was coded as a function. Specifically, this tells us whether practices are clear or ambiguous in the minds of evaluators. For instance, a checklist or workflow relates to specific procedural innovation so it creates some certainty in what is happening and it coded as a process, while a well-written report or inspection strategy is more of an operational activity that is not spe-

Table A5.1. SRF Program Element Descriptive Statistics

	Mean	St. dev.	% Area for improvement	% Area for attention	% Meets expectations	N
Data completeness	1.188	0.816	43.75	31.25	25.00	48
Data accuracy	0.675	0.798	20.48	26.51	53.01	83
Timeliness of data entry	0.814	0.861	29.07	23.26	47.67	86
Completion of commitments	1.596	0.748	75.00	9.62	15.38	52
Inspection coverage	1.690	0.556	73.56	21.84	4.60	87
Quality of inspection reports	1.326	0.850	57.30	17.98	24.72	89
Identification of alleged violations	1.267	0.845	52.22	22.22	25.56	90
Identification of SNF and HPV	1.344	0.850	58.89	16.67	24.44	90
Enforcement promotes compliance	1.780	0.593	86.81	4.40	8.79	91
Timely and appropriate action	1.126	0.900	47.13	18.39	34.48	87
Penalty calculation method	1.250	0.921	57.61	9.78	32.61	92
Final penalty assessment	1.570	0.744	72.09	12.79	15.12	86

Source: Author.

cifically defined or a direct result of a formalized procedure so it is left ambiguous and coded as a function.

SRF reports are a crucial data source for this methodological approach, because it indicates not just what practices are being used but also how those practices are being interpreted by third parties (e.g., is this a good practice that can be copied by others or is it just well executed?). For instance, good practices of inspector training could be due to processes if they are based on formalized programs, or they could be based on unwritten rules and cultural norms that cannot be easily defined or replicated, making them more akin to functions (Fowler, 2021). Given that most practices are unlikely to perfectly fit the ideal type of functions or processes, many practices contain elements of both, which led to portions of some good practices being coded as processes and other portions as functions. As similar practices were described across multiple states or programs, comparing reports provided additional data points to triangulate which practices skewed toward processes and which toward functions. In all, I identified 16 practices across nine program elements as being predominantly function-based, and 22 practices across nine program elements as being predominantly process-based (see table 5.2).

In stage 2, I use a structural equation model (SEM) to confirm that the theoretical structure of program elements and latent concepts identified through the qualitative analysis was empirically present in the data, and to test the causal relationship with program outcomes (see figure A5.1 for a diagram and table 5.3 for results). In general, SEM allows one to estimate unobserved latent variables based on observed variables, so that inferences can be made about latent dimensions present within a group of observed variables (Bollen, Rabe-Hesketh, & Skrondal, 2008; Coursey, 2008). Here, the unobserved latent variables are functions and processes and the observed variables are program elements.

While data is available for the Virgin Islands and District of Columbia, there are missing reports for five states/territories during the 2009 to 2013 cycle (Arizona, California, Maine, Nevada, and Puerto Rico), and eight states/territories (California, Maine, Minnesota, Nevada, Ohio, Puerto Rico, South Dakota, and Wisconsin) during the 2015 to 2019 cycle. EPA Region 9 used an alternative evaluation strategy that focused on local and regional efforts, so its data is not comparable to other states'. Additionally, some reports either were not available or had entry errors that made the data unusable; most fitting the latter category were concentrated in EPA Region 5. Given that there is randomly occurring missing data throughout

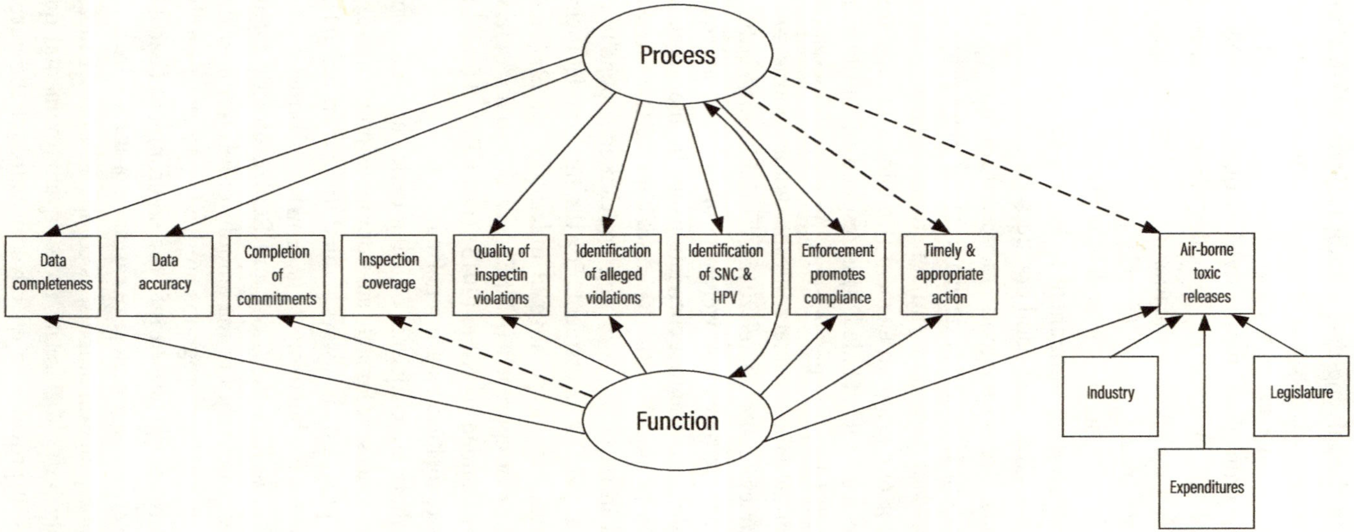

Figure A5.1 Diagram of SEM Relationships for SRF Program Elements. *Source:* Author-created image.

the dataset, I use the missing data setting in Stata 14's Maximum Likelihood Estimation for SEM to maximize the amount of observations in the analysis. This feature imputes missing observations when calculating the model by assuming joint normality (i.e., observed exogenous, latent exogenous, and latent endogenous variables are jointly normally distributed). In general, it makes an estimation of missing data points based on other observations in the dataset (StataCorp, 2015).

I initially fit a measurement model for processes and functions, and then added in a regression component to test the causal relationship with program outcomes. Given that good practices were not identified for three program elements, I reviewed good practices from SRF reports for CWA and RCRA programs in order to determine how those program elements fit into the model of processes and functions; however, there were no good practices for one program element (timeliness of data entry) across any program, so it is not included. This resulted in an initial theoretical model that included 11 program elements. As is common with SEM models, the initial model failed to meet thresholds for goodness-of-fit (GOF) indicators (Coursey, 2008; Kline, 2015). Thus, I refined the model by removing program elements that were a poor fit based on equation-level GOF indicators (e.g., R^2), so that correlations for both observed and latent variables iteratively adjust until the model met GOF thresholds. This process resulted in removing two program elements: penalty calculation method and final penalty assessment. For the final model including nine program elements, the comparative fit index (CFI) is .957 and the root mean square error of approach (RMSEA) is .065; both were within the thresholds recommended by Kline (2015) (i.e., CFI > .90 and RMSEA < .08). Standardized coefficients are reported.

Although there are criticisms of using toxic chemical releases as an output or outcome measure for state environmental programs (e.g., assumes that the goal of programs is always reduction of chemical releases), it is common in previous scholarship (e.g., Fowler & Birdsall, 2021). Logically, the CAA, as well as the CWA and RCRA, directly regulates toxic chemical releases, so changes in the amount of releases over time should be an indicator of whether programs are having an effect on the amount of toxic chemicals being released into the environment (Bacot & Dawes, 1997). In this way, toxic chemical releases are a more direct measure of implementation on program outputs, as compared to other measures such as the air quality index that relate more to environmental quality (i.e., outcomes). Thus, it provides an effective measure for the purposes here;

specifically, it tells us whether there is a correlation between the process and function ratings for state environmental agencies and the amount of toxic chemical waste released into the air on an annual basis.

Methods Memo for Chapter 6

I follow the analytical strategy of Fowler (2022), as it tests the same set of hypotheses. In general, the argument for using states as a unit of analysis is that the federalism arrangement for environmental policy in the US allows 50 natural experiments in policymaking and implementation. To this end, most of the research on state environmental policy relies on the contention that interstate differences in policy outcomes are largely a result of a combination of the context of program management and the capacity to administer programs (e.g., Konisky & Woods, 2012; Woods, 2021). On the one hand, this includes federal environmental programs, such as the CAA, CWA, and RCRA, which states tend to have primary implementation authority over; on the other hand, it also includes state initiatives to go above and beyond the federal minimums or to address unique environmental problems through innovative approaches (Fowler, 2020b). Thus, rather than looking specifically at how a single policy is implemented, this analysis is looking holistically at how the environment is governed through a group of policies at both federal and state levels, which state policy actors have control over through both policymaking and implementation processes. This controls for a core set of structures within governance arrangements, but allows for fluctuation in policy adoption and implementation processes across states.

The two dependent variables are change in environmental expenditures and toxic chemical releases. Most states do not regularly make substantive changes to environmental programs, leaving budgets as the core policy tool for state legislators making decisions about environmental governance. Importantly, federal funding only partially supports state environmental programs and appropriations of any federal funds still goes through legislative approval, so agencies are reliant on state legislatures to approve any resource allocations (Clark & Whitford, 2011; Fowler, 2022). To this end, state expenditures are part of an annual process that represents agenda setting and policy adoption as it relates to environmental governance.

Additionally, toxic chemical releases are broadly indicative of the operations of environmental regulatory regimes. Specifically, programs like the CAA or CWA are designed to constrain the amount of pollution released, and it is assumed that pollution is directly related to environmental quality. Thus, environmental program performance is often examined by looking at the rate at which chemical releases occur (e.g., Bacot & Dawes, 1997; Fowler & Birdsall, 2021; Fowler & Kettler, 2021). Notably, I am not assuming that fewer releases equates to better environmental governance or a more efficient management of program; I am, however, assuming that the number of releases should be indicative of whether programs are following established patterns of management. Specifically, if status quos are retained, then one could assume that toxic releases should remain stable over time, but if policy norms change, then it would be likely that substantive differences in toxic releases will also emerge over time. Nevertheless, by measuring implementation outputs this way, I am not directly observing implementation behaviors or policy norms; instead, I am assuming a direct correlation between those behaviors and toxic releases. While this approach is consistent with previous scholarship (e.g., Fowler, 2019b, 2022), leaving implementation outputs unobserved in the model creates some analytical limitations here, as one must infer a causal link with policy outputs.

Changes in environmental expenditures and toxic releases are also used to measure policy and problems streams, respectively. Notably, these are measured as change over previous years, and there is no reason to believe that changes in previous expenditures or toxic releases should predict future changes in either. Again, if one accepts that expenditures are a measure of policy outputs, then it is only reasonable that they would also be a measure of the policy stream; same for toxic releases, as this is a common problem indicator used to judge environmental pollution. Additionally, the LCV scorecards rate congressional delegates based on pro-environmental votes on key legislation. In using this measure of politics, I am assuming that inferences can be made from voting patterns of congressional delegation about the ideological tendencies of citizens from those states, which is the same basic logic employed by others who have constructed state ideological measures using interest group ratings (e.g., Berry et al., 2010, 2013; Hopper, 2017). Specifically, I am making an inference that how Congressional delegations are voting is indicative of the general mood of the public toward the environment. While this modeling strategy is in keeping with previous scholarship, it does not explicitly account for the social construction of how policy actors identify problems, interpret policies, or decode politics in ambiguous situations (Schneider and Sidney, 2009; Pierce et al., 2014).

In order to incorporate process and function capacity into this analysis, I expanded the methodology from chapter 5 by collecting data from SRF evaluations across CWA and RCRA programs in addition to the CAA programs, and rerunning the SEM (see the "Methods Memo for Chapter 5" for more information). I then estimated state-level average score for processes and functions for each round of SRF evaluations. Since SRF evaluations are performed intermittently and do not cover every year in the dataset, I assumed that estimates were valid measurements across a five-year span (i.e., the data year, two years prior to the data year, and two years following the data year). In the cases where the five-year spans for rounds 2 and 3 overlapped, scores were averaged. However, this did reduce the analytical sample, as there is missing data from several states (again, see the "Methods Memo for Chapter 5" for more discussion). Given that analyses from chapter 5 indicated that process capacity likely has a causal relationship with policy outputs, I also examine a factorial inter-action with process capacity recoded from a count variable to a dummy variable comparing states with above- and below-average process capacity. Findings for process capacity in model 1 and functions in models 1 and 2 were not statistically significant.

For control variables, in the policymaking equation, state expenditures for the initial year of observation accounts for the baseline amount of spending in any given year; in the implementation equation, toxic releases serves the same purpose. Additionally, mini-EPA controls for the organizational mission of state agencies, specifically comparing those with a focus on pollution prevention to those with other missions (e.g., public health, natural resource conservation) (Hopper, 2020). Finally, program authority is a dummy variable comparing states with and without primary implementation authority (i.e., primacy) over the CAA, CWA, and RCRA. While 44 states have primacy over those programs, six states have a lower level of both budget control and implementation responsibility in relation to environmental governance, as the federal government retains authority over one or more major programs (US EPA, 2021a). Findings indicate that only mini-EPA in model 2 (states with a mini-EPA agency tend to experience decreases in toxic releases as compared to other agency types) and toxic releases in models 1 and 2 are statistically significant (states with higher toxic releases tend to experience larger increases); however, model comparisons indicate that including these control factors improves the efficiency of models. See table A6.1 for variable descriptives.

Table A6.1. Variable Descriptives for SUR Models

Variable	Description	Mean	St. Dev.
Expenditures (t_1)	State spending on natural resources in thousands of (2009 real) dollars per capita	.092	.090
Expenditures (t_1-t_0)	One-year change in state spending on natural resources in (real 2009) dollars per capita	−.077	20.432
Expenditures (t_2-t_1)		−.402	19.584
Toxic releases (t_1)	Total toxic chemical releases per capita in pounds per capita	37.304	156.623
Toxic releases (t_1-t_0)	One-year change in total toxic chemical releases per capita in pounds per capita	1.442	87.667
Toxic releases (t_2-t_1)		−.321	94.594
LCV (t_1-t_0)	One-year change in state average on LCV scorecards	−.228	10.499
Process	Estimate of process capacity in state agencies based on SRF evaluations	.0063	.216
Functions	Estimate of function capacity in state agencies based on SRF evaluations	.0057	.296
Program authority	Dummy variable comparing states with primary implementation authority over CAA, CWA, & RCRA to states without	.874	.332
Mini-EPA	Dummy variable comparing states with a mini-EPA-type environmental agency to states with other agency types	.624	.485
(t_0)	Year prior to initial observation year		
(t_1)	Initial year of data observation		
(t_2)	Year following initial observation year		
(t_1-t_0)	Change from t_0 to t_1		
(t_2-t_1)	Change from t_1 to t_2		

Source: Author.

SUR is an extension of ordinary least squares (OLS regression), but is more efficient than fitting two separate equations by utilizing relevant information from cross-regression correlations when estimating parameters for both equations jointly (Mintz & Huang, 1990; Andrews & Van de Walle, 2013; Fowler, 2022). According to Martin and Smith (2005), "SUR estimation transforms the errors so that they all have the same variance and are uncorrelated. This transformation is then applied to the other variables in each equation, and OLS is applied to these transformed variables. This procedure . . . offers more precise parameter estimates than single equation least squares because it incorporates the additional information provided by the correlation between the individual equation errors" (p. 604). Nevertheless, SUR is only more efficient if both equations are correlated; otherwise, most software packages default to OLS. Fortunately, the correlation of residuals and Breusch-Pagan test indicates that this is not the case in either model presented in chapter 6.

References

Aberbach, J.D., & T. Christensen. (2014). Why Reforms So Often Disappoint. *American Review of Public Administration* 44(1): 3–16.

Aberbach, J.D., & B.A. Rockman. (2017). Conducting and Coding Elite Interviews. *PS: Political Science & Politics* 35(4): 673–676.

Agranoff, R., & M. McGuire. (2001). American Federalism and the Search for Models of Management. *Public Administration Review* 61(6): 671–681.

Aldrich, H.E. (1972). Technology and Organizational Structure: A Reexamination of the Findings of the Aston Group. *Administrative Science Quarterly* 17(1): 26–43.

Alter, A.L., D.M. Oppenheimer, N. Epley, & R.N. Eyre. (2007). Overcoming Intuition: Metacognitive Difficulty Activates Analytic Reasoning. *Journal of Experimental Psychology: General* 136(4): 569–576.

An, S. (2019). Employee Voluntary and Involuntary Turnover and Organizational Performance: Revisiting the Hypothesis from Classical Public Administration. *International Public Management Journal* 22(3): 444–469.

Anderson, S.E., R.A. DeLeo, & K. Taylor. (2020). Policy Entrepreneurs, Legislators, and Agenda Setting: Information and Influence. *Policy Studies Journal* 48(3): 587–611.

Andrews, R., & T. Entwistle. (2010). Does Cross-Sectoral Partnership Deliver? An Empirical Exploration of Public Service Effectiveness, Efficiency, and Equity. *Journal of Public Administration Research and Theory* 20(3): 679–701.

Andrews, R. (2012). Social Capital and Public Service Performance: A Review of the Evidence. *Public Policy and Administration* 27(1): 49–67.

Andrews, R., & S. Van de Walle. (2013). New Public Management and Citizens' Perceptions of Local Service Efficiency, Responsiveness, Equity, and Effectiveness. *Public Management Review* 15(5): 762–783.

Ansell, C., & A. Gash. (2008). Collaborative Governance in Theory and Practice. *Journal of Public Administration Research and Theory* 18(4): 543–571.

Antonacopoulou, E.P., & W.H. Guttel. (2010). Staff Induction Practices and Organizational Socialization: A Review and Extension of the Debate. *Society & Business Review* 5(1): 22–47.

Arendt, H. (1994). *Eichmann in Jerusalem: A Report on the Banality of Evil*. New York: Penguin Books.

Arnold, G. (2021). Does Entrepreneurship Work? Understanding What Policy Entrepreneurs Do and Whether It Matters. *Policy Studies Journal* 49(4): 968–991.

Ashford S., & J. Black. (1996). Productivity during Organizational Entry: The Role of Desire for Control. *Journal of Applied Psychology* 81(2): 199–214.

Ashforth, B.E., & F. Mael. (1989). Social Identity Theory and the Organization. *Academy of Management Review* 14(1): 20–39.

Auspurg, K., & T. Hinz. (2015). *Factorial Survey Experiments*. Thousand Oaks, CA: Sage Publications.

Avery, G. (2004). Bioterrorism, Fear, and Public Health Reform: Matching a Policy Solution to the Wrong Window. *Public Administration Review* 64(3): 275–288.

Bacot, A.H., & R.A. Dawes. (1997). State Expenditures and Policy Outcomes in Environmental Program Management. *Policy Studies Journal* 25(3): 355–370.

Baekgaard, M., & S. Serritzlew. (2016). Interpreting Performance Information: Motivated Reasoning or Unbiased Comprehension. *Public Administration Review* 76(1): 73–82.

Balla, S.J. (1998). Administrative Procedures and Political Control of the Bureaucracy. *American Political Science Review* 92(3): 663–673.

Barbas, J., & J. Jerit. (2010). Are Survey Experiments Externally Valid? *American Political Science Review* 104(2): 226–242.

Barnard, C.I. (1968). *The Functions of the Executive*, 30th Anniversary edition. Cambridge, MA: Harvard University Press.

Battaglio, R.P., P. Belardinelli, N. Belle, & P. Cantarelli. (2019). Behavioral Public Administration ad fontes: A Synthesis of Research on Bounded Rationality, Cognitive Biases, and Nudging in Public Organizations. *Public Administration Review* 79(3): 304–320.

Baum, M.A., and A.S. Jamison. (2006). The Oprah Effect: How Soft News Helps Inattentive Citizens Vote Consistently. *Journal of Politics* 68(4): 946–959.

Baumgartner, F.R., B.D. Jones, & P.B. Mortensen. (2018). Punctuated Equilibrium Theory: Explaining Stability and Change in Public Policymaking. In *Theories of the Policy Process*, 4th ed., edited by C.M. Weible & P.A. Sabatier (pp. 55–102). Boulder, CO: Westview Press.

Beck, M. (2020). States Roll Back COVID-19 Precautions as Troubling News Strains Start to Spread. *Boise State Public Radio News*, February 16.

Beck, N., and J.N. Katz. (1995). What to Do (and Not to Do) with Time Series Cross-Section Data. *American Political Science Review* 89(3): 634–647.

Beck, N., and J.N. Katz. (1996). Nuisance vs. Substance: Specifying and Estimating Time-Series-Cross-Section Models. *Political Analysis* 6(1): 1–36.

Beland, D., & M. Howlett. (2016). The Role and Impact of the Multiple-Streams Approach in Comparative Policy Analysis. *Journal of Comparative Policy Analysis: Research & Practice* 18(3): 221–227.

Beland, D., P. Rocco, & A. Waddan. (2016). *Obamacare Wares: Federalism, State Politics, and the Affordable Care Act.* Lawrence: University Press of Kansas.

Belle, N., P. Cantarelli, & P. Belardinelli. (2017). Cognitive Biases in Performance Appraisal: Experimental Evidence on Anchoring and Halo Effects with Public Sector Managers and Employees. *Review of Public Personnel Administration* 37(3): 275–294.

Berrey, S.A. (2015). *The Jim Crow Routine: Everyday Performances of Race, Civil Rights, and Segregation in Mississippi.* Chapel Hill: University of North Carolina Press.

Berry, H. (2020). Starting Monday, the City of Boise Will Begin Enforcing Its Health Orders and Face Mask Mandate. *Idaho Press*, November 19.

Berry, J.M. (2017). Validity and Reliability Issues in Elite Interviewing. *PS: Political Science & Politics* 35(4): 679–682.

Berry, W.D., R.C. Fording, E.J. Ringquist, R.L. Hanson, & C. Klarner. (2010). Measuring Citizen and Government Ideology in the U.S. States: A Re-appraisal. *State Politics & Policy Quarterly* 10(2): 117–135.

Berry, W.D., R.C. Fording, E.J. Ringquist, R.L. Hanson, & C. Klarner. (2013). A New Measure of State Government Ideology, and Evidence that Both the New Measure and an Old Measure Are Valid. *State Politics & Policy Quarterly* 13(2): 164–182.

Bhanot, S.P., & E. Linos. (2020). Behavioral Public Administration: Past, Present, and Future. *Public Administration Review* 80(1): 168–171.

Birkland, T.A. (1997). *After Disaster: Agenda Setting, Public Policy, and Focusing Events.* Washington, DC: Georgetown University Press.

Birkland, T.A., & M.K. Warnement. (2016). Refining the Idea of Focusing Events in the Multiple-Streams Framework. In *Decision-Making under Ambiguity and Time Constraints: Assessing the Multiple-Streams Framework*, edited by R. Zohlnhöfer & F.W. Rüb (pp. 91–108) Colchester, UK: ECPR Press.

Blum, S. (2018). The Multiple-Streams Framework and Knowledge Utilization: Argumentative Couplings of Problem, Policy, and Politics Issues. *European Policy Analysis* 4(1): 94–117.

Bollen, K.A., S. Rabe-Hesketh, & A. Skrondal. (2008). Structural Equation Models. In *The Oxford Handbook of Political Methodology* edited by J.M. Box-Steffensmeier, H.E. Brady, & D. Collier. Oxford: Oxford University Press.

Boswell, C., & E. Rodrigues. (2016). Policies, Politics, and Organisational Problems: Multiple Streams and the Implementation of Targets in UK Government. *Policy & Politics* 44(4): 507–524.

Bovens, M., & P. 't Hart. (1996). *Understanding Policy Fiascoes.* New Brunswick, NJ: Transaction.

Bovens, M., & S. Zouridis. (2002). From Street-Level to System-Level Bureaucracies: How Information and Communication Technology is Transforming Administrative Discretion and Constitutional Control. *Public Administration Review* 62(2): 174–184.

Bozeman, B. (1993). A Theory of Government "Red Tape." *Journal of Public Administration Research and Theory* 3(3): 273–303.

Bozeman, B., & M.K. Feeney. (2011). *Rules and Red Tape: A Prism for Public Administration Theory and Research.* Armonk, NY: ME Sharpe.

Bozeman, B., & G. Kingsley. (1998). Risk Culture in Public and Private Organizations. *Public Administration Review* 58(2): 109–118.

Bradbury, M., J.E. Sowa, & J.E. Kellough. (2013). Employee Turnover in Public Agencies: Examining the Extent and Correlates. In *Human Resource Management in the Public Sector*, edited by R.J. Burke, A.J. Noblet, & C.L. Cooper (pp. 177–195). Northampton, MA: Edward Elgar.

Brandsen, T., & M. Honingh. (2016). Distinguishing Different Types of Coproduction: A Conceptual Analysis Based on the Classical Definitions. *Public Administration Review* 76(3): 427–435.

Brehm, J., & S. Gates. (1999). *Working, Shirking, & Sabotage: Bureaucratic Response to a Democratic Public.* Ann Arbor: University of Michigan Press.

Brewer, G.A. (2003). Building Social Capital: Civic Attitudes and Behavior of Public Servants. *Journal of Public Administration Research and Theory* 13(1): 5–26.

Bright, L. (2009). Why Do Public Employees Desire Intrinsic Nonmonetary Opportunities? *Public Personnel Management* 38(3): 15–37.

Bright, L. (2018). Government Career Interests, Perceptions of Fit, and Degree Orientations: Exploring Their Relationships in Public Administration Graduate Programs. *Teaching Public Administration* 36(1): 63–80.

Brown, T.L., & M. Potoski. (2005). Transaction Costs and Contracting: The Practitioner Perspective. *Public Performance & Management Review* 28(3): 326–351.

Brudney, J.L. (1985). Coproduction: Issues in Implementation. *Administration & Society* 17(3): 243–256.

Brunjes, B.M., & J.E. Kellough. (2018). Representative Bureaucracy and Government Contracting: A Further Examination of Evidence from Federal Agencies. *Journal of Public Administration Research and Theory* 28(4): 519–534.

Brunsson, N. (1990). Deciding for Responsibility and Legitimation: Alternative Interpretations of Organizational Decision-Making. *Accounting, Organizations, and Society* 15(1–2): 47–59.

Brunsson, N. (2007). *The Consequences of Decision-Making.* Oxford: Oxford University Press.

Bushouse, B.K., W.S. Jacobson, K.T. Lambright, J.J. Llorens, R.S. Morse, & O. Poocharoen. (2011). Crossing the Divide: Building Bridges between Public Administration Practitioners and Scholars. *Journal of Public Administration Research and Theory* 21(s1): i99–i112.

Cairney, P., & M.D. Jones. (2016). Kingdon's Multiple Streams Approach: What Is the Empirical Impact of this Universal Theory? *Policy Studies Journal* 44(1): 37–58.

Chaiken, S. (1980). Heuristic versus Systematic Information Processing and the Use of Source versus Message Cues in Persuasion. *Journal of Personality and Social Psychology* 39(5): 752–776.

Chappell, A.T., & L. Lanza-Kaduce. (2010). Police Academy Socialization: Understanding the Lessons Learned in a Paramilitary-Bureaucratic Organization. *Journal of Contemporary Ethnography* 39(2): 187–214.

Chen, C., E.M. Berman, & C. Wang. (2017). Middle Managers' Upward Roles in the Public Sector. *Administration & Society* 49(5): 700–729.

Chollette, L., & S. Harrison. (2020). Unintended Consequences: Ambiguity Neglect and Policy Ineffectiveness. Working Paper. https://papers.ssrn.com/sol3/papers.cfm?abstract_id=3513644

Chong, D., & J.N. Druckman. (2007). Framing Public Opinion in Competitive Democracies. *American Political Science Review* 101(4): 637–655.

Christensen, T., & M. Painter. (2004). The Politics of SARS—Rational Responses or Ambiguity, Symbols and Chaos? *Policy and Society* 23(2): 18–48.

Christian, C.W. (1994). Voluntary Compliance with the Individual Income Tax: Results from the 1988 TCMP Study. *IRS Research Bulletin* 1500.

Chun, Y.H., & H.G. Rainey. (2005a). Goal Ambiguity in Organizational Performance in U.S. Federal Agencies. *Journal of Public Administration Research and Theory* 15(4): 529–557.

Chun, Y.H., & H.G. Rainey. (2005b). Goal Ambiguity in U.S. Federal Agencies. *Journal of Public Administration Research and Theory* 15(1): 1–30.

Clark, B.Y., and A.B. Whitford. (2011). Does More Federal Environmental Funding Increase or Decrease States' Efforts? *Journal of Policy Analysis and Management* 30(1): 136–152.

Cohen, M.D., J.G. March, & J.P. Olsen. (1972). A Garbage Can Model of Organizational Choice. *Administrative Science Quarterly* 17(1): 1–25.

Compton, M.E. (2019). The 'Social Warfare State': Americans' Making of a Civic Generation. In *Great Policy Successes*, edited by M.E. Compton & P. 't Hart (pp. 104–121). Oxford: Oxford University Press.

Cook, B.J., & B.D. Wood. (1989). Principal-Agent Models of Political Control of Bureaucracy. *American Political Science Review* 83(3): 965–978.

Coppock, A., & O.A. McClellan. (2019). Validating the Demographic, Political, Psychological, and Experimental Results Obtained From a New Source of Online Survey Respondents. *Research & Politics* 6(1).

Coursey, D.H. (2008). Confirmatory Factor Analysis: A Practical Introduction. In *Handbook of Research Methods in Public Administration*, 2nd ed., edited by K. Yang and G.J. Miller. Boca Raton, FL: CRC Press.

Crank, J., & R. Langworthy. (1996). Fragmented Centralization and the Organization of the Police. *Policing and Society* 6(3): 213–229.

Crow, D., & M. Jones. (2018). Narratives as Tools for Influencing Policy Change. *Policy & Politics* 46(2): 217–234.

Dahl, R.A. (1998). *On Democracy*. New Haven, CT: Yale University Press.

Damanpour, F., & M. Schneider. (2009). Characteristics of Innovation and Innovation Adoption in Public Organizations: Assessing the Role of Managers. *Journal of Public Administration Research and Theory* 19(3): 495–522.

Danzinger, J.N., & K.V. Andersen. (2002). The Impacts of Information Technology on Public Administration: An Analysis of Empirical Research from the "Golden Age" of Transformation. *International Journal of Public Administration* 25(5): 591–627.

Das, T.K., & B. Teng. (1999). Cognitive Biases and Strategic Decision Processes: An Integrative Perspective. *Journal of Management Studies* 36(6): 757–778.

Daugherty, B.J., & C.C. Bolton. (2008). *With All Deliberate Speed: Implementing Brown v. Board of Education*. Fayetteville: University of Arkansas Press.

Davis, R.C. (2010). A New Approach in Dallas. *Police Practice & Research* 11(2): 129–131.

Davis, R.S., & E.C. Stazyk. (2015). Developing and Testing a New Goal Taxonomy: Accounting for the Complexity of Ambiguity and Political Support. *Journal of Public Administration Research and Theory* 25(3): 751–775.

Davis, R.S., & E.C. Stazyk. (2022). Ambiguity, Appraisal, and Affect: Examining the Connections between Goal Perceptions, Emotional Labour, and Exhaustion. *Public Management Review* 24(10): 1499–1520.

Dawson, J. (2020). Callers Demand Statewide Mask Mandate in Idaho from Gov. Brad Little. *Boise State Public Radio*, September 30. https://www.boise statepublicradio.org/post/callers-demand-statewide-mask-mandate-idaho-gov-brad-little#stream/0

de Paulo, C.J.N., P. Messina, & M. Stier. (2005). *Ambiguity in the Western Mind*. New York: Lang.

DeHart-Davis, L. (2009a). Green Tape: A Theory of Effective Organizational Rules. *Journal of Public Administration Research and Theory* 19(2): 361–384.

DeHart-Davis, L. (2009b). Green Tape and Public Employee Rule Abidance: Why Organizational Rule Attributes Matter. *Public Administration Review* 69(5): 901–910.

DeHart-Davis, L. (2017). *Creating Effective Rules in Public Sector Organizations*. Washington, DC: Georgetown University Press.

DeHart-Davis, L., J. Chen, & T.D. Little. (2013). Written versus Unwritten Rules: The Role of Rule Formalization in Green Tape. *International Public Management Journal* 16(3): 331–356.

DeLeo, R.A. (2018). Indicators, Agendas and Streams: Analysing the Politics of Preparedness. *Policy & Politics* 46(1): 27–45.

DeLeo, R.A., & A. Duarte. (2022). Does Data Drive Policymaking? A Multiple Streams Perspective on the Relationship Between Indicators and Agenda Setting. *Policy Studies Journal* 50(3): 701–724.

deLeon, P., & L. deLeon. (2002). What Ever Happened to Policy Implementation? An Alternative Approach. *Journal of Public Administration Research and Theory* 12(4): 467–492.

Derthick, M.A. (2011). *Up in Smoke: From Legislation to Litigation in Tobacco Politics*, 3rd ed. Washington, DC: CQ Press.

Downs, A. (1991). Up and Down with Ecology: The 'Issue-Attention Cycle.' In *Agenda-Setting: Readings on Media, Public Opinion, and Policymaking*, edited by D.L. Protess & M. McCombs (pp. 27–34). New York: Routledge.

Durose, C., & L. Richardson. (2016). *Designing Public Policy for Co-Production: Theory, Practice, and Change*. Chicago, IL: Policy Press.

Edwards, K., & E.E. Smith. (1996). A Disconfirmation Bias in the Evaluation of Arguments. *Journal of Personality and Social Psychology* 71(1): 5–24.

Ellsberg, D. (2001). *Risks, Ambiguity, and Decision*. New York: Garland.

Elmore, R.F. (1979). Backward Mapping: Implementation Research and Policy Decisions. *Political Science Quarterly* 94(4): 601–616.

Elmore, R.F. (1985). Forward and Backward Mapping: Reversible Logic in the Analysis of Public Policy. In *Policy Implementation in Federal and Unitary Systems*, edited by K. Hanf and T.A.J. Toonen. Dordrecht, Netherlands: Springer.

Emerson, K., T. Nabatchi, & S. Balogh. (2012). An Integrative Framework for Collaborative Governance. *Journal of Public Administration Research and Theory* 22(1): 1–29.

Empson, W. (1966). *Seven Types of Ambiguity*. New York: New Directions.

Engler, F., & N. Herweg. (2019). Of Barriers to Entry for Medium and Large n Multiple Streams Applications: Methodological and Conceptual Considerations. *Policy Studies Journal* 47(4): 905–926.

Epley, N., & T. Gilovich. (2004). Are Adjustments Insufficient? *Personality and Social Psychology Bulletin* 30(4): 447–460.

Epstein, D., & S. O'Halloran. (1994). Administrative Procedures, Information, and Agency Discretion. *American Journal of Political Science* 38(3): 697–722.

Epstein, S. (1994). Integration of the Cognitive and Psychodynamic Unconscious. *American Psychology* 49: 709–724.

Evans, J.S.B.T. (2003). In Two Minds: Dual-Process Accounts of Reasoning. *Trends in Cognitive Sciences* 7(1): 454–459.

Executive Office of the President. (2021). Executive Order on Protecting the Federal Workforce and Requiring Mask-Wearing. https://www.whitehouse.gov/briefing-room/presidential-actions/2021/01/20/executive-order-protecting-the-federal-workforce-and-requiring-mask-wearing/

Exworthy, M., & M. Powell. (2004). Big Windows and Little Windows: Implementation in the "Congested State." *Public Administration* 82(2): 263–281.

Fairholm. G.W. (2009). *Organizational Power Politics: Tactics in Organizational Leadership*, 2nd ed. Santa Barbara, CA: ABC-CLIO.

Farber, D.A. (2007). *Retained by the People: The "Silent" Ninth Amendment and the Constitutional Rights Americans Don't Know They Have*. New York: Basic Books.

Farmer, D.J. (1994). Social Construction of Concepts: The Case of Efficiency. *Administrative Theory & Praxis* 16(2): 254–262.

Feiock, R.C., & J.T. Sholtz. (2009). Self-Organizing Governance of Institutional Collective Action Dilemmas: An Overview. In *Self-Organizing Federalism: Collective Mechanisms to Mitigate Institutional Collective Action Dilemmas*, edited by R.C. Feiock & J.T. Sholtz (pp. 3–32). Cambridge: Cambridge University Press.

Festinger, L. (1957). *A Theory of Cognitive Dissonance*. Stanford, CA: Stanford University Press.

Fiorino, D.J. (1997). Strategies for Regulatory Reform: Forward Compared to Backward Mapping. *Policy Studies Journal* 25(2): 249–265.

Fishman, D.A. (1999). ValuJet Flight 592: Crisis Communication Theory Blended and Extended. *Communication Quarterly* 47(4): 345–375.

Fowler, L. (2015). Management Matters in Renewable Portfolio Standards. *International Journal of Organization Theory & Behavior* 18(2): 206–230.

Fowler, L. (2019a). Obstacles and Motivators for Partnership Formation in a Multidimensional Environment. *Politics & Policy* 47(2): 267–299.

Fowler, L. (2019b). Problems, Politics, and Policy Streams in Policy Implementation. *Governance* 32(3): 403–420.

Fowler, L. (2020a). Best Practices for Implementing Federal Environmental Policies: A Principal-Agent Perspective. *Journal of Environmental Planning and Management* 63(8): 1453–1469.

Fowler, L. (2020b). *Environmental Federalism: Old Legacies and New Challenges*. New York: Routledge.

Fowler, L. (2020c). Governance, Federalism, and Organizing Institutions to Manage Complex Problems. *Public Administration* 98(3): 713–729.

Fowler, L. (2021). How to Implement Policy: Coping with Ambiguity and Uncertainty. *Public Administration* 99(3): 581–597.

Fowler, L. (2022). Using the Multiple Streams Framework to Connect Policy Adoption to Implementation. *Policy Studies Journal* 50(3): 615–639.

Fowler, L., & C. Birdsall. (2020). Are the Best and Brightest Joining the Public Service? *Review of Public Personnel Administration* 40(3): 532–554.

Fowler, L., & C. Birdsall. (2021). Does the Primacy System Work? State versus Federal Implementation of the Clean Water Act. *Publius* 51(1): 131–160.

Fowler, L., & A.T. Johnson. (2017). Overlapping Authorities in US Energy Policy. *The Electricity Journal* 30(9): 1–5.

Fowler, L., & J. Kettler. (2021). Are Republicans Bad for the Environment? *State Politics & Policy Quarterly* 21(2): 195–219.

Fowler, L., & J. Vallett. (2021). Conditional Nature of Policy as a Stabilizing Force: Erin's Law and Teacher Child Abuse Reporting Practices. *Administration & Society* 53(6): 937–962.

Frankel, J. (2020). Officials Leave It to Stores to Navigate Gray Areas of Mask Orders. This Is the Results. *Idaho Statesman*, August 11.

Frederickson, H.G., K.B. Smith, C.W. Larimer, & M.J. Licari. (2015). *Public Administration Theory Primer*. New York: Routledge.

French, J.R.P., & B. Raven. (2015). The Based of Social Power. In *Classics of Organizational Theory*, 8th ed. edited by J.M. Shafritz, J.S. Ott & Y.S. Jang (pp. 251–260). Boston: Cengage.

Frisch-Aviram, N., I. Beeri, & N. Cohen. (2020). Entrepreneurship in the Policy Process: Linking Behavior and Context through a Systematic Review of the Policy Entrepreneurship Literature. *Public Administration Review* 80(2): 188–197.

Frisch-Aviram, N., N. Cohen, & I. Beeri. (2020). Policy Entrepreneurship in Developing Countries: A Systematic Review of the Literature. *Public Administration and Development* 40(1): 35–48.

Furnham, A., & J. Marks. (2013). Tolerance of Ambiguity: A Review of the Recent Literature. *Psychology* 4(9): 717–728.

Furnham, A., & T. Ribchester. (1995). Tolerance of Ambiguity: A Review of the Concept, Its Measurement and Applications. *Current Psychology* 14(3): 179–199.

Gajduschek, G. (2003). Bureaucracy: Is It Efficient? Is It Not? Is That the Question?: Uncertainty Reduction: An Ignored Element of Bureaucracy Rationality. *Administration & Society* 34(6): 700–723.

George, B., S.K. Pandey, B. Steijn, A. Decramer, & M. Audenaert. (2021). Red Tape, Organizational Performance, and Employee Outcomes: Meta-analysis, Meta-regression, and Research Agenda. *Public Administration Review* 81(4): 638–651.

Gerrish, E. (2016). The Impact of Performance Management on Performance in Public Organizations: A Meta-Analysis. *Public Administration Review* 76(1): 48–66.

Gioia, D.A., & H.P. Sims. (1983). Perceptions of Managerial Power as a Consequence of Managerial Behavior and Reputation. *Journal of Management* 9(1): 7–24.

Goggin, M.L. (1986). The "Too Few Cases/Too Many Variables" Problem in Implementation Research. *Western Political Quarterly* 39(2): 328–347.

Goggin, M.L., A. O'M. Bowman, J.P. Lester, & L.J. O'Toole. (1990). *Implementation Theory and Practice: Toward a Third Generation*. Glenwood, IL: Scott Foreman/Little Brown.

Gollwitzer, A., & G. Oettingen. (2019). Paradoxical Knowledge. *Social Psychological* 50(3): 145–161.

Goyal, N., M. Howlett, & N. Chindarkar. (2020). Who Coupled Which Stream(s)? Policy Entrepreneurship and Innovation in the Energy-Water Nexus in Gujarat, India. *Public Administration and Development* 40(1): 49–64.

Gray, P. (1998). Policy Disasters in Europe: An Introduction. In *Policy Disasters in Western Europe*, edited by P. Gray & P. 't Hart (pp. 3–20). London: Routledge.

Greenhouse, L. (2012). *The U.S. Supreme Court: A View Short Introduction*. Oxford: Oxford University Press.

Grimmelikhuijsen, S., S. Jilke, A.L. Olsen, & L. Tummers. (2017). Behavioral Public Administration: Combining Insights from Public Administration and Psychology. *Public Administration Review* 77(1): 45–56.

Gritter, M. (2015). *The Policy and Politics of Food Stamps*. New York: Palgrave MacMillan.

Grossman, G., S. Kim, J.M. Rexer, & H. Thirumurthy. (2020). Political Partisanship Influences Behavioral Responses to Governors' Recommendations for COVID-19 Prevention in the United States. *Proceedings of the National Academy of Sciences* 117(39): 24144–24153.

Grundfest, J.A., & A.C. Pritchard. (2002). Statutes with Multiple Personality Disorders: The Value of Ambiguity in Statutory Design and Interpretation. *Stanford Law Review* 54(4): 627–736.

Gunitsky, S. (2019). Rival Visions of Parsimony. *International Studies Quarterly* 63(3): 707–716.

Gupta, S., T.D. Nguyen, F.L. Rojas, S. Raman, B. Lee, A. Bento, K.I. Simon, & C. Wing. (2020). Tracking Public and Private Responses to the COVID-19 Epidemic: Evidence from State and Local Government Actions. *National Bureau of Economic Research Working Paper* No. 27027.

Habermas, J. (1998). *On the Pragmatics of Communication*. Cambridge, MA: MIT Press.

Hall, T.E. (2002). Live Bureaucrats and Dead Public Servants: How People in Government are Discussed on the Floor of the House. *Public Administration Review* 62(2): 242–251.

Hall, W. (2010). What are the Policy Lessons of National Alcohol Prohibition in the United States, 1920–1933? *Addiction* 105(7): 1164–1173.

Hammond, K.R. (1996). *Human Judgement and Social Policy: Irreducible Uncertainty, Inevitable Error, Unavoidable Injustice*. Oxford: Oxford University Press.

Harding, H., & J. Scholl. (2020). Coronavirus: Boise-Area Officials Meet to Talk Mask Enforcement; Hospitalizations Up. *Idaho Statesman*, October 29.

Hargreaves, I.S., P.M. Pexman, D.J. Pittman, & B.G. Goodyear. (2011). Tolerating Ambiguity: Ambiguous Words Recruit the Left Inferior Frontal Gyrus in Absence of a Behavioral Effect. *Experimental Psychology* 58(1): 19–30.

Harvey, W.S. (2011). Strategies for Conducting Elite Interviews. *Qualitative Research* 11(3): 431–441.

Haselton, M.G., D. Nettle, & D.R. Murray. (2016). The Evolution of Cognitive Bias. In *Handbook of Evolutionary Psychology*, 2nd ed., edited by D.M. Buss (pp. 968–987). Hoboken, NJ: John Wiley & Sons.

Henderson, A.C. (2013). Examining Policy Implementation in Health Care: Rule Abidance and Deviation in Emergency Medical Services. *Public Administration Review* 73(6): 799–809.

Hendriks, C.M., & J. Lees-Marshment. (2019). Political Leaders and Public Engagement: The Hidden World of Informal Elite-Citizen Interaction. *Political Studies* 67(3): 597–617.

Herman, R.B., & D.O. Renz. (1997). Multiple Constituencies and the Social Construction of Nonprofit Organization Effectiveness. *Nonprofit and Voluntary Sector Quarterly* 26(2): 185–206.

Herweg, N. (2016). Clarifying the Concept of Policy-Communities in the Multiple-Streams Framework. In *Decision-Making under Ambiguity and Time Constraints: Assessing the Multiple-Streams Framework*, edited by R. Zohlnhöfer & F.W. Rüb (pp. 125–146). Colchester, UK: ECPR Press.

Herweg, N., C. Rüb, & R. Zohlnhöfer. (2015). Straightening the Three Streams: Theorising Extensions of the Multiple Streams Framework. *European Journal of Political Research* 54(3): 435–449.

Herweg, N., N. Zahariadis, & R. Zohlnhöfer. (2018). The Multiple Streams Framework: Foundations, Refinements, and Empirical Applications. In *Theories of the Policy Process*, 4th ed., edited by C.M. Weible & P.A. Sabatier (pp. 25–58). Boulder, CO: Westview Press.

Hill, M., & P. Hupe. (2014). *Implementing Public Policy: An Introduction to the Study of Operational Governance*, 3rd ed. Thousand Oaks, CA: Sage.

Hjern, B. (1982). Implementation Research—the Link Gone Missing. *Journal of Public Policy* 2(3): 301–308.

Holzer, M., & K. Yang. (2005). Administrative Discretion in a Turbulent Time: An Introduction. *Public Administration Quarterly* 29(1–2): 128–139.

Hopper, J.A. (2017). The Regulation of Combination: The Implications of Combining Natural Resource Conservation and Environmental Protection. *State Politics & Policy Quarterly* 17(1): 105–124.

Hopper, J.A. (2020). *Environmental Agencies in the United States: The Enduring Power of Organizational Design and State Politics.* Lanham, MD: Rowman & Littlefield.

Howlett, M. (2011). Public Managers as the Missing Variable in Policy Studies: An Empirical Investigation Using Canadian Data. *Review of Policy Research* 28(3): 247–263.

Howlett, M. (2019). Moving Policy Implementation Theory Forward: A Multiple Streams/Critical Juncture Approach. *Public Policy and Administration* 34(4): 405–430.

Howlett, M., A. McConnell, & A. Perl. (2015). Streams and Stages: Reconciling Kingdon and Policy Process Theory. *European Journal of Political Research* 54(3): 419–434.

Howlett, M., & R.M. Walker. (2012). Public Managers in the Policy Process: More Evidence on the Missing Variable? *Policy Studies Journal* 40(2): 211–233.

Hudson, B., D. Hunter, & S. Peckham. (2019). Policy Failure and the Policy-Implementation Gap: Can Policy Support Programs Help? *Policy Design & Practice* 2(1): 1–14.

Hupe, P., & A. Buffat. (2014). A Public Service Gap: Capturing Contexts in a Comparative Approach of Street-Level Bureaucracy. *Public Management Review* 16(4): 548–569.

Hupe, P & M. Hill. (2007). Street-Level Bureaucracy and Public Accountability. *Public Administration* 85(2): 279–299.

Huy, Q.N. (2001). In Praise of Middle Managers. *Harvard Business Review* 79(8): 72–79.

Hvidman, U., & S.C. Andersen. (2014). Impact of Performance Management in Public and Private Organizations. *Journal of Public Administration Research and Theory* 24(1): 35–58.

Idaho Press Staff. (2020). Boise to Mandate Masks in Public Starting Saturday. *Idaho Press*, July 2.

Internal Revenue Service (IRS). (2016). Tax Gap Estimates for Tax Years 2008–2010. https://www.irs.gov/pub/newsroom/tax%20gap%20estimates%20for%20 2008%20through%202010.pdf

Jackson, J., B. Bradford, M. Hough, A. Myhill, P. Quinton, & T.R. Tyler. (2012). Why Do People Comply with the Law? Legitimacy and the Influence of Legal Institutions. *British Journal of Criminology* 52(6): 1051–1071.

Jacobsen, C.B., & M.L. Jakobsen. (2018). Perceived Organizational Red Tape and Organizational Performance in Public Services. *Public Administration Review* 78(1): 24–36.

Jaskyte, K. (2011). Predictors of Administrative and Technological Innovations in Nonprofit Organizations. *Public Administration Review* 71(1): 77–86.

Jennings, M.K. (2007). Political Socialization. In *The Oxford Handbook of Political Behavior*, edited by R.J. Dalton & H. Kingermann. Oxford: Oxford University Press.

Johansen, M. (2013). The Impact of Managerial Quality on Employee Turnover. *Public Management Review* 15(6): 858–877.

Jones, B.D. (2003). Bounded Rationality and Political Science: Lessons from Public Administration and Public Policy. *Journal of Public Administration Research and Theory* 13(4): 395–412.

Jones, M.D., H.L. Peterson, J.J. Pierce, N. Herweg, A. Bernal, H.L. Raney, & N. Zahariadis. (2016). A River Runs Through It: A Multiple Streams Meta-Review. *Policy Studies Journal* 44(1): 13–36.

Jones, M.D., & G. Song. (2014). Making Sense of Climate Change: How Story Frames Shape Cognition. *Political Psychology* 35(4): 447–476.

Jung, C.S. (2014). Extending the Theory of Goal Ambiguity to Programs: Examining the Relationship between Goal Ambiguity and Performance. *Public Administration Review* 74(2): 205–219.

Kahn, W.A., & K.E. Kram. (1994). Authority at Work: Internal Models and Their Organizational Consequences. *Academy of Management Review* 19(1): 17–50.

Kahneman, D. (1981). The Framing of Decisions and the Psychology of Choice. *Science* 221(448): 453–458.

Kahneman, D. (2011). *Thinking, Fast and Slow*. New York: Farrar, Straus, and Giroux.

Kahneman, D., & Tversky, A. (1979). Prospect Theory: An Analysis of Decision under Risk. *Econometrica* 47: 263–291.

Kaufmann, H. (2015). *Red Tape: Its Origins, Uses, and Abuses*. Washington, DC: Brookings Institute Press.

Kaufmann, W., G. Taggart, & B. Bozeman. (2018). Administrative Delay, Red Tape, and Organizational Performance. *Public Performance & Management Review* 42(3): 529–553.

Kennedy, B. (2014). Unraveling Representative Bureaucracy: A Systematic Analysis of the Literature. *Administration & Society* 46(4): 395–421.

Kingdon, J. (1984). *Agendas, Alternatives, and Public Policies*, 1st ed. New York: HarperCollins.

Kingdon, J. (1995). *Agendas, Alternatives, and Public Policies*, 2nd ed. New York: HarperCollins

Klayman, J. (1995). Varieties of Confirmation Bias. *Psychology of Learning & Motivation* 32: 385–418.

Kline, R.B. (2015). *Principles and Practice of Structural Equation Modeling*, 4th ed. New York: Guilford Press.

Konisky, D.M. and N.D. Woods. (2012). Measuring State Environmental Policy. *Review of Policy Research* 29(4): 544–569.

Krislov, S. (2012). *Representative Bureaucracy*. New Orleans: Quid Pro Books.

Kuhberger, A., M. Schulte-Mecklenbeck, & J. Perner. (2002). Framing Decisions: Hypothetical and Real. *Organizational Behavior and Human Decision Processes* 89(2): 1162–1175.

Kuhn, T.S. (2012). The *Structure of Scientific Revolutions*, 4th ed. Chicago: University of Chicago Press.

Lasswell, H. (2018). *Politics: Who Gets What, When, How*. New York: Whittlesey House.

League of Conservation Voters. (2021). National Environmental Scorecard. https://scorecard.lcv.org/scorecard/archive

Lee, Y., & H.L. Schachter. (2019). Exploring the Relationship between Trust in Government and Citizen Participation. *International Journal of Public Administration* 42(5): 405–416.

Leland, S., & D.C. Read. (2013). Representative Bureaucracy, Public-Private Partnerships and Urban Development. *Journal of Place Management and Development* 6(2): 86–101.

Levitan, D.M. (1942). The Neutrality of the Public Service. *Public Administration Review* 2(4): 317–323.

Liang, J. (2018). Latinos and Environmental Justice: Examining the Link between Degenerative Policy, Political Representation, and Environmental Policy Implementation. *Policy Studies Journal* 46(1): 60–89.

Lieder, F., T.L. Griffiths, Q.J.M. Huys, & N.D. Goodman. (2018). The Anchoring Bias Reflects Rational Use of Cognitive Resources. *Psychonomic Bulletin & Review* 25(1): 322–349.

Light, P.C. (1999a). *The New Public Service*. Washington, DC: Brookings Institute Press.

Light, P.C. (1999b). *The True Size of Government*. Washington, DC: Brookings Institute Press.

Light, P.C. (2020). The True Size of Government is Nearing a Record High. Brookings Institute. https://www.brookings.edu/blog/fixgov/2020/10/07/the-true-size-of-government-is-nearing-a-record-high/

Lipsky, M. (2010). *Street-Level Bureaucracy: Dilemmas of the Individual in Public Services*, 30th Anniversary Expanded Edition. New York: Russell Sage Foundation.

Long, E., & A.L. Franklin. (2004). The Paradox of Implementing the Government Performance and Results Act: Top-Down Direction for Bottom-Up Implementation. *Public Administration Review* 64(3): 309–319.

Lovenheim, M.F., & D.P. Steefel. (2011). Do Blue Laws Save Lives? The Effect of Sunday Alcohol Sales Bans on Fatal Vehicle Accidents. *Journal of Policy Analysis and Management* 30(4): 798–820.

Mahler, J. (1997). Influences of Organizational Culture on Learning in Public Agencies. *Journal of Public Administration Research and Theory* 7(4): 519–540.

Mahoney, J., K. Mohamedali, & C. Nguyen. (2016). Causality and Time in Historical Institutionalism. In *Oxford Handbook of Historical Institutionalism*, edited by O. Fioretos, T.G. Falleti, & A. Sheingate (pp. 71–88). Oxford: Oxford University Press.

Manhire, J.T. (2015). What Does Voluntary Tax Compliance Mean: A Government Perspective. *University of Pennsylvania Law Review* 11.

Manna, P., & S.L. Moffitt. (2021). Traceable Tasks and Complex Policies: When Politics Matter for Policy Implementation. *Policy Studies Journal* 49(1): 190–218.

March, J.G., & J.P. Olsen. (2009). The Logic of Appropriateness. ARENA Working Papers 9. https://ideas.repec.org/p/erp/arenax/p0026.html

March, J.G., & J.P. Olsen. (2011). Elaborating the 'New Institutionalism.' In *The Oxford Handbook of Political Science*, edited by R.E. Goodin (pp. 159–175). Oxford: Oxford University Press.

Marchington, M., D. Grimshaw, J. Rubery, & H. Willmott (eds.). (2005). *Fragmenting Work: Blurring Organizational Boundaries and Disordering Hierarchies.* Oxford: Oxford University Press.

Martin, S., & P.C. Smith. (2005). Multiple Public Service Performance Indicators: Toward an Integrated Statistical Approach. *Journal of Public Administration Research and Theory* 15(4): 599–613.

Matland, R.E. (1995). Synthesizing the Implementation Literature: The Ambiguity-Conflict Model of Policy Implementation. *Journal of Public Administration Research and Theory* 5(2): 145–174.

May, P.J. (1992). Policy Learning and Failure. *Journal of Public Policy* 12(4): 331–354.

May, P.J., & S.C. Winter. (2009). Politicians, Managers, and Street-Level Bureaucrats: Influences on Policy Implementation. *Journal of Public Administration Research and Theory* 19(3): 453–476.

McConnell, A. (2010). Policy Success, Policy Failure, and Grey Areas In-between. *Journal of Public Policy* 30(3): 345–362.

Meier, K.J. (1997). Bureaucracy and Democracy: The Case for More Bureaucracy and Less Democracy. *Public Administration Review* 57(3): 193–199.

Meier, K.J. (1999). Are We Sure Lasswell Did It This Way? Lester, Goggin, and Implementation Research. *Policy Currents* 9(1): 5–8.

Meier, K.J. (2019). Theoretical Frontiers in Representative Bureaucracy: New Directions for Research. *Perspectives on Public Management and Governance* 2(1): 39–56.

Meier, K.J., & A. Hicklin. (2008). Employee Turnover and Organizational Performance: Testing a Hypothesis from Classical Public Administration. *Journal of Public Administration Research and Theory* 18(4): 573–590.

Meier, K.J., & L.J. O'Toole. (2002). Public Management and Organizational Performance: The Effect of Managerial Quality. *Journal of Policy Analysis and Management* 21(4): 629–643

Meier, K.J., & L.J. O'Toole. (2006). *Bureaucracy in a Democratic State: A Governance Perspective.* Baltimore: Johns Hopkins University Press.

Meier, K.J., & L.J. O'Toole. (2007). Modeling Public Management: Empirical Analysis of the Management-Performance Nexus. *Public Management Review* 9(4): 503–527.

Meier, K.J., L.J. O'Toole, & S. Nicholson-Crotty. (2004). Multilevel Governance and Organizational Performance: Investigating the Political-Bureaucratic Labyrinth. *Journal of Policy Analysis and Management* 23(1): 31–47.

Menard, S. (2001). *Applied Logistic Regression Analysis.* Thousand Oaks, CA: Sage Publications.

Mettler, S. (2005). *Soldiers to Citizens: The G.I. Bill and the Making of the Greatest Generation.* Oxford: Oxford University Press.

Miller, L.S., K.M. Hess, & C.M.H. Orthmann. (2013). *Community Policing: Partnerships for Problem Solving.* Boston: Cengage Learning.

Mintrom, M., & R. O'Connor. (2020). The Importance of Policy Narrative: Effective Government Responses to COVID-19. *Policy Design & Practice* 3(3): 205–227.

Mintz, A., & C. Huang. (1990). Defense Expenditures, Economic Growth, and the "Peace Dividend." *American Political Science Review* 84(4): 1283–1293.

Miron, J.A., & J. Zwiebel. (1991). Alcohol Consumption during Prohibition. *American Economic Review* 81(2): 242–247.

Moffitt, S.L. (2014). *Making Policy Public: Participatory Bureaucracy in American Democracy.* Cambridge: Cambridge University Press.

Mohr, L.B. (1971). Organizational Technology and Organizational Structure. *Administrative Science Quarterly* 16(4): 444–459.

Monahan, T., & J.A. Fisher. (2010). Benefits of 'Observer Effects': Lessons from the Field. *Qualitative Research* 10(3): 357–376.

Montjoy, R.S., & L.J. O'Toole. (1979). Toward a Theory of Policy Implementation: An Organizational Perspective. *Public Administration Review* 39(5): 465–476.

Moon, M.J. (1999). The Pursuit of Managerial Entrepreneurship: Does Organization Matter? *Public Administration Review* 59(1): 31–43.

Morgan, D., K.G. Bacon, R. Bunch, C.D. Cameron, & R. Deis. (1996). What Middle Managers Do in Local Government: Stewardship of the Public Trust and the Limits of Reinventing Government. *Public Administration Review* 56(4): 359–366.

Moynihan, D.P. (2008). *The Dynamics of Performance Management: Constructing Information and Reform.* Washington, DC: Georgetown University Press.

Moynihan, D.P., & J. Soss. (2014). Policy Feedback and the Politics of Administration. *Public Administration Review* 74(3): 320–332.

Moynihan, D.P., & S. Lavertu. (2012). Cognitive Biases in Governing: Technology Preferences in Election Administration. *Public Administration Review* 72(1): 68–77.

Moyson, S., N. Raaphorst, S. Groeneveld, & S. Van de Walle. (2018). Organizational Socialization in Public Administration Research: A Systematic Review and Directions for Future Research. *American Review of Public Administration* 48(6): 610–627.

Mulgan, R. (2000). Accountability: An Ever-Expanding Concept? *Public Administration* 78(3): 555–573.

Mullinix, K.J., T.J. Leeper, J.N. Druckman, & J. Freese. (2015). The Generalizability of Survey Experiments. *Journal of Experimental Political Science* 2(2): 109–138.

Nakamura, R.T. (1987). The Textbook Policy Process and Implementation Research. *Review of Policy Research* 7(1): 142–154.

National Conference of State Legislatures. (2021). State Partisan Composition. https://www.ncsl.org/research/about-state-legislatures/partisan-composition. aspx

Nelson, R.R. (1959). The Economics of Invention: A Survey of the Literature. *Journal of Business* 32(2): 101–127.

Nelson, R.R. (2003). On the Uneven Evaluation of Human Know-How. *Research Policy* 32(6): 909–922.

Nelson, R.R., A. Peterhansl, & B. Sampat. (2004). Why and How Innovations Get Adopted: A Tale of Four Models. *Industrial & Corporate Change* 13(5): 679–699.

Nelson, T.E., & Z.M. Oxley. (1999). Issue Framing Effects on Belief Importance and Opinion. *Journal of Politics* 61(4): 1040–1067.

Nicholson-Crotty, S., & J. Nicholson-Crotty. (2004). Interest Group Influence on Managerial Priorities in Public Organizations. *Journal of Public Administration Research and Theory* 14(4): 571–583.

Nicholson-Crotty, S., J. Nicholson-Crotty, & S. Webeck. (2019). Are Public Managers More Risk Averse? Framing Effects and Status Quo Bias across the Sectors. *Journal of Behavioural Public Administration* 2(1).

Nickerson, R.S. (1998). Confirmation Bias: A Ubiquitous Phenomenon in Many Guises. *Review of General Psychology* 2(2): 175–220.

Nisbett, R.E., & T.D. Wilson. (1977). The Halo Effect: Evidence for Unconscious Alteration of Judgements. *Journal of Personality and Social Psychology* 35(4): 250–256.

O'Toole, L.J. (1997). Treating Networks Seriously: Practical and Research-Based Agendas in Public Administration. *Public Administration Review* 57(1): 45–52.

O'Toole, L.J. (2000). Research on Policy Implementation: Assessment and Prospects. *Journal of Public Administration Research and Theory* 10(2): 263–288.

O'Toole, L.J. (2015). Networks and Networking: The Public Administrative Agendas. *Public Administration Review* 75(3): 361–371.

Oberfield, Z.W. (2014). *Becoming Bureaucrats: Socialization at the Front Lines of Government Service.* Philadelphia: University of Pennsylvania Press.

Ogletree, C.J. (2004). *All Deliberate Speed: Reflections on the First Half Century of Brown v. Board of Education.* New York: W.W. Norton & Co.

Okten, I.O., A. Gollwitzer, & G. Oettingen. (2022). When Knowledge Is Blinding: The Dangers of Being Certain about the Future during Uncertain Societal Events. *Personality and Individual Differences* 195: 111606.

Osborne, S.P. and L. Brown. (2011). Innovation, Public Policy, and Public Services Delivery in the UK: The Word That Would Be King? *Public Administration* 89(4): 1335–1350.

Ostrom, E., M. Cox, & E. Schlager. (2014). An Assessment of the Institutional Analysis and Development Framework and Introduction to the Social-Ecological

Systems Framework. In *Theories of the Policy Process*, 3rd ed., edited by P.A. Sabatier & C.M. Weible (pp. 267–306). Boulder, CO: Westview Press.

Ostrom, E., & V. Ostrom. (2014). *Choice, Rules, and Collective Action: The Ostroms on the Study of Institutions and Governance*. Colchester, UK: ECPR Press.

Overeem, P. (2005). The Value of the Dichotomy: Politics, Administration, and the Political Neutrality of Administrators. *Administrative Theory & Praxis* 27(2):: 311–329.

Page, B.I. (1976). The Theory of Political Ambiguity. *American Political Science Review* 70(3): 742–752.

Pandey, S.K., and G.A. Kingsley. (2000). Examining Red Tape in Public and Private Organizations: Alternative Explanations from a Social Psychological Model. *Journal of Public Administration Research and Theory* 10(4): 779–799.

Pandey, S.K., & B.E. Wright. (2006). Connecting the Dots in Public Management: Political Environment, Organizational Goal Ambiguity, and the Public Manager's Role Ambiguity. *Journal of Public Administration Research and Theory* 16(4): 511–532.

Peters, B.G. (2010). Bureaucracy and Democracy in the Modern State. *Public Administration Review* 70(4): 642–643.

Peters, B.G. (2015). State Failure, Governance Failure and Policy Failure: Exploring the Linkages. *Public Policy and Administration* 30(3–4): 261–276.

Peters, B.G., & B.W. Hogwood. (1985). In Search of the Issue-Attention Cycle. *Journal of Politics* 47(1): 238–253.

Peters, B.G., & J. Pierre. (1998). Governance without Government? Rethinking Public Administration. *Journal of Public Administration Research and Theory* 8(2): 223–243.

Petty, R.E., & J.T. Cacioppo. (1986). The Elaboration Likelihood Model of Persuasion. In *Advances in Experimental Social Psychology*, edited by L. Berkowitz (pp. 123–205). New York: Academic Press.

Picchi, A. (2020). Taxes 2020. These Two Groups of Taxpayers Face the Highest Audit Rates. *USA Today*, January 31.

Pierce, J.J., S. Siddiki, M.D. Jones, K. Schumacher, A. Pattison, & H. Peterson. (2014). Social Construction and Policy Design: A Review of Past Applications. *Policy Studies Journal* 42(1): 1–29.

Potoski, M. (1999). Managing Uncertainty through Bureaucratic Design: Administrative Procedures and State Air Pollution Control Agencies. *Journal of Public Administration Research and Theory* 9(4): 623–640.

Potoski, M. (2002). Designing Bureaucratic Responsiveness: Administrative Procedures and Agency Choice in State Environmental Policy. *State Politics & Policy Quarterly* 2(1): 1–23.

Pressman, J.L., & A. Wildavsky. (1984). *Implementation: How Great Expectations in Washington Are Dashed in Oakland; Or, Why It's Amazing that Federal Programs Work at All*, 3rd ed. Berkeley: University of California Press.

Primo, D.M., M.L. Jacobsmeier, and J. Milyo. (2007). Estimating the Impact of State Policies and Institutions with Mixed-Level Data. *State Politics & Policy Quarterly* 7(4): 446–459.

Provan, K.G., & K. Huang. (2012). Resource Tangibility and the Evolution of a Publicly Funded Health and Human Services Network. *Public Administration Review* 72(3): 366–375.

Provan, K.G., & P. Kenis. (2008). Modes of Network Governance: Structure, Management, and Effectiveness. *Journal of Public Administration Research and Theory* 18(2): 229–252.

Quattrone, G.A., & A. Tversky. (1988). Contrasting Rational and Psychological Analyses of Political Choice. *American Political Science Review* 82(3): 719–736.

Quratulain, S., & A.K. Khan. (2015). Red Tape, Resigned Satisfaction, Public Service Motivation, and Negative Employee Attitudes and Behaviors: Testing a Model of Moderated Mediation. *Review of Public Personnel Administration* 35(4): 307–322.

Rainey, H.G. (1983). Public Agencies and Private Firms. *Administration & Society* 15(2): 207–242.

Rainey, H.G. (2014). *Understanding and Managing Public Organizations*, 5th ed. San Francisco, CA: Jossey-Bass.

Rainey, H.G., S. Pandey, & B. Bozeman. (1995). Research Note: Public and Private Managers' Perceptions of Red Tape. *Public Administration Review* 55(6): 567–574.

Ran, B., & T.J. Golden. (2011). Who Are We? The Social Construction of Organizational Identity through Sense-Exchanging. *Administration & Society* 43(4): 417–445.

Rawat, P., & J.C. Morris. (2016). Kingdon's "Streams" Model at Thirty: Still Relevant in the 21st Century? *Politics & Policy* 44(4): 608–638.

Reed, D.S. (2014). *Building the Federal Schoolhouse: Localism and the American Education State*. Oxford: Oxford University Press.

Reed, W.E. (1999). *The Politics of Community Policing: The Case of Seattle*. New York: Routledge.

Riddle, V. (2009). Policy Implementation in an Africa State: An Extension of Kingdon's Multiple-Streams Approach. *Public Administration* 87(4): 938–954.

Robinson, O.C. (2014). Sampling in Interview-Based Qualitative Research: A Theoretical and Practical Guide. *Qualitative Research in Psychology* 11(1): 25–41.

Robinson, S.E., & W.E. Eller. (2010). Participation in Policy Streams: Testing the Separation of Problems and Solution in Subnational Policy Systems. *Policy Studies Journal* 38(2): 199–215.

Robertson, M., & J. Swan. (2003). 'Control—What Control?' Culture and Ambiguity Within a Knowledge Intensive Firm. *Journal of Management Studies* 40(4): 831–858.

Rossmann, D., & E.A. Shanahan. (2012). Defining and Achieving Normative Democratic Values in Participatory Budgeting Processes. *Public Administration Review* 72(1): 56–66.

Roulston, K. (2013). Analysing Interviews. In *The Sage Handbook of Qualitative Data Analysis*, edited U. Flick (pp. 297–312). Thousand Oaks, CA: Sage Publications.

Rutledge, P.E. (2020). Trump, COVID-19, and the War on Expertise. *American Review of Public Administration* 50(6–7): 505–511.

Saetren, H. (2005). Facts and Myths about Research on Public Policy Implementation: Out-of-Fashion, Allegedly Dead, But Still Very Much Alive and Relevant. *Policy Studies Journal* 33(4): 559–582.

Saetren, H. (2014). Implementing the Third Generation Research Paradigm in Policy Implementation Research: An Empirical Assessment. *Public Policy and Administration* 29(2): 84–105.

Samuelson, W., & R. Zeckhauser. (1988). Status Quo Bias in Decision Making. *Journal of Risk and Uncertainty* 1(1): 7–59.

Schafer, J.G. (2019). A Systematic Review of the Public Administration Literature to Identify How to Increase Public Engagement and Participation with Local Governance. *Journal of Public Affairs* 19(2): e1873.

Schein, E.G. (2017). *Organizational Culture and Leadership*, 5th ed. Hoboken, NJ: Wiley & Sons.

Scheufele, D.A., & D. Tewksbury. (2007). Framing, Agenda Setting, and Priming: The Evolution of Three Media Effects Models. *Journal of Communication* 57(1): 9–20.

Schlager, E., & M. Cox. (2018). The IAD Framework and the SES Framework: An Introduction and Assessment of the Ostrom Workshop Frameworks. In *Theories of the Policy Process*, 4th ed., edited by C.M. Weible & P.A. Sabatier. Boulder, CO: Westview Press.

Schneider, A.L., H. Ingram, & P. deLeon. (2018). Democratic Policy Design: Social Construction of Target Populations. In *Theories of the Policy Process*, 4th ed., edited by C.M. Weible & P.A. Sabatier (pp. 105–150). Boulder, CO: Westview Press.

Schneider, A., and M. Sidney. (2009). What is Next for Policy Design and Social Construction Theory. *Policy Studies Journal* 37(1): 103–119.

Scott, C. (2000). Accountability in the Regulatory State. *Journal of Law & Society* 27(1): 38–60.

Scott, P.G. (1997). Assessing Determinants of Bureaucratic Discretion: An Experiment in Street-Level Decision Making. *Journal of Public Administration Research and Theory* 7(1): 35–58.

Simon, H.A. (1997). *Administrative Behavior: A Study of Decision-Making Processes in Administrative Organizations*, 4th ed. New York: Free Press.

Simon, H.A. (2004). Science Seeks Parsimony, Not Simplisticity: Searching for Patterns in Phenomena. In *Simplicity, Inference, and Modelling*, edited by A. Zellner, H.A. Keuzenkamp, & M. McAleer (pp. 32–72). Cambridge: Cambridge University Press.

Shaffer, D.R., & C. Hendrick. (1974). Dogmatism and Tolerance for Ambiguity as Determinants of Differential Reactions to Cognitive Inconsistency. *Journal of Personality and Social Psychology* 29(5): 601–608.

Slothuus, R., & C.H. de Vreese. (2010). Political Parties, Motivated Reasoning, and Issue Framing Effects. *Journal of Politics* 72(3): 630–645.

Smith, K.B., & C. Larimer. (2016). *The Public Policy Theory Primer*, 3rd ed. New York: Routledge.

Smylie, M.A., & A.E. Evans. (2006). Social Capital and the Problem of Implementation. In *New Directions in Education Policy Implementation: Confronting Complexity*, edited by M. Honig (pp. 187–208). Albany, NY: State University of New York Press.

Sowa, J.E., & S.C. Selden. (2003). Administrative Discretion and Active Representation: An Expansion of the Theory of Representative Bureaucracy. *Public Administration Review* 63(6): 700–710.

Sowell, T. (2011). *Economic Facts and Fallacies*, 2nd ed. New York: Basic Books.

Spano, R. (2006). Observer Behavior as a Potential Source of Reactivity: Describing and Quantifying Observer Effects in a Large-Scale Observational Study of Police. *Sociological Methods & Research* 34(4): 521–553.

StataCorp. (2015). *Stata 14 Base Reference Material*. College Station, TX: Stata Press.

Stazyk, E.C., & H.T. Goerdel. (2011). The Benefits of Bureaucracy: Public Managers' Perceptions of Political Support, Goal Ambiguity, and Organizational Effectiveness. *Journal of Public Administration Research and Theory* 21(4): 645–672.

Sterling, B. (2011). Post-Idea World. *Wired*, August 15.

Stewart, D.W. (1985). Professionalism vs. Democracy: Friedrich vs. Finer Revisited. *Public Administration Quarterly* 9(1): 13–25.

Stoker, G., C. Hay, & M. Barr. (2016). Fast Thinking: Implications for Democratic Politics. *European Journal of Political Research* 55(1): 3–21.

Stone, D. (2011). *Policy Paradox: The Art of Political Decision Making*, 3rd ed. New York: W.W. Norton & Co.

Svara, J.H. (1998). The Politics-Administration Dichotomy Model as Aberration. *Public Administration Review* 58(1): 51–58.

Svara, J.H. (2001). The Myth of the Dichotomy: Complementarity of Politics and Administration in the Past and Future of Public Administration. *Public Administration Review* 61(2): 176–183.

Sveningsson, S., & M. Alvesson. (2003). Managing Managerial Identities: Organizational Fragmentation, Discourse and Identity Struggle. *Human Relations* 56(10): 1163–1193.

Taber, C.S., & M. Lodge. (2006). Motivated Skepticism in the Evaluation of Political Beliefs. *American Journal of Political Science* 50(3): 755–769.

Tankersley, J., & A. Rappeport. (2021). Biden Seeks $80 Billion to Beef Up I.R.S. Audit of High-Earners. *New York Times*, July 7.

Taylor, J. (2014). Organizational Culture and the Paradox of Performance Management. *Public Performance & Management Review* 38(1): 7–22.

Teisman, G.R., & E. Klijn. (2002). Partnership Arrangements: Governmental Rhetoric or Governance Scheme? *Public Administration Review* 62(2): 197–205.

Terry, L.D. (1990). Leadership in the Administrative State: The Concept of Administrative Conservatorship. *Administration & Society* 21(4): 395–412.

Terry, L.D. (1998). Administrative Leadership, Neo-Managerialism, and the Public Management Movement. *Public Administration Review* 58(3): 194–200.

Terry, L.D. (2003). *Leadership of Public Bureaucracies: The Administrator as Conservator*. Thousand Oaks, CA: Sage Publications.

Terry, L.D., & M.G. Levin. (1998). Organizational Scepticism, the Modern Conception of Leadership and the Obsession with New. *Journal of Management History* 4(4): 303–317.

Thaler, R.H., & C. Sunstein. (2008). *Nudge: Improving Decisions about Health, Wealth, and Happiness*. New Haven, CT: Yale University Press.

Thelen, K. (1999). Historical Institutionalism in Comparative Politics. *Annual Review of Political Science* 2: 369–404.

Thompson, T. (2015). *The Affordable Care Act*. Farmington Hills, MI: Greenhaven Press.

Triantafillou, P. (2015). The Politics of Neutrality and the Changing Role of Expertise in Public Administration. *Administrative Theory & Praxis* 37(3): 174–187.

Tversky, A., & D. Kahneman. (1974). Judgment Under Uncertainty: Heuristics and Biases. *Science* 185(4157): 1124–1131.

Tyler, T.R., J. Fagan, & A. Geller. (2014). Street Stops and Police Legitimacy: Teachable Moments in Young Urban Men's Legal Socialization. *Journal of Empirical Legal Studies* 11(4): 751–785.

US Bureau of Economic Analysis (US BEA). (2021). Regional Data. https://apps.bea.gov/itable/iTable.cfm?ReqID=70&step=1

US Census Bureau. (2021). Annual Survey of State Government Finance Datasets. https://www.census.gov/programs-surveys/state/data/datasets.All.html

US Department of the Treasury. (2022). Monthly Statement of the Public Debt (MSPD) Balancing Worksheet, June 30, 2022. https://www.treasurydirect.gov/govt/reports/pd/mspd/mspd_balsht.pdf

US Environmental Protection Agency (US EPA). (2005). Evaluation of the OECA/ECOS State Review Framework in Pilot States. https://www.epa.gov/sites/production/files/2015-09/documents/eval-oeca-ecos-state-review-framework-pilot-projects.pdf

US Environmental Protection Agency. (2010). State Review Framework (SRF) Definitions of the Status of Identified Recommendations. https://www.epa.gov/sites/production/files/2013-08/documents/srf-rd2-definitions.pdf

US Environmental Protection Agency. (2021a). State Review Framework for Compliance and Enforcement Performance. https://www.epa.gov/compliance/state-review-framework-compliance-and-enforcement-performance

US Environmental Protection Agency. (2021b). Toxic Releases Inventory. https://www.epa.gov/toxics-release-inventory-tri-program/tri-basic-data-files-calendar-years-1987-2019?

US Environmental Protection Agency. (2021c). What is the Toxics Release Inventory? https://www.epa.gov/toxics-release-inventory-tri-program/what-toxics-release-inventory

Utych, S.M. (2022). Race, Dehumanization, and the NFL National Anthem Protests. *Journal of Experimental Political Science* 9(1): 88–103.

Utych, S.M., & L. Fowler. (2021). More Human than Human: The Consequences of Positive Dehumanization. *Administrative Theory & Praxis* 43(2): 190–208.

Valentino, C.L. (2004). The Role of Middle Managers in the Transmission and Integration of Organizational Culture. *Journal of Healthcare Management* 49(6): 393–404.

Van der Velde, M., & M.D. Class. (1995). The Relationship of Role Conflict and Ambiguity to Organizational Culture. In *Organizational Risk Factors for Job Stress*, edited by S.L. Sauter & L.R. Murphy (pp. 53–59). Washington, DC: American Psychology Association.

Van Hiel, A., & I. Mervielde. (2002). Effects of Ambiguity and Need for Closure on the Acquisition of Information. *Social Cognition* 20(5): 380–408.

Voorn, B., M. van Genugten, & S. van Thiel. (2019). Multiple, Principals, Multiple Problems: Implications for Effective Governance and a Research Agenda for Joint Service Delivery. *Public Administration* 97(3): 671–685.

Wagenaar, H. (2004). "Knowing" the Rules: Administrative Work as Practice. *Public Administration Review* 64(6): 643–656.

Walker, R.M., Y. Chandra, J. Zhang, & A. van Witteloostuijn. (2019). Topic Modeling the Research-Practice Gap in Public Administration. *Public Administration Review* 79(6): 931–937.

Wallenstein, P. (2005). *Blue Laws and Black Codes: Conflict, Courts, & Change in Twentieth-Century Virginia*. Charlottesville: University of Virginia Press.

Wallner, J. (2008). Legitimacy and Public Policy: Seeing Beyond Effectiveness, Efficiency, and Performance. *Policy Studies Journal* 36(3): 421–443.

Wang, X.H., & M.W. Wart. (2007). When Public Participation in Administration Leads to Trust: An Empirical Assessment of Managers' Perceptions. *Public Administration Review* 67(2): 265–278.

Wanous, J.P., A.E. Reichers, & S.D. Malik. (1984). Organizational Socialization and Group Development: Toward an Integrative Perspective. *Academy of Management Review* 9(4): 670–683.

Waterman, R.W., & K.J. Meier. (1998). Principal-Agent Models: An Expansion? *Journal of Public Administration Research and Theory* 8(2): 173–202.

West, W.F. (1984). Structuring Administrative Discretion: The Pursuit of Rationality and Responsiveness. *American Journal of Political Science* 28(2): 340–360.

Westley, F.R. (1990). Middle Managers and Strategy: Microdynamics of Inclusion. *Strategic Management Journal* 11(5): 337–351.

Williamson, O.E. (1997). Transaction Cost Economics and Public Administration. In *Public Priority Setting: Rules and Costs*, edited by P.B. Boorsma, K. Aarts, & A.E. Steenge. Dordrecht, Netherlands: Springer.

Williamson, O.E. (1999). Public and Private Bureaucracies: A Transaction Cost Economics Perspective. *Journal of Law, Economics, & Organization* 15(1): 306–342.

Williamson, O.E. (2015). The Economics of Organization: The Transaction Cost Approach. In *Classics of Organizational Theory*, 8th ed. edited by J.M. Shafritz, J.S. Ott, & Y.S. Jang (pp. 210–207). Boston: Cengage.

Willingham, A.J. (2017). An Oxford Comma Changed This Court Case Completely. *CNN*. https://www.cnn.com/2017/03/15/health/oxford-comma-maine-court-case-trnd/index.html

Wilson, W. (1887). The Study of Administration. *Political Science Quarterly* 2(2): 197–222.

Winter, S. (2012). Implementation. In *Handbook of Public Policy*, edited by B.G. Peters & J. Pierre (pp. 151–166). London: Sage.

Wood, B.D., & J. Bohte. (2004). Political Transaction Costs and the Politics of Administrative Design. *Journal of Politics* 66(1): 176–202.

Wood, B.D., & R.W. Waterman. (1991). The Dynamics of Political Control of the Bureaucracy. *American Political Science Review* 85(3): 801–828.

Woods, N.D. (2006). Primacy Implementation of Environmental Policy in the U.S. States. *Publius* 36(2): 259–276.

Woods, N.D. (2021). The State of State Environmental Policy Research: A Thirty-Year Progress Report. *Review of Policy Research* 38(3): 347–369.

Wright, B.E. (2001). Public-Sector Work Motivation: A Review of the Current Literature and a Revised Conceptual Model. *Journal of Public Administration Research and Theory* 11(4): 559–586.

Wright, R.E., & T.W. Zeiler (Eds.). (2014). *Guide to US Economic Policy*. Washington, DC: CQ Press.

Yarrow, A. (2008). *Forgive Us Our Debts: The Intergenerational Dangers of Fiscal Irresponsibility*. New Haven, CT: Yale University Press.

Zahariadis, N. (1995). *Markets, States, & Public Policy: Privatization in Brian and France*. Ann Arbor: University of Michigan Press.

Zahariadis, N. (2003). *Ambiguity and Choice in Public Policy: Political Decision Making in Modern Democracies*. Washington, DC: Georgetown University Press.

Zahariadis, N. (2005). *Essence of Political Manipulation: Emotions, Institutions, and Greek Foreign Policy.* New York: Lang.

Zahariadis, N. (2007). The Multiple Streams Framework: Structure, Limitations, Prospects. In *Theories of the Policy Process,* edited by P. Sabatier. Boulder, CO: Westview Press.

Zahariadis, N. (2014). Ambiguity and Multiple Streams. In *Theories of the Policy Process,* 3rd ed., edited by P.A. Sabatier & C.M. Weible (pp. 25–58). Boulder, CO: Westview Press.

Zahariadis, N., & T. Exadaktylos. (2016). Policies that Succeed and Programs that Fail: Ambiguity, Conflict, and Crisis in Greek Higher Education. *Policy Studies Journal* 44(1): 59–82.

Zaller, J.R. (1992). *The Nature and Origins of Mass Opinion.* Cambridge: Cambridge University Press.

Zey, M. (1998). *Rational Choice Theory and Organizational Theory: A Critique.* Thousand Oaks, CA: Sage.

Ziller, R.C. (1964). Individual and Socialization: A Theory of Assimilation in Large Organizations. *Human Relations* 17(4): 341–360.

Zohlnhöfer, R., & C. Rüb. (2016). How Well Does the Multiple Streams Framework Travel? Evidence from German Case Studies. In *Decision-Making under Ambiguity and Time Constraints: Assessing the Multiple-Streams Framework,* edited by R. Zohlnhöfer & F.W. Rüb (pp. 169–188). Colchester, UK: ECPR Press.

Index

www.ingramcontent.com/pod-product-compliance
Lightning Source LLC
Chambersburg PA
CBHW020346270326
41926CB00007B/326